TOP 10
PARIS

W9-CRB-883

MIKE GERRARD & DONNA DAILEY

EYEWITNESS TRAVEL

Left **Glass Pyramid, Musée du Louvre** Right **Crypt vaults, Sacré-Coeur**

LONDON, NEW YORK,
MELBOURNE, MUNICH AND DELHI
www.dk.com

Printed and bound in China by Leo Paper Products Ltd
First American Edition, 2002
13 14 15 16 10 9 8 7 6 5 4 3 2

Published in the United States by DK Publishing,
345 Hudson Street, New York, New York 10014

Copyright 2002, 2013 © Dorling Kindersley
Limited, London

**Reprinted with revisions 2003, 2004, 2005, 2006,
2007, 2008, 2009, 2010, 2011, 2012, 2013**

All rights reserved. Without limiting the rights under
copyright reserved above, no part of this publication
may be reproduced, stored in or introduced into
a retrieval system, or transmitted, in any form, or
by any means (electronic, mechanical, photocopying,
recording, or otherwise), without the prior written
permission of both the copyright owner and the
above publisher of this book.

Published in Great Britain by Dorling
Kindersley Limited.

A catalog record for this book is available
from the Library of Congress

ISSN 1479-344X
ISBN: 978-0-75669-657-3

Within each Top 10 list in this book, no hierarchy of quality
or popularity is implied. All 10 are, in the editor's
opinion, of roughly equal merit.

Floors are referred to throughout in
accordance with French usage; i.e. the "first floor"
is the floor above ground level.

MIX
Paper from
responsible sources
FSC™ C018179
www.fsc.org

Contents

Paris Top 10

The information in this DK Eyewitness Top 10 Travel Guide is checked annually.
Every effort has been made to ensure that this book is as up-to-date as possible at the time of
going to press. Some details, however, such as telephone numbers, opening hours, prices,
gallery hanging arrangements and travel information are liable to change. The publishers
cannot accept responsibility for any consequences arising from the use of this book, nor for
any material on third party websites, and cannot guarantee that any website address in this
book will be a suitable source of travel information. We value the views and suggestions of
our readers very highly. Please write to: Publisher, DK Eyewitness Travel Guides,
Dorling Kindersley, 80 Strand, London, Great Britain WC2R 0RL, or email: travelguides@dk.com.

Cover: All photographs specially commissioned except: Front – **Getty Images**: Sylvain Sonnet main; **Dorling
Kindersley**: Max Alexander clb. Spine – **Dorling Kindersley**: Robert O'Dea b. Back – **Dorling Kindersley**: cra;
Max Alexander ca; Eric Meacher cla.

Left **Rose window, Notre-Dame** Right **Stone carvings, Arc de Triomphe**

Left **Bois de Boulogne** Right **Montmartre**

PARIS
TOP 10

PARIS TOP 10

TOP 10 Paris Highlights

From Notre-Dame to the Eiffel Tower, Paris holds some of the world's most famous sights and these ten attractions should be top of the list for any first-time visitor. With the exception of the overtly modern Pompidou Centre, they have been landmarks of this elegant and romantic capital for centuries and remain awe-inspiring sights, no matter how often you visit the city.

1 Musée du Louvre

The world's largest museum unsurprisingly also contains one of the world's finest collections of art and antiquities (up to 1848). To complete the superlatives, the building was once France's largest royal palace *(see pp8–11)*.

2 Musée d'Orsay

This former railway station is one of the world's leading art galleries *(above)* and, for many, reason alone to visit Paris *(see pp12–15)*.

3 Eiffel Tower

Some six million visitors a year ascend to the top of this most famous Paris landmark for the spectacular views. It was erected for the Universal Exhibition of 1889 *(see pp16–17)*.

4 Notre-Dame

This great Gothic cathedral, founded on the site of a Gallo-Roman temple, is a repository of French art and history. It also represents the geographical "heart" of France *(see pp18–21)*.

Share your travel recommendations on traveldk.com

Sacré-Coeur
The terrace in front of this monumental white-domed basilica in Montmartre affords one of the finest free views over Paris *(see pp22–3)*.

Arc de Triomphe
Napoleon's triumphal arch, celebrating battle victories, stands proudly at the top of the Champs-Elysées and, along with the Eiffel Tower, is one of the city's most enduring images *(see pp24–5)*.

Centre Georges Pompidou
Home to France's National Museum of Modern Art, the building itself is a work of contemporary art. There are also extensive research facilities *(see pp26–7)*.

— miles ─ 0 ─ km — 1

Panthéon
The great and the good of France are buried in the Panthéon *(above)*, including Voltaire *(see pp28–9)*.

Sainte-Chapelle
Called "a gateway to heaven", this splendid medieval church *(left)* was built to house the relics collected by St Louis on his many Crusades *(see pp30–31)*.

Hôtel des Invalides
The glowing golden dome of the Hôtel des Invalides church *(right)* is unmistakable across the rooftops of Paris *(see pp32–3)*.

Map labels: Montmartre, Clichy, Belleville, Les Halles, Marais, Île de la Cité, Île St-Louis, Latin Quarter, Jardin du Luxembourg, Jardin des Plantes

🔟 Musée du Louvre

One of the world's most impressive museums, the Louvre contains some 35,000 priceless objects. Built as a fortress by King Philippe-Auguste in 1190, Charles V (1364–80) was the first king to make it his home. In the 16th century François I replaced it with a Renaissance-style palace and founded the royal art collection with 12 paintings from Italy. Revolutionaries opened the collection to the public in 1793. Shortly after, Napoleon renovated the Louvre as a museum.

Musée du Louvre façade

🍽 Try out Le Café Marly in the Richelieu Wing or the food court in Carrousel du Louvre. For a special option make a reservation at the Grand Louvre restaurant below the pyramid.

🎫 Beat the queues and buy tickets online or at machine kiosks at the Porte des Lions entrance at the west end of the Denon Wing (except Friday).

- Musée du Louvre, 75001
- Map L2
- 01 40 20 53 17
- www.louvre.fr
- Open 9am–6pm Mon, Thu, Sat & Sun, 9am–10pm Wed & Fri; closed Tue & public hols
- Admission €10 (subject to change); free 1st Sun of month; under 18s free; under 26s (EU only) free • Partial disabled access

Top 10 Sights

1. Venus de Milo
2. Mona Lisa
3. Glass Pyramid
4. Marly Horses
5. The Raft of the Medusa
6. The Winged Victory of Samothrace
7. The Lacemaker
8. Slaves
9. Medieval Moats
10. Perrault's Colonnade

1 Venus de Milo

The positioning of this statue, dramatically lit at the end of a hallway, enhances its beauty. Believed to represent the goddess Aphrodite, it dates from the end of the 2nd century BC and was discovered on the Greek island of Milos in 1820.

2 Mona Lisa

Arguably the most famous painting in the world, Leonardo's portrait of the woman with the enigmatic smile *(see p11)* has been beautifully restored. Visit early or late in the day.

3 Glass Pyramid

The unmistakable pyramid, designed by I.M. Pei, became the Louvre's new entrance in 1989. Stainless steel tubes form the 21-m-high (69-ft) frame *(below)*.

4 Marly Horses

Coustou's rearing horses being restrained by horse-tamers were sculpted in 1745 for Louis XIV's Château de Marly. Replicas stand near the Place de la Concorde.

For more Paris museums **See pp34–5**

5 The Raft of the Medusa

A shipwreck three years earlier inspired this early Romantic painting *(right)* by Théodore Géricault (1791–1824) in 1819. The work depicts a moment when the survivors spot a sail on the horizon.

6 The Winged Victory of Samothrace

This Hellenistic treasure (3rd–2nd century BC) stands atop a stone ship radiating grace and power. It commemorates a naval triumph at Rhodes.

7 The Lacemaker

Jan Vermeer's masterpiece *(below)*, painted around 1665, gives a simple but beautiful rendering of everyday life and is the highlight of the Louvre's Dutch collection.

8 Slaves

Michelangelo sculpted these two slaves (1513–20) for the tomb of Pope Julius II in Rome. The unfinished figures seem to be emerging from their "prisons" of stone.

9 Medieval Moats

An excavation in the 1980s uncovered the remains of the medieval fortress. You can see the base of the towers and the drawbridge support.

10 Perrault's Colonnade

The majestic east façade by Claude Perrault (1613–88), with its columns *(below)*, was part of an extension plan commissioned by Louis XIV.

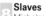

Key

- ▨ Ground floor
- ▨ First floor
- ▨ Second floor

Gallery Guide

The foyer is under the pyramid. Visitors who have tickets are given priority access at the pyramid. Alternatively, buy tickets at the Carrousel du Louvre entrance (99 rue de Rivoli) and Porte des Lions. The Sully, Denon and Richelieu wings lead off from the foyer. Painting and sculpture are displayed by country, plus galleries for *objets d'art*, antiquities, prints and drawings. Don't miss the temporary shows, contemporary and tribal art (Pavilion des Sessions, Denon).

Above **Sleeping Hermaphrodite, Greek Antiquities**

Louvre Collections

1 French Paintings
This superb collection ranges from the 14th century to 1848 and includes works by such artists as Jean Watteau, Georges de la Tour and JH Fragonard.

2 French Sculpture
Highlights include the Tomb of Philippe Pot by Antoine le Moiturier, the Marly Horses (see p8) and works by Pierre Puget in the glass-covered courtyards.

3 Egyptian Antiquities
The finest collection outside Cairo, featuring a Sphinx in the crypt, the Seated Scribe of Sakkara, huge sarcophagi, mummified animals, funerary objects and intricate carvings depicting everyday life in Ancient Egypt.

4 Greek Antiquities
Akhenaton and Nefertiti, Egypt

The wondrous art of Ancient Greece here ranges from a Cycladic idol from the third millennium BC to Classical Greek marble statues (c.5th century BC) to Hellenistic works (late 3rd–2nd century BC).

Basement floor

Collections floorplan

5 Oriental Antiquities
A stunning collection includes a re-created temple of an Assyrian king and the Codex of Hammurabi (18th century BC), mankind's oldest written laws.

6 Italian Paintings
French royalty adored the art of Italy and amassed much of this collection (1200–1800). There are many works by da Vinci including the Mona Lisa.

7 Italian Sculpture
Highlights of this collection, dating from the early Renaissance, include a 15th-century Madonna and Child by Donatello and Michelangelo's Slaves (see p9).

8 Dutch Paintings
Rembrandt works take pride of place in this section, along with domestic scenes by Vermeer and portraits by Frans Hals.

9 Objets d'Art
The ceramics, jewellery and other items in this collection span many countries and centuries.

10 Islamic Art
This exquisite collection, which spans 13 centuries and three continents, is covered by an ultra-modern glass veil.

For more Paris museums See pp34–5

Top 10 Louvre Residents

1. Charles V (1364–80)
2. Henri II (1547–49)
3. Catherine de' Medici (1519–89)
4. Henri IV (1589–1610)
5. Louis XIII (1610–43)
6. Louis XIV (1643–1715)
7. Anne of Austria (1601–66)
8. Guillaume Coustou, sculptor (1677–1746)
9. Edmé Bouchardon, sculptor (1698–1762)
10. François Boucher, artist (1703–70)

Leonardo da Vinci and the Mona Lisa

Mona Lisa, Leonardo da Vinci's enigmatic portrait

Leonardo da Vinci
A Renaissance man extraordinaire, Leonardo was not only an artist but a sculptor, engineer, architect and scientist. His many achievements included the study of anatomy and aerodynamics.

Born in Vinci to a wealthy family, Leonardo da Vinci (1452–1519) first took up an apprenticeship under the Florentine artist Andrea del Verrocchio, then served the Duke of Milan as an architect and military engineer, during which time he painted the acclaimed Last Supper *mural (1495). On his return to Florence, to work as architect to Cesare Borgia, he painted his most celebrated portrait, the* Mona Lisa *(1503–06). It is also known as* La Gioconda, *allegedly the name of the model's aristocratic husband, although there is ongoing speculation regarding the identity of the subject. The masterpiece, particularly the sitter's mysterious smile, shows mastery of two techniques: chiaroscuro, the contrast of light and shadow, and sfumato, subtle transitions between colours. It was the artist's own favourite painting and he took it with him everywhere. In 1516 François I brought them both to France, giving da Vinci the use of a manor house in Amboise in the Loire Valley, where he died three years later. The* Mona Lisa *is the Renaissance master's only known surviving work of portraiture.*

🔟 Musée d'Orsay

This wonderful collection covers a variety of art forms from the 1848–1914 period, including a superb Impressionists section. Its setting, in a converted railway station, is equally impressive. Built in 1900, in time for the Paris Exposition, the station was in use until 1939, when it was closed and largely ignored, bar its use as the location for Orson Welles' 1962 film, The Trial. It was later used as a theatre and as auction rooms, and in the mid-1970s was considered for demolition. In 1977, the Paris authorities decided to save the imposing station building by converting it into this striking museum.

Musée d'Orsay façade

🍽 The busy museum restaurant serves lunch and dinner on Thursdays. For a snack or a drink try the upper level café (Café Campana) or the self-service mezzanine café just above.

🎵 Regular music concerts are held. Call 01 40 49 47 50.

• 1 rue de la Légion-d'Honneur, 75007
• Map J2
• 01 40 49 48 14
• www.musee-orsay.fr
• Open 9:30am–6pm Tue–Sun (Thu till 9:45pm); closed 1 Jan, 1 May, 25 Dec
• Admission €9 (under 18s free, under 26s EU only free), €6.50 18–25s non-EU. Tickets can be bought online

Top 10 Features

1. The Building
2. Van Gogh Paintings
3. Le Déjeuner sur l'Herbe
4. Olympia
5. Blue Waterlilies
6. Degas' Statues of Dancers
7. Jane Avril Dancing
8. Dancing at the Moulin de la Galette
9. La Belle Angèle
10. Café Campana

The Building

The former railway station which houses this museum is almost as stunning as the exhibits. The light and spacious feel when one first steps inside, after admiring the magnificent old façade, takes one's breath away.

Van Gogh Paintings

The star of the collection is Vincent Van Gogh (1853–90) and the most striking of the canvases on display is the 1889 work showing the artist's *Bedroom at Arles (below)*. Also on display are self-portraits, painted with the artist's familiar intensity (Middle Level).

Le Déjeuner sur l'Herbe

Edouard Manet's (1832–83) controversial painting (1863) was first shown in an "Exhibition of Rejected Works". Its bold portrayal of a classically nude woman *(below)* enjoying the company of 19th-century men in suits brought about a wave of criticism (Galerié Seine).

Olympia
Another Manet portrayal (1865) of a naked courtesan, receiving flowers sent by an admirer, was also regarded as indecent and shocked the public and critics, but it was a great influence on later artists (Room 14).

Blue Waterlilies
Claude Monet (1840–1926) painted this stunning canvas (1919) on one of his favourite themes. His love of waterlilies led him to create his own garden at Giverny to enable him to paint them in a natural setting. This experimental work *(below)* inspired many abstract painters later in the 20th century (Room 34).

Degas' Statues of Dancers
The museum possesses an exceptional collection of works by Edgar Degas (1834–1917). Focusing on dancers and the world of opera, his sculptures range from the innocent to the erotic. The striking *Young Dancer of Fourteen* (1881) was the only one exhibited in the artist's lifetime *(right)* (Upper Level).

Jane Avril Dancing
Toulouse-Lautrec's (1864–1901) paintings define Paris's *belle époque*. Jane Avril was a famous Moulin Rouge dancer and featured in several of his works, like this 1895 canvas *(below)*, which Toulouse-Lautrec drew from life, in-situ at the cabaret (Room 47).

Dancing at the Moulin de la Galette
One of the best-known paintings of the Impressionist era (1876), this work was shown at the Impressionist exhibition in 1877. The exuberance of Renoir's (1841–1919) work captures the look and mood of Montmartre and is undeniably one of the artist's masterpieces (Middle Level).

La Belle Angèle
This portrait of a Brittany beauty (1889) by Paul Gauguin (1848–1903) shows the influence of Japanese art on the artist. It was bought by Degas, to finance Gauguin's first trip to Polynesia (Room 43).

Café Campana
As a rest from all the impressive art, the Musée d'Orsay's café, renovated by the Campana Brothers, is delightfully situated behind one of the former station's huge clocks. A break here is an experience in itself and the food is good too.

Gallery Guide
As soon as you enter the gallery, collect a map of its layout. The ground floor houses fine works from the early to mid-19th century, as well as striking Oriental works, decorative arts and a bookshop. The middle level includes Naturalist, Symbolist and Post-Impressionist paintings and sculpture terraces. The upper level is home to the Impressionist galleries. The museum also features temporary exhibits focusing on 19th-century artists, such as Manet and Degas.

For more Paris art galleries **See pp36–7**

Left *Blue Dancers* (1890), Degas Right *La Belle Angèle* (1889), Gauguin

Musée d'Orsay Collections

The Impressionists
One of the best Impressionist collections in the world. Admirers of Manet, Monet and Renoir will not be disappointed.

The Post-Impressionists
The artists who moved on to a newer interpretation of Impressionism are equally well represented, including Matisse, Toulouse-Lautrec and the towering figure of Van Gogh.

School of Pont-Aven
Paul Gauguin *(see p13)* was at the centre of the group of artists associated with Pont-Aven in Brittany. His work here includes the carved door panels known as the *House of Pleasure* (1901).

Art Nouveau
Art Nouveau is synonymous with Paris, with many metro stations retaining entrances built in that style. Pendants and bottles by René-Jules Lalique (1860–1945) are among the examples.

Symbolism
This vast collection includes works by Gustav Klimt (1862–1918), Edvard Munch (1863–1944) and James Whistler's (1834–1903) 1871 portrait of his mother.

Romanticism
The Romantics wanted to heighten awareness of the spiritual world. One striking work is *The Tiger Hunt* (1854) by Eugène Delacroix (1798–1863).

Floorplan: the collections

Key

- Ground floor
- Middle level
- Upper level

Sculpture
The collection includes pieces by Rodin *(see p111)* and satirical carvings of politicians by Honoré Daumier (1808–79).

Naturalism
Naturalist painters intensified nature in their work. *Haymaking* (1877) by Jules Bastien-Lepage (1848–84) is a fine example.

Nabis
The Nabis Movement moved art into a more decorative form. Pierre Bonnard (1867–1947) is one of its exponents.

Photography Collection
Some 10,000 early photographs include work by Bonnard, Degas and photographer Julia Margaret Cameron (1815–79).

Sign up for DK's email newsletter on traveldk.com

Top 10 Impressionists

(Prices for Impressionist paintings are considered a financial barometer for the art world. One of Monet's Waterlily paintings fetched almost US$80 million in 2008.)

The Impressionist Movement

Regarded as the starting point of modern art, the Impressionist Movement is probably the best-known and best-loved art movement in the world – certainly if prices at auction and the crowds in the Musée d'Orsay's galleries are anything to go by. The movement started in France, and almost all its leading figures were French, including the

Cathedral at Rouen (1892–3), Claude Monet

Parisian-born British artist Alfred Sisley. Impressionism was a reaction against the formality and Classicism insisted upon by the Académie des Beaux-Arts in Paris, who were very much the art establishment and decided what would or would not be exhibited at the Paris Salon. The term "impressionism" was actually coined by a critic of the style, who dismissed the 1872 Monet painting Impression: Sunrise, *which is now on display at the Musée Marmottan (see p153). The artists themselves then adopted the term. The style influenced painters such as Van Gogh and was to have a lasting influence on 19th- and 20th-century art.*

Dancing at the Moulin de la Galette (1876), Renoir

⭐10 Eiffel Tower

The most distinctive symbol of Paris, the Eiffel Tower (Tour Eiffel) was much maligned by critics when it rose on the city's skyline in 1889 as part of the Universal Exhibition, but its graceful symmetry soon made it the star attraction. At 312 m (1,023 ft) high, it was the world's tallest building until it was surpassed by New York's Empire State Building in 1931. Despite its delicate appearance, it weighs 10,100 metric tons and engineer Gustave Eiffel's construction was so sound that it never sways more than 9 cm (3.5 in) in strong winds.

Eiffel Tower from the Trocadéro

Top 10 Features

1. Viewing Gallery
2. Ironwork
3. Lighting
4. View from the Trocadéro
5. Gustave Eiffel's Office
6. First Level
7. Second Level
8. Hydraulic Lift Mechanism
9. Bust of Gustave Eiffel
10. Champ-de-Mars

🍴 There are restaurants and snack bars on levels 1 and 2 and a champagne bar on level 3, plus food kiosks around the base.

🎫 Beat the queues by booking your visit in advance either by phone or online.

• *Champ-de-Mars, 7e*
• *Map B4* • *08 92 70 12 39* • *www.tour-eiffel.com*
• *Open: Lift 9:30am– 11:45pm daily; last adm for top 10:30pm (mid-Jun– 1 Sep: 9am–12:45am; last adm for top 11pm); Stairs 9:30am–6:30pm daily; last adm 6pm (mid-Jul–1 Sep: 9am– 12:45am; last adm midnight)* • *Admission: €4.70 (stairs); €8.10–€13.10 (lift)*
• *Disabled access first and second levels only*

Viewing Gallery
At 276 m (906 ft), the view is stupendous, stretching for 80 km (50 miles) on a clear day. You can also see Gustave Eiffel's sitting room on this level.

Ironwork
The complex pattern of the girders, held together by 2.5 million rivets, stabilizes the tower in high winds. The 18,000 metal parts can expand up to 15 cm (6 in) on hot days.

For more on the Eiffel Tower Quarter See pp110–17

First Level
You can walk the 345 steps to the 57 m (187 ft) high first level and enjoy a meal at the restaurant 58 Tour Eiffel. Renovation of this floor is currently underway until late 2013.

Second Level
At 116 m (380 ft) high, this is the location of the Jules Verne Restaurant, one of the finest in Paris for both food and views (see p117). It is reached by a private lift in the south pillar.

Hydraulic Lift Mechanism
The 1899 lift mechanism is still in operation and travels some 103,000 km (64,000 miles) a year. The uniformed guard clinging to the outside is a model.

Bust of Gustave Eiffel
This bust of the tower's creator, by Antoine Bourdelle, was placed below his remarkable achievement, by the north pillar, in 1929.

Champ-de-Mars
The long gardens of this former parade ground (right) stretch from the base of the tower to the École Militaire (military school).

Caricature of Gustave Eiffel with his tower

The Life of Gustave Eiffel
Born in Dijon, Gustave Eiffel (1832–1923) was an engineer and builder who made his name building bridges and viaducts. Eiffel was famous for the graceful designs and master craftsmanship of his wrought-iron constructions. He once remarked that his famous tower was "formed by the wind itself". In 1890 he became immersed in the study of aerodynamics, and kept an office in the tower until his death, using it for experiments. In 1889, when the Eiffel Tower was erected, its creator was awarded the Légion d'Honneur for the achievement.

Lighting
A 200,000-watt lighting system makes the Eiffel Tower a spectacular night-time sight. It sparkles like a giant Christmas tree for 5 minutes every hour from dusk until 1am.

View from the Trocadéro
Day or night, the best approach for a first-time view of the tower is from the Trocadéro (see p136), which affords a monumental vista from the terrace across the Seine.

Gustave Eiffel's Office
Located at the top of the tower is Gustave Eiffel's office, which has been restored to its original condition. It displays wax models of Thomas Edison and Eiffel himself.

TOP 10 Notre-Dame

The "heart" of the country, both geographically and spiritually, the Cathedral of Notre-Dame (Our Lady) stands majestic on the Ile de la Cité. After Pope Alexander III laid the foundation stone in 1163, an army of craftsmen toiled for 170 years to realize Bishop Maurice de Sully's magnificent design. Almost destroyed during the Revolution, the Gothic masterpiece was restored in 1841–64 by architect Viollet-le-Duc. Some 130 m (430 ft) in length with a high-vaulted nave and double side aisles, it also contains France's largest organ.

Flying Buttresses
The striking buttresses supporting the cathedral's east façade are by Jean Ravy. The best view is from Square Jean XXIII.

Notre-Dame seen from the River Seine

🍴 There are cafés opposite the Square Jean XXIII.

🎵 Free organ recitals on Sunday afternoons.

• 6 Parvis Notre-Dame-Place Jean-Paul II, 75004 • Map N4 • 01 53 10 07 00 (towers); 01 42 34 56 10 (cathedral)
• Open: cathedral 7:45am–6:45pm daily (to 7:30pm Sat–Sun); towers Apr–Sep: 10am–6:30pm daily (to 11pm Sat–Sun Jun–Aug); Oct–Mar: 10am–5:30pm daily
• Adm (towers): €8.50 (€5.50 18–25s, under-18s free, free 1st Sun of month)

Top 10 Features

1. West Front
2. Portal of the Virgin
3. Flying Buttresses
4. The Towers
5. Galerie des Chimières
6. The Spire
7. Rose Windows
8. Statue of the Virgin and Child
9. Choir Stalls
10. Treasury

West Front
The glorious entrance to the cathedral *(right)* is through three elaborately carved portals. Biblical scenes, sculpted in the Middle Ages, represent the life of the Virgin, the Last Judgment and the Life of St Anne. Above is the Gallery of Kings of Judaea and Israel.

Portal of the Virgin
The splendid stone tympanum *(left)* was carved in the 13th century and shows the Virgin Mary's death and glorious coronation in heaven. However, the Virgin and Child carving seen between the doors is a modern replica.

The Towers
The twin towers are 69 m (226 ft) high; climb the 387 steps of the north tower for splendid vistas. The south tower houses the Emmanuel Bell, weighing 13 tonnes.

For more Paris churches See pp40–41

5 Galerie des Chimères

Lurking between the towers are the famous gargoyles (chimères), placed here by Viollet-le-Duc to ward off evil.

Floorplan of the Cathedral

7 Rose Windows

Three great rose windows adorn the north, south and west façades, but only the north window (below) retains its 13th-century stained glass, depicting the Virgin surrounded by figures from the Old Testament. The south window shows Christ encircled by the Apostles.

8 Statue of the Virgin and Child

Also known as Notre-Dame de Paris (Our Lady of Paris), this beautiful 14th-century statue was brought to the cathedral from the chapel of St Aignan. It stands against the southeast pillar of the transept, at the entrance to the chancel.

9 Choir Stalls

More than half of the original stalls commissioned by Louis XIV survive. Among the beautifully carved work on the 78 stalls are scenes from the Life of the Virgin.

10 Treasury

Ancient manuscripts, reliquaries and religious garments are housed in the sacristy. The Crown of Thorns is on public view on the first Friday of every month.

Cathedral Guide

Enter through the West Front. The stairs to the towers are outside to your left. Ahead, the central nave soars to a height of 35 m (115 ft), while 24 side chapels line the walls. These contain the "May" paintings by Charles le Brun, donated by the goldsmiths' guild each May in the 17th–18th centuries. The fine transept across the nave is the best place to admire the three rose windows. Remnants of the 14th-century stone screen can be seen on the north and south bays of the chancel. Nicolas Coustou's *Pietà* stands behind the high altar, flanked by statues of Louis XIII by Coustou and Louis XIV by Antoine Coysevox.

6 The Spire

The 96-m (315-ft) spire was added by Viollet-le-Duc. Next to the Apostles statues on the roof is one of the architect, admiring his work.

Left **Joan of Arc** Centre **Empress Josephine** Right **Napoleon**

Famous Visitors to Notre-Dame

Joan of Arc
1 The French patriot Jeanne d'Arc (1412–31), who defended her country against the invading English, had a posthumous trial here in 1455, despite having been burnt at the stake 24 years earlier. At the re-trial she was found to be innocent of heresy.

François II and Mary Stuart
2 Mary Stuart (1542–87) (Mary Queen of Scots) had been raised in France and married the Dauphin in 1558. He ascended the throne as François II in 1559 and the king and queen were crowned in Notre-Dame.

Napoleon
3 The coronation of Napoleon (1769–1821) in Notre-Dame in 1804 saw the eager general seize the crown from Pope Pius VII and crown himself emperor and his wife Josephine, empress.

Josephine
4 Josephine's (1763–1814) reign as Empress of France lasted only five years; Napoleon divorced her in 1809.

Pope Pius VII
5 In 1809 Pope Pius VII (1742–1823), who oversaw the Notre-Dame coronation, was taken captive when the emperor declared the Papal States to be part of France. The pope was imprisoned at Fontainebleau, 50 km (30 miles) south of Paris.

Philip the Fair
6 In 1302 the first States General parliament was formally opened at Notre-Dame by Philip IV (1268–1314), otherwise known as Philip the Fair. He greatly increased the governing power of the French royalty.

Henry VI of England
7 Henry VI (1421–71) became King of England at the age of one. Like his father, Henry V, he also claimed France and was crowned in Notre-Dame in 1430.

Marguerite of Valois
8 In August 1572, Marguerite (1553–1589), sister of Charles IX, stood in the Notre-Dame chancel during her marriage to the protestant Henri of Navarre (1553–1610), while he stood alone by the door.

Henri of Navarre
9 As a Protestant Huguenot, Henri's marriage to the Catholic Marguerite resulted in uprising and massacres. In 1589 he became Henri IV, the first Bourbon king of France, and converted to Catholicism, declaring that "Paris is well worth a mass".

Charles de Gaulle
10 On 26 August 1944, Charles de Gaulle entered Paris and attended a Magnificat service to celebrate the liberation of Paris, despite the fact that hostile snipers were still at large outside the cathedral.

For more historic events in Paris **See pp44–5**

Top 10 Events in Notre-Dame History

The Man Who Saved Notre-Dame

By 1831, when Victor Hugo's novel Notre-Dame de Paris *(The Hunchback of Notre-Dame) was published, the cathedral was in a sorry state of decay. Even for the crowning of Emperor Napoleon in 1804, the setting for such ceremonious state occasions was crumbling and had to be disguised with wall*

Novelist Victor Hugo

hangings and ornamentation. During the Revolution, the cathedral was even sold to a scrap dealer, but was never actually demolished. Hugo was determined to save the country's spiritual heart and helped mount a successful campaign to restore Notre-Dame before it was too late; the man chosen to design and oversee the restoration was Eugène Emmanuel Viollet-le-Duc (1814–1879). Paris-born, Viollet-le-Duc had already proved his skill in restoration work, as evidenced by the cathedrals in Amiens and Laon, and on the spectacular walled city of Carcassonne in southern France. Work began in 1841 and continued for 23 years until the building was finished more or less as we see it today. Viollet-le-Duc later went on to restore Sainte-Chapelle nearby (see pp30–31).

The Hunchback of Notre-Dame

Hugo's 1831 novel tells the story of Quasimodo, a hunchbacked bell-ringer at Notre-Dame, who falls in love with gypsy girl Esmeralda.

For more novels set in Paris **See pp46–7**

🔟 Sacré-Coeur

One of the most photographed images of the city, the spectacular white outline of Sacré-Coeur (Sacred Heart) watches over Paris from its highest point. The basilica was built as a memorial to the 58,000 French soldiers killed during the Franco-Prussian War (1870–71). It took 46 years to build and was finally completed in 1923 at a cost of 40 million francs (6 million euros). Priests still pray for the souls of the dead here, 24 hours a day, as they have since 1885. People flock here for the panoramic views – at sunset, in particular, there are few sights in Paris more memorable.

Sacré-Coeur dome

🍴 Avoid the crowds and head to 23 rue des Abbesses and grab a bite at the St Jean or try Café Arrosé at 123 rue Caulaincourt.

🎵 An evocative sung Mass takes place on Sundays at 11am.

- Parvis de la Basilique du Sacré-Coeur, 75018
- Map F1
- 01 53 41 89 00
- www.sacre-coeur-montmartre.com
- Open 6am–10:30pm, last entry 10:15pm (basilica), 9:30am–5:30pm (dome) daily. Crypt opening times vary.
- Admission €8 (dome and crypt only)

Top 10 Features

1. Great Mosaic of Christ
2. Crypt Vaults
3. Bronze Doors
4. Dome
5. Statue of Christ
6. Bell Tower
7. Equestrian Statues
8. Stained-Glass Gallery
9. Façade
10. The Funicular

Great Mosaic of Christ

A glittering Byzantine mosaic of Christ *(right)*, created by Luc Olivier Merson between 1912–22, decorates the vault over the chancel. It represents France's devotion to the Sacred Heart.

Crypt Vaults

The arched vaults of the crypt house a chapel containing the heart of Alexandre Legentil, one of the advocates of Sacré-Coeur.

Bronze Doors

The doors of the portico entrance are beautifully decorated with bronze relief sculptures depicting the Last Supper *(right)* and other scenes from the life of Christ

For more Paris churches See pp40–41

The Dome

The distinctive egg-shaped dome of the basilica is the second-highest viewpoint in Paris after the Eiffel Tower. Reached via a spiral staircase, vistas can stretch as far as 48 km (30 miles) on a clear day.

Statue of Christ

The basilica's most important statue shows Christ giving a blessing. It is symbolically placed in a niche over the main entrance, above the two equestrian statues.

Bell Tower

The *campanile*, designed by Lucien Magne and added in 1904, is 80 m (262 ft) high. One of the heaviest bells in the world, the 19-ton La Savoyarde hangs in the belfry. Cast in Annecy in 1895, it was donated by the dioceses of Savoy.

Equestrian Statues

Two striking bronze statues of French saints stand on the portico above the main entrance, cast by H Lefêbvre *(below)*. One is of Joan of Arc, the other of Saint Louis.

Stained-Glass Gallery

One level of the great dome is encircled by stained-glass windows. From here there is a grand view over the whole interior.

The Franco-Prussian War

In 1870, as Prussia made moves to take over Germany, France was also threatened by its military power. Two Catholic businessmen in Paris vowed to build a church dedicated to the Sacred Heart if France were spared the Prussian onslaught. France declared war on Prussia in July, but she was ill-prepared and in September Napoleon III was captured. Parisians held fast, however, defending their city with home-made weapons and eating dogs, cats and rats. But by January 1871 they surrendered.

Captured French soldier taking leave of his wife

Façade

Architect Paul Abadie (1812–1884) employed a mix of domes, turrets and Classical features in his design. The Château-Landon stone secretes calcite when wet and bleaches the façade white.

The Funicular

To avoid the steep climb up to Sacré-Coeur, take the *funiculaire* cable railway and enjoy the views at leisure. It runs from the end of rue Foyatier, near Square Willette.

Arc de Triomphe

The best day to visit the world's most familiar triumphal arch is 2 December, the date that marks Napoleon's victory at the Battle of Austerlitz in 1805, when the sun, setting behind the Champs-Elysées and the Arc de Triomphe, creates a spectacular halo around the building. Work began on the 50-m (164-ft) arch in 1806 but was not completed until 1836, due, in part, to Napoleon's fall from power. Four years later, Napoleon's funeral procession passed beneath it, on its way to his burial in Les Invalides (see pp32–3). Today the arch is a focal point for numerous public events.

Arc de Triomphe pediment

🕐 Try to get here early, as the morning light shows the golden tone of the stonework at its best.

☕ Enjoy a coffee and the old-world charm of Le Fouquet (99 av des Champs-Elysées) – expensive, but worth the treat.

• Place Charles-de-Gaulle, 75008 • 01 55 37 73 77 (enquiries)
• http://arc-de-triomphe.monuments-nationaux.fr
• Map B2 • Open Apr–Sep: 10am–11pm daily; Oct–Mar: 10am–10:30pm daily (last adm 45 mins before closing). Closed 1 Jan, 1 May, 8 May (am), 14 Jul (am), 11 Nov, 25 Dec and for major events
• Admission €9.50

Top 10 Features

1. Viewing Platform
2. Tomb of the Unknown Soldier
3. Museum
4. Departure of the Volunteers in 1792
5. Frieze
6. Triumph of Napoleon
7. Battle of Austerlitz
8. Battle of Aboukir
9. General Marceau's Funeral
10. Thirty Shields

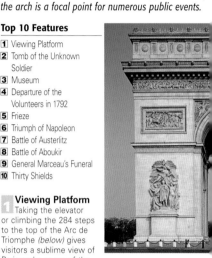

Viewing Platform

Taking the elevator or climbing the 284 steps to the top of the Arc de Triomphe *(below)* gives visitors a sublime view of Paris and a sense of the arch's dominant position in the centre of the Place de l'Etoile. To the east is the magnificent Champs-Elysées *(see p103)* and to the west is the Grande Arche of La Défense *(see p151)*. There are another 40 steps after the lift.

Tomb of the Unknown Soldier

In the centre of the arch flickers the eternal flame on the Tomb of the Unknown Soldier, a victim of World War I buried on 11 November 1920. It is symbolically re-ignited every day at 6:30pm.

Museum
Within the arch is a small but interesting museum which tells the history of its construction and gives details of various celebrations and funerals that the arch has seen over the years. The more recent of these are shown in a short video.

Triumph of Napoleon
As you look at the arch from the Champs-Elysées, the relief on the left base shows the restored *Triumph of Napoleon*. This celebrates the Treaty of Vienna peace agreement signed in 1810, when Napoleon's empire was in its heyday.

Battle of Austerlitz
Another battle victory is shown on a frieze *(above)* on the arch's northern side. It depicts Napoleon's heavily outnumbered troops breaking the ice on Lake Satschan in Austria, a tactic which drowned thousands of enemy troops.

Battle of Aboukir
Above the *Triumph of Napoleon* carving is this scene showing Napoleonic victory over the Turks in 1799. The same victory was commemorated on canvas in 1806 by the French painter Antoine Gros and is now on display at the Palace of Versailles *(see p151)*.

General Marceau's Funeral
Marceau died in battle against the Austrian army in 1796, after a famous victory against them only the previous year. His funeral is depicted in this frieze *(right)*, which is located above the *Departure of the Volunteers in 1792*.

Departure of the Volunteers in 1792
One of the most striking sculptures is on the front right base *(right)*. It shows French citizens leaving to defend their nation against Austria and Prussia.

Thirty Shields
Immediately below the top of the arch runs a row of 30 shields, each carrying the name of a Napoleonic victory.

Frieze
A frieze running around the arch shows French troops departing *(or battle (east)* and their victorious return *(west)*.

The Great Axis
The Arc de Triomphe is at the centre of three arches and together they create a grand vision of which even Napoleon would have been proud. The emperor was responsible for the first two, placing the Arc de Triomphe directly in line with the Arc de Triomphe du Carrousel in front of the Louvre *(see pp8–11)*, which also celebrates the 1805 victory at Austerlitz. In 1989, the trio was completed with the Grande Arche at La Défense. The 8km-long (5-mile) *Grand Axe* (Great Axis) runs from here to the Glass Pyramid at the Louvre.

Centre Georges Pompidou

Today one of the world's most famous pieces of modern architecture, the Pompidou Centre opened in 1977, when architects Richard Rogers and Renzo Piano startled everyone by turning the building "inside out", with brightly coloured pipes displayed on the façade. Designed as a cross-cultural arts complex, it houses the excellent Musée National d'Art Moderne (Modern Art Museum) as well as a cinema, library, shops and performance space. The outside forecourt is a popular gathering-spot for tourists and locals alike.

Centre Georges Pompidou façade

🏠 The centre's café is pleasant and has free Wi-Fi access. For something grander, head to Georges, the roof-top brasserie.

🎟 Buy tickets online to avoid the queues.

• Place Georges Pompidou 75004 • Map P2 • www.centre pompidou.fr • 01 44 78 12 33 • Open 11am–9pm Wed–Mon (11pm Thu); closed 1 May • Adm (museum) €8–13; Brancusi's Studio free (open 2–6pm Wed–Mon). Free 1st Sun of the month, under 18s free, under 26s free (EU only).

Top 10 Features

1. Escalator
2. Top-Floor View
3. The Piazza
4. Stravinsky Fountains
5. Pipes
6. Bookshop
7. Brancusi's Studio
8. Man with a Guitar
9. Violinist at the Window
10. La Baigneuse

Escalator
One of the building's most striking and popular features is the external escalator *(right)*, which climbs, snake-like, up the front of the centre in its plexi-glass tube. The view gets better and better as you rise high above the activity in the Centre's forecourt, before arriving at the top for the best view of all.

Top-Floor View
The view from the top of the Pompidou Centre is spectacular. The Eiffel Tower is visible, as is Montmartre in the north and the Tour Montparnasse to the south. On clear days views can stretch as far as La Défense *(see p151).*

The Piazza
Visitors and locals gather in the open space in front of the Centre to enjoy the variety of street performers and changing installations of monumental sculptures, which are often related to shows at the Centre.

4 Stravinsky Fountain

This colourful fountain in Place Igor Stravinsky was designed by Niki de Saint-Phalle and Jean Tinguely as part of the Pompidou Centre development. Inspired by composer Stravinsky's ballet *The Firebird* (1910), the bird spins and sprays water!

9 Violinist at the Window

French artist Henri Matisse (1869–1964) was one of the proponents of the short-lived Fauvist Movement, which advocated the use of bold, strong colours. *Violinist at the Window* was painted in 1917–18 and can be interpreted as a self-portrait.

10 La Baigneuse

Joan Miró (1893–1983) was born in Barcelona but moved to Paris in 1920. His simplistic yet evocative *La Baigneuse (The Swimmer)* (1924) depicts an immense blue ocean, watched over by a crescent moon. A woman's form is almost lost amid the waves; her tendrils of yellow hair reflect their serpentine lines.

5 Pipes

Part of the shock factor of the Pompidou Centre is that the utility pipes are outside the building. Not only that, they are vividly coloured: bright green for water, yellow for electricity and blue for air conditioning.

6 Bookshop

The ground-floor bookshop sells a range of postcards, posters of major works in the Modern Art Museum and books on artists associated with Paris.

7 Brancusi's Studio

The studio of revolutionary Romanian sculptor Constantin Brancusi (1876–1957) is to the north of the centre, displaying his abstract works.

8 Man with a Guitar

Within the Modern Art Museum, this 1914 work by artist Georges Braque (1882–1963) is one of the most striking of the Cubist Movement.

Centre Guide

The Centre is home to various institutions. The Museum of Modern Art (Mnam) is on levels 4 and 5, the cinema on level 1. Check at the information desk or on the website for details about the temporary shows, rehangs of works on level 5 and the contemporary art "happenings". Displays at the Mnam often change and some works are now shared with its sister institution in Metz.

The Panthéon

Today Paris's beautiful Panthéon building is a fitting final resting place for the nation's great figures. However, it was originally built as a church, on the instigation of Louis XV to celebrate his recovery from a serious bout of gout in 1744. Dedicated to Sainte Geneviève, the structure was finished in 1790 and was intended to look like the Pantheon in Rome, hence the name; in fact it more closely resembles St Paul's Cathedral in London. During the Revolution it was turned into a mausoleum, but Napoleon gave it back to the church in 1806. It was later deconsecrated, handed back to the church once more, before finally becoming a public building in 1885.

Panthéon façade

🍴 Crêpes à Gogo (12 rue Soufflot, open 7am–11pm) is an ideal pit stop for a crêpe, coffee and an ice cream.

⏱ Ticket sales stop 45 minutes before closing time, so arrive on time.

• Place du Panthéon, 75005 • Map N6
• 01 44 32 18 00
• http://pantheon.monuments-nationaux.fr
• Open Apr–Sep: 10am–6:30pm daily; Oct–Mar: 10am–6pm daily. Closed 1 Jan, 1 May, 25 Dec
• Admission €8.50 (under 25s €5.50, under 18s and EU under 25s free)
• No dis access

Top 10 Features

1. Dome
2. Dome Galleries
3. Crypt
4. Frescoes of Sainte Geneviève
5. Foucault's Pendulum
6. Monument to Diderot
7. Façade
8. Pediment Relief
9. Tomb of Voltaire
10. Tomb of Victor Hugo

Dome
Inspired by Sir Christopher Wren's design of St Paul's Cathedral in London, as well as by the Dôme Church at Les Invalides *(see p32)*, this iron-framed dome *(below left)* is made up of three layers. At the top a narrow opening only lets in a tiny amount of natural light, in keeping with the building's sombre purpose.

Dome Galleries
A staircase leads to the galleries immediately below the dome, affording spectacular 360-degree panoramic views of Paris. The pillars surrounding the galleries are both decorative and functional, providing essential support for the dome.

Crypt
The crypt is eerily impressive in its scale compared to most tiny, dark church crypts. Here lie the tombs and memorials to worthy French citizens, including the prolific French writer Emile Zola *(see p47)*

For more Paris burial sites **See p156**

4 Frescoes of Sainte Geneviève

Delicate murals by 19th-century artist Pierre Puvis de Chavannes, on the south wall of the nave, tell the story of Sainte Geneviève, the patron saint of Paris. In 451 she is believed to have saved the city from invasion by the barbaric Attila the Hun and his hordes due to the power of her prayers.

6 Monument to Diderot

French philosopher Denis Diderot (1713–84) is honoured by this grand 1925 monument by Alphonse Terroir.

7 Façade

The Panthéon's façade was inspired by Roman design. The 22 Corinthian columns support both the portico roof and *bas-reliefs*.

Panthéon Floorplan

5 Foucault's Pendulum

In 1851 French physicist Jean Foucault (1819–68) followed up an earlier experiment to prove the earth's rotation by hanging his famous pendulum from the dome of the Panthéon. The plane of the pendulum's swing rotated 11° clockwise each hour in relation to the floor, thereby proving Foucault's theory.

8 Pediment Relief

The *bas-relief* above the entrance *(below)* shows a female figure, representing France, handing out laurels to the great men of the nation – the same way that Greeks and Romans honoured their heroes.

9 Tomb of Voltaire

A statue of the great writer, wit and philosopher Voltaire (1694–1788) stands in front of his tomb.

10 Tomb of Victor Hugo

The body of the French author *(see p46)* was carried to the Panthéon in a pauper's hearse, at his own request.

Louis Braille

One of the most influential citizens to be buried in the Panthéon is Louis Braille. Born in France in 1809, Braille became blind at the age of three; at nine he attended the National Institute for the Young Blind in Paris and proved to be a gifted student. He continued at the Institute as a teacher and, in 1829, had the idea of adapting a coding system in use by the army, by turning words and letters into raised dots on card. Reading braille transformed the lives of blind people forever. Its inventor died in 1852.

🔟 Sainte-Chapelle

*This Gothic masterpiece, built by Louis IX (1214–70)
as a shrine for his holy relics of the passion and
completed in 1248, is considered the most beautiful
church in Paris, not least for its 15 stained-glass
windows soaring 15 m (50 ft) to a star-covered
vaulted roof. The church was damaged during the
Revolution but restored in the mid-19th century.*

Sainte-Chapelle façade

🚇 For a little 1920s-
style elegance, try
**Brasserie des Deux
Palais** on the corner
of boulevard du Palais
and rue de Lutèce.

👓 A pair of binoculars
comes in handy if
you want to see
the uppermost
glass panels.

• 6 blvd du Palais, 75001
• Map N3
• 01 53 40 60 97
• Open Mar–Oct:
9:30am–6pm (mid-May–
mid-Sep: till 9pm Wed);
Nov–Feb: 9am–5pm;
closed 1 Jan, 1 May,
25 Dec
• Admission €8.50, €5.50
for under 25s (free 1st
Sun of month Nov–Mar).
€11 joint adm to
Conciergerie (see p69).
Temp exhibitions €1.50
extra. Ticket sales stop
30 mins before closing.
• Restricted disabled
access (48 hrs advance
notice for wheelchairs)
• http://sainte-chapelle.
monuments-nationaux.fr

Top 10 Features

1. Upper Chapel Entrance
2. Rose Window
3. Window of Christ's Passion
4. Apostle Statues
5. Window of the Relics
6. The Spire
7. Main Portal
8. St Louis' Oratory
9. Seats of the Royal Family
10. Evening Concerts

1 Upper Chapel Entrance

As you emerge, via a spiral
staircase, into this airy
space *(right)*, the effect of
light and colour is utterly
breathtaking. The 13th-
century stained-glass
windows, the oldest extant
in Paris, separated by stone
columns *(below)*, depict
Biblical scenes from
Genesis through to the
Crucifixion. To "read" the
windows, start in the lower
left panel and follow each
row left to right, from
bottom to top.

2 Rose Window

The Flamboyant-style
rose window, depicting
St John's vision of the
Apocalypse in 86 panels,
was replaced by Charles
VIII in 1485. The green
and yellow hues are at
their brightest at sunset.

5 Window of the Relics

Another striking window *(below)*, this tells the story of St Helena and the True Cross and of St Louis bringing his many relics to Sainte-Chapelle.

6 The Spire
The open latticework and pencil-thin shape give the 75-m (245-ft) *flèche* (spire) a delicate appearance. Three earlier church spires burned down – this one was erected in 1853.

Relics of the Passion

Louis IX, later St Louis, was the only French king to be canonized. While on his first Crusade in 1239, he purchased the alleged Crown of Thorns from the Emperor of Constantinople, and subsequently other relics, including pieces of the True Cross, nails from the Crucifixion and a few drops of Christ's blood, paying almost three times more for them than for the construction of Sainte-Chapelle itself. The relics reside in Notre-Dame and are only displayed on religious holidays.

7 Main Portal
Like the Upper Chapel, the main portal has two tiers. Its pinnacles are decorated with a crown of thorns as a symbol of the relics within.

3 Window of Christ's Passion
Located above the apse, this stained-glass depiction of the Crucifixion is the chapel's most beautiful window.

4 Apostle Statues
Beautifully carved medieval statues of 12 apostles stand on pillars along the walls. Badly damaged in the Revolution, most have been restored: the bearded apostle *(right)*, fifth on the left, is the only original statue.

8 St Louis' Oratory
In the late 14th century Louis XI added an oratory where he could watch Mass through a small grille in the wall. The chapel originally adjoined the Conciergerie, the former royal palace on the Ile de la Cité *(see p69)*.

9 Seats of the Royal Family
During Mass, the royal family sat in niches located in the fourth bays on both sides of the chapel, away from the congregation.

10 Evening Concerts
Sainte-Chapelle has excellent acoustics. From March to November classical concerts are held here several evenings a week.

🔟 Hôtel des Invalides

*The "invalides" for whom this imposing Hôtel was built were wounded
soldiers of the late 17th century. Louis XIV had the building constructed
between 1671 and 1678, and veterans are still housed here, although
only a dozen or so compared to the original 4,000. They share their
home with the greatest French soldier of them all, Napoleon Bonaparte,
whose body rests in a crypt directly below the golden dome of the
Dôme Church. Other buildings accommodate military offices, the
Musée de l'Armée and smaller military museums.*

Musée de l'Armée façade

🍷 Le Café du Musée,
between the Varenne
metro station and the
Musée Rodin *(see
p111)* is a lovely
spot for a drink.

🎟 A ticket provides
access to all
attractions.

• 129 rue de Grenelle,
75007
• Map D4
• 08 10 11 33 99
• www.invalides.org
• Open Apr–Sep:
10am–6pm daily, until
9pm Tue (Oct–Mar: until
5pm); closed first Mon
of month (except
Jul–Sep), 1 Jan, 1 May,
1 Nov, 25 Dec
• Admission €9 adults;
€7 concessions; under
18s free; under 26s (EU
only) free • Limited
disabled access

Top 10 Features

1. Napoleon's Tomb
2. Golden Dome
3. Musée de l'Armée
4. Dôme Church Ceiling
5. Hôtel des Invalides
6. Church Tombs
7. St-Louis-des-Invalides
8. Invalides Gardens
9. Musée de l'Ordre de la Libération
10. Musée des Plans-Reliefs

Golden Dome
The second church at
the Hôtel was begun in
1677 and took 27 years
to build. Its magnificent
dome stands 107 m
(351 ft) high and
glistens as much
now as it did when
Louis XIV, the
Sun King, had
it first gilded
in 1715.

Napoleon's Tomb
Napoleon's body was
brought here from St Helena
in 1840, some 19 years after
he died. He
rests in splen-
did grandeur in
a cocoon of six
coffins *(left)*,
almost situated
"on the banks
of the Seine"
as was his
personal wish.

Musée de l'Armée
The Army Museum
is one of the largest
collections of militaria in
the world. Enthusiasts will
be absorbed for hours, and
even the casual visitor
will be fascinated. The
"Department Moderne,"
which traces military
history from Louis XIV to
Napoleon III, has been
revamped and is especially
worth a visit *(see p111)*.

4 Dôme Church Ceiling

The colourful, circular painting on the interior of the dome above the crypt is the *Saint Louis in Glory* painted in 1692 by the French artist, Charles de la Fosse. Near the centre is St Louis, who represents Louis XIV, presenting his sword to Christ in the presence of the Virgin and angels.

Hôtel des Invalides Floorplan

9 Musée de l'Ordre de la Libération

The Order of Liberation, France's highest military honour, was created by Général de Gaulle in 1940 to acknowledge contributions during World War II. The museum details the history of the honour and the wartime Free French movement.

5 Hôtel des Invalides

One of the loveliest sights in Paris *(above)*, the Classical façade of the Hôtel is four floors high and 196 m (645 ft) end to end. Features include the dormer windows with their variously shaped shield surrounds.

7 St-Louis-des-Invalides

Adjoining the Dôme Church is the Invalides complex's original church. It is worth seeing for its 17th-century organ, on which the first performance of Berlioz's *Requiem* was given.

10 Musée des Plans-Reliefs

Maps and models of French forts and fortified towns are displayed here and some of them are beautifully detailed, such as the oldest model on display, of Perpignan in 1686.

Hôtel Guide

Approach the Hôtel des Invalides from the Seine for the best view, and then walk around to the south side (by the Dôme Church) to reach the ticket office. You will need a ticket for the museums and to see Napoleon's Tomb. If time is short, concentrate on the Musée de l'Armée, before walking through to the front of the buildings and reaching the impressive cobbled courtyard that is directly in front of the Dôme Church.

6 Church Tombs

Encircling the Dôme Church are the imposing tombs of great French military men, such as Marshal Foch and Marshal Vauban, who revolutionized military fortifications and siege tactics.

8 Invalides Gardens

The approach to the Hôtel is across public gardens and then through a gate into the Invalides Gardens themselves. Designed in 1704, their paths are lined by 17th- and 18th-century cannons.

Left **Mona Lisa**, Musée du Louvre Centre **Musée Carnavalet** Right **Cannons, Musée de l'Armée**

Museums

1 Musée du Louvre
French and Italian sculpture, Greek and Roman antiquities and paintings from the 12th to the 19th centuries are just some of the highlights of the world's largest museum *(see pp8–11)*.

2 Musée Carnavalet
Housed in a grand Marais mansion, this museum presents the history of Paris. The collection includes painting, sculpture and antique furniture, re-creating private residences of the 16th and 17th centuries. There is also a collection of mementoes from the Revolution as well as a wonderful French garden.

3 Musée des Arts Décoratifs
Set over nine levels, adjoining the west end of the Louvre's Richelieu Wing, this decorative arts museum showcases furniture and tableware from the 12th century to the present. The breathtaking anthology of pieces includes Gothic panelling and Renaissance porcelain, to 1970s carpets and chairs by Philippe Starck. Also in the museum is the Musée de la Mode et du Textile, which mounts fashion exhibitions and the Musée de la Publicité, which has exhibitions on advertising *(see p95)*.

4 Musée National du Moyen Age
This splendid museum dedicated to the art of the Middle Ages is known by several names, including the Musée de Cluny after the beautiful mansion in which it is housed, and the Thermes de Cluny after the Roman baths adjoining the museum. Highlights include the famous "Lady and the Unicorn" tapestries, medieval stained glass and exquisite gold crowns and jewellery *(see p120)*.

Muséum National d'Histoire Naturelle garden

5 Muséum National d'Histoire Naturelle
Paris's Natural History Museum in the Jardin des Plantes contains a fascinating collection of animal skeletons, plant fossils, minerals and gemstones. Its highlight is the magnificent Grande Galerie de l'Evolution, which depicts the changing interaction between man and nature during the evolution of life on Earth *(see pp60 & 129)*.

6 musée du quai Branly

In a city dominated by Western art, this museum housing 300,000 artifacts (of which 3,500 are on display at any one time) tips the balance in favour of arts from Africa, Asia, Oceania and the Americas. Must-sees include the African instruments. The striking Jean Nouvel-designed building is an attraction in itself *(see p112)*.

7 Musée de l'Armée

France's proud military history is on display in this museum, housed in a wing of the Hôtel des Invalides. Exhibits include military art and artifacts from ancient times through to the 20th century, with a large modern exhibit devoted to World War II. Napoleon's campaign tent, his stuffed dog, and suits of armour and weapons from medieval times are among the many highlights *(see p111)*.

8 Musée Cognacq-Jay

The Hôtel Donon is a fine setting for this superb collection of 18th-century art, furniture, porcelain and other decorative arts, amassed by the wealthy founders of the Samaritaine department store. Paintings by Rembrandt, Reynolds and other masters alone are worth the visit *(see p85)*.

Venus with Doves, Musée Cognacq-Jay

9 Cité de l'Architecture et du Patrimoine

In the east wing of the Palais Chaillot, the Cité de l'Architecture and the Musée des Monuments Français showcase French architectural heritage and has become one of the world's great architectural centres. The Galeries des Moulages houses models of great French cathedrals *(see pp135–6)*.

10 Musée Jacquemart-André

Set in an elegant private mansion, this museum was once the home of Edouard André and his artist wife Nélie Jacquemart. The museum houses their spectacular personal art collection, which features works by Boucher, Botticelli, Rembrandt and Fragonard, as well as excellent temporary exhibits *(see p105)*.

Left *Bedroom at Arles* (1889), Van Gogh, Musée d'Orsay Right **L'Orangerie**

Art Galleries

Musée d'Orsay
See pp12–15.

Musée Picasso
A favourite of Parisians and visitors alike. The beautifully restored Hôtel Salé *(see p90)* in the Marais is a splendid setting for this extensive collection of paintings, sculptures, drawings and other works by Pablo Picasso (1881–1973), including works from his Cubist period. Large sculptures also adorn the garden and courtyard. The museum is due to reopen in mid-2013, after closing for extensive renovation work *(see p85)*.

Musée Rodin
On a sunny day, head straight for the gardens of the Musée Rodin, next to the Hôtel des Invalides complex, where you can enjoy some of the French sculptor's most famous works, including *The Thinker* and *The Burghers of Calais*, while strolling among the shady trees and rose bushes. Then go inside the beautiful 18th-century mansion, the Hôtel Biron, where Auguste Rodin (1840–1917) lived and worked for nine years, until his death. An extensive collection of his works from throughout his career is on display, plus temporary exhibitions *(see p111).*

Musée National d'Art Moderne
The revolutionary Pompidou Centre is the perfect home for France's outstanding Modern Art Museum. It features some 1,400 works on two levels, one focusing on the artists and movements of the first half of the 20th century, the other featuring art from the 1960s to the present day. The museum often rotates changing displays of works *(see pp26–7).*
◈ Pl Georges Pompidou, 75004 • Map P2
• Open 11am–9pm, Wed–Mon
• Admission charge

Jeu de Paume
This gallery is one of the finest exhibition spaces in the city, being set within a 19th-century real tennis court *(jeu de paume)*. It is a showcase for outstanding photography, film and video.
◈ 1 pl de la Concorde, 75008 • Map D3
• Open noon–9pm Tue, noon–7pm Wed–Fri, 10am–7pm Sat, Sun • Closed 1 Jan, 1 May, 25 Dec • Admission charge

The Thinker, Musée Rodin

 For more on Paris artists See p144

Musée de L'Orangerie

The prime exhibits here are eight of Monet's huge waterlily canvases (see p13) and the gallery, located in a corner of the Tuileries, was renovated to improve their display. The Walter-Guillaume collection covers works by Matisse, Picasso, Modigliani and other modern masters from 1870 to 1930.

⊗ Jardin des Tuileries, 75001 • Map D3
• www.musee-orangerie.fr • Open 9am–6pm Wed–Mon • Admission charge

Espace Montmartre Salvador Dalí

This underground museum with its black walls, lighting effects and soundtrack

Lip Sofa, Salvador Dalí

features some of Dalí's lesser-known works, including bronzes and book illustrations (see p141).

Musée Marmottan-Claude Monet

The Impressionist paintings of Claude Monet are the star attraction at this museum, featuring

some 165 works donated by his son and perhaps the finest collection of his works in the world. They include a series of his late waterlily paintings. Other Impressionist and Realist painters are also represented, and there is a fine collection of illuminated medieval manuscripts (see p153).

Musée Maillol

Works of the French artist Aristide Maillol, including his drawings, engravings, paintings and plastercasts, are the focal point of this museum which was created by his model, Dina Vierny. Other major artists feature in temporary exhibitions (see p121).

Maison Européenne de la Photographie

If you're a photography fan, don't miss this splendid gallery in the Marais. Its exhibitions range from portraits to documentary work, retrospectives to contemporary photographers (see p87).

Left **Jardin du Luxembourg** Centre **Jardin des Plantes** Right **Bois de Boulogne**

🔟 Parks and Gardens

1 Jardin du Luxembourg
Parisians love this centrally located park, set around the Palais du Luxembourg. The sweeping terrace is a great place for people-watching, while locals sunbathe around the Octagonal Lake or sail toy boats in the water. Statues are dotted throughout the grounds, and there is a café *(see p119)*.

2 Jardin des Tuileries
Now officially part of the Louvre, these gardens were laid out in the 17th century as part of the old Palais de Tuileries. They stretch along the Seine between the Louvre and Place de la Concorde. The walkways are lined with lime and chestnut trees. Statues include bronze figures by Aristide Maillol *(see p95)*.

3 Jardin des Plantes
Established as a medicinal herb garden for the king in 1635, these vast botanical gardens are a wonderfully tranquil spot. Paths are lined with statuary and mature trees, including the oldest in Paris, grown from the stump of an *Acacia robinia* dating from 1636 *(see p129)*.

4 Bois de Boulogne
At the weekends, Parisians head for this vast park on the western edge of the city, with a boating lake and paths for cycling, jogging and strolling. There are three formal gardens, lakes and waterfalls, and even two horse-racing tracks. A good spot for a break from the city bustle *(see p152)*.

5 Bois de Vincennes
Another great escape from the city, this park is to the east of Paris what the Bois de Boulogne is to the west. A former royal hunting ground, it was landscaped in the 1860s. Now it features ornamental lakes and waterfalls, a zoo, a funfair and horse-racing tracks *(see p151)*.

6 Parc Monceau
The most fashionable green space in Paris, full of well-heeled residents of the nearby mansions and apartments. The lush landscaping dates from the 18th century, and some architectural follies, such as the Classical colonnade, survive *(see p153)*.

Bois de Boulogne

Share your travel recommendations on traveldk.com

7 Jardins du Palais-Royal
These lovely gardens are enclosed by the 18th-century arcades of the Palais-Royal (see p96). Contemporary sculptures include Daniel Buren's controversial striped columns. ◈ Pl du Palais Royal, 75001 • Map L1

8 Versailles
There are gardens galore at this famous royal palace, from the formal French gardens with their geometric paths and shrubberies, to the wandering paths through the rural-style English garden north of the Petit Trianon. In summer, you can row boats on the lovely cross-shaped Grand Canal (see p151).

9 Parc Montsouris
Located south of Montparnasse, this is the second-largest park in central Paris and very popular with city residents. It was laid out in the English style atop an old granite quarry by landscape architect Adolphe Alphand between 1865 and 1878. Hemingway (see p47) and other writers and artists frequented the park in the mid-20th century. It has a jogging path, lake and a bandstand. ◈ Blvd Jourdan, 75014 • Metro Cité Universitaire

10 Parc des Buttes Chaumont
The great city planner Baron Haussmann created this wonderful retreat northeast of the city centre in 1867, from what was formerly a rubbish dump (see p61). His architects built artificial cliffs, waterfalls, streams and a lake complete with an island crowned by a Roman-style temple. There is also boating available, a café and lovely views of Sacré-Coeur (see pp22–3). ◈ Rue Manin, 75019 • Metro Buttes-Chaumont

Top 10 Fountains

1 Agam Fountain
Jewish architect Yaacov Agam designed this fountain of water and lights. ◈ La Défense • RER La Défense

2 Four Seasons Fountain
Paris looks down on figures representing the Seine and Marne rivers, designed in 1739 by sculptor Edme Bouchardon. ◈ Rue de Grenelle • Map C4

3 Fontaine des Innocents
Carved by Jean Goujon in 1547, this is Paris's only Renaissance fountain. ◈ Square des Innocents • Map N2

4 Medici Fountain
This ornate 17th-century fountain with a pond was built for Marie de Médicis. ◈ Jardin du Luxembourg • Map L6

5 Molière Fountain
This 19th-century fountain honours the French playwright. ◈ Rue de Richelieu • Map E3

6 Observatory Fountain
Four bronze statues representing the continents hold aloft a globe. ◈ Jardin du Luxembourg • Map L6

7 Châtelet Fountain
The two sphinxes of this 1808 fountain commemorate Napoleon's victory in Egypt. ◈ Pl du Châtelet • Map N2

8 Stravinsky Fountain
Birds squirt water from this colourful fountain (see p27).

9 Trocadéro Fountains
Spouting towards the Eiffel Tower, these fountains are illuminated at night (see p17).

10 Versailles Fountains
The fountains at Versailles (see p154) flow to music at weekends in spring and in summer.

Left **Notre-Dame** Centre **Sacré-Coeur** Right **Sainte-Chapelle**

🔟 Places of Worship

1 Notre-Dame
See pp18–21.

2 Sacré-Coeur
See pp22–3.

3 Sainte-Chapelle
Although the chapel is no longer used for worship, the soaring stained-glass windows encourage reverence *(see pp30–31).*

4 Eglise du Dôme
The final resting place of Napoleon Bonaparte is the beautiful Dôme Church in the Hôtel des Invalides complex – an elaborate monument to French Classical style. Built as the chapel for the resident soldiers of the Invalides, its ornate high altar is in stark contrast to the solemn marble chapels surrounding the crypt, which hold the tombs of French military leaders. Its golden dome can be seen for miles around *(see pp32–3).*

5 Panthéon
Patterned after the Pantheon in Rome, this domed late 18th-century church only served as a house of worship for two years, before becoming a monument and burial place for the great and the good of the Revolution era. Later distinguished citizens are also buried here *(see pp28–9).*

6 St-Eustache
For centuries, this monumental Gothic edifice was the "market church" serving the traders of Les Halles. Taking more than 100 years to build, it was finally completed in 1637 and its cavernous interior displays the architectural style of the early Renaissance. Popular Sunday afternoon organ recitals and other classical concerts take place in this wonderfully atmospheric setting *(see p75).*

7 La Madeleine
Designed in the style of a Greek temple in 1764, this prominent church in Paris's financial district, on the edge of the Opéra Quarter, is one of the city's most distinctive sights, spectacularly surrounded by 52 Corinthian columns. The church was consecrated to Mary Magdalene in 1845. The bronze doors,

Baptism of Christ, La Madeleine

which include *bas-reliefs* of the Ten Commandments, and the *Last Judgment* on the south pediment are exterior highlights, while the ornate marble and gold interior has many fine statues, including François Rude's *Baptism of Christ*. It is also a popular venue for classical concerts.
Ⓢ Pl de la Madeleine, 75008 • Map D3 • Open 9:30am–7pm daily (services vary) • Free

Grande Synagogue de la Victoire

8 Built in the late 19th century, this elaborate synagogue is the second-largest in Europe. The building is open only to those wishing to attend services and to groups who have arranged a visit in advance. Other smaller synagogues can be found in the Marais, which has a large Jewish community, including one at 10 rue Pavée, built in 1913 by Hector Guimard, the architect who designed the city's Art Nouveau metro stations. ◈ 44 rue de la Victoire, 75009 • Map E2

Mosquée de Paris

9 The city's Grand Mosque was built during the 1920s as a tribute to North African Muslims who gave military support to France during World War I. It features beautiful Moorish architecture, executed by craftsmen brought over from North Africa, and a peaceful interior courtyard (see p129).

St-Sulpice

10 Outstanding frescoes in the Chapel of the Angels by Eugène Delacroix are the highlight of this 17th-century church's otherwise sober interior. With more than 6,500 pipes, its organ, designed by Jean-François Chalgrin in 1776, is one of the largest in the world. The novelist Victor Hugo married Adèle Foucher here in 1822 (see p119).

St-Sulpice façade

Left **Conciergerie** Right **Hôtel de Ville**

Historic Buildings

Hôtel des Invalides
See pp32–3.

Versailles
Louis XIV turned his father's old hunting lodge into the largest palace in Europe and moved his court here in 1678. It was the royal residence for more than a century until Louis XVI and his queen Marie-Antoinette fled during the Revolution (see p151).

Conciergerie
Originally home to the care-taker and guards of the Palais de Justice, the Conciergerie was turned into a jail at the end of the 14th century. It took its place in history during the Revolution, when more than 4,000 citizens (including Marie-Antoinette) were held prisoner here, half of whom were guillotined. It remained a prison until 1914 (see p69).

Palais de Justice
The enormous building that now houses the French law courts and judiciary dates back to Roman times and was the royal palace until the 14th century, when Charles V moved the court to the Marais. During

Palais de Justice

the Revolution, thousands were sentenced to death in the Première Chambre Civile, allegedly the former bedroom of Louis IX (see p70).

Hôtel Dieu
The Hôtel Dieu, now the hospital for central Paris, was built on the site of a foundling home in 1866–78; the original 12th-century building on the Ile de la Cité was demolished during the urban renewal schemes of the 19th century. A monument in the courtyard commemorates a courageous battle here in 1944 when Paris police held out against the Nazis. ⊗ 1 pl du Parvis Notre-Dame, 75004 • Map N4

Palais de l'Elysée
This imposing palace has been the official residence of the President of the French Republic since 1873. It was built as a private mansion in 1718 and subsequently owned by Madame de Pompadour, mistress of Louis XV, who extended the English-style gardens to the Champs-Elysées. Napoleon signed his abdication here in 1815 (see p105).

Hôtel de Ville
Paris's city hall sports an elaborate façade, with ornate stonework, statues and a turret-ed roof. It is a 19th-century re-construction of the original town hall, which was burned down in the Paris Commune of 1871

(see p45). Though the pedestrianized square in front is pleasant now, it was once the site of gruesome executions: Ravaillac, assassin of Henri IV, was quartered alive here in 1610. ◎ *4 pl de l'Hôtel de Ville, 75001 • Map P3 • 01 42 76 40 40 • Open for group tours only (booking essential: 01 42 76 54 04) • Free*

Palais-Royal
This former royal palace now houses State offices. Built by Cardinal Richelieu in 1632, it passed to the Crown on his death 10 years later and was the childhood home of Louis XIV. The dukes of Orléans acquired it in the 18th century. ◎ *Pl du Palais Royal, 75005 • Map L1 • Closed to the public*

La Sorbonne
The city's great university had humble beginnings in 1253 as a college for 16 poor students to study theology. France's first printing house was also established here in 1469. After suppression during the Revolution it became the University of Paris *(see p119).*

Palais du Luxembourg
Marie de Médicis had architect Salomon de Brosse model this palace after her childhood home, the Pitti Palace in Florence. Shortly after its completion she was exiled by her son, Louis XIII. It was seized from the Crown during the Revolution to become a prison and it now houses the French Senate. Nearby is the Musée du Luxembourg. ◎ *15 rue de Vaugirard, 75006 • Map L6 • 01 44 54 19 49 • Open for reserved tours only; gardens open dawn-dusk*

Palais du Luxembourg

Left **Charlemagne crowned as Holy Roman Emperor** Right **Paris Commune burning of the city**

Historical Events in Paris

1 Arrival of the Parisii

Although the remains of Neolithic settlements have been found dating back to 4500 BC, the first inhabitants are considered to be a Celtic tribe called the Parisii, who settled on the Ile de la Cité in the 3rd century BC. Hunters and fishermen, they named their village Lutetia, meaning "boatyard on a river". The tribe minted their own gold coins and a pagan altar was found beneath Notre-Dame.

2 Roman Settlement

The Romans conquered the Parisii in 52 BC and destroyed their city. After rebuilding it as their administrative centre, they founded their own town on the Left Bank. The baths in the Hôtel de Cluny *(see p34)* and the amphitheatre in rue Monge are the only remains. In AD 360 the Roman prefect was declared emperor and Lutetia was renamed Paris, after its original inhabitants.

3 Founding of France

Roman rule weakened under Barbarian attacks. In 450 the prayers of a young nun, Geneviève, were credited with saving the city from invasion by Attila the Hun. She became the patron saint of Paris. But in 476 the Franks captured the city, Christianity became the official religion and Paris the capital of their new kingdom, France.

4 Charlemagne, Holy Roman Emperor

In 751 the Carolingian dynasty became rulers of France when Pepin the Short ascended the throne. His heir Charlemagne was crowned Holy Roman Emperor in 800 and moved the capital to Aix-La-Chapelle (Aachen). Paris fell into decline until Hugues Capet became king in 987, moving the capital back to his home city.

5 St Bartholomew's Day Massacre

Catherine de'Medici, Henri II's queen, bore three French kings and one queen, Marguerite de Valois, who married the Protestant Henri of Navarre in August 1572. Many Protestants came to Paris for the wedding and Catherine plotted their massacre. The killings began on 24 August and thousands died. Henri of Navarre survived and later became Henri IV, the first Bourbon king.

Succession of Louis XIII

6 French Revolution

Following decades of royal excess and the growing gulf between rich and poor, Paris erupted with the storming of the Bastille prison in 1789 *(see box)*.

7 Napoleon's Coronation

As Paris rose from the ashes of the Revolution, a young general from Corsica, Napoleon Bonaparte, saved the city from a royalist revolt, then led military victories in Italy and Egypt. He crowned himself Emperor of France in Notre-Dame in 1804 *(see p20)*.

8 The Second Empire

In 1851, Napoleon's nephew, Louis-Napoleon, seized power as Emperor Napoleon III. He appointed Baron Haussmann to oversee massive building works that transformed Paris into the most glorious city in Europe. The wide boulevards, many public buildings, parks, sewer system and the first department stores date from 1852 to 1870.

9 The Paris Commune

Following France's defeat in the Franco-Prussian War in 1871 *(see p23)*, many citizens rejected the harsh terms of the surrender and a left-wing group revolted, setting up the Paris Commune. But, after 72 days, government troops marched on the city. In a week of street fighting (21–28 May), much of the city burned and thousands of rebellious citizens were killed.

10 Liberation of Paris

The occupation of France by Germany during World War II was a dark period for Paris. However, the city was also the centre for the French Resistance. Allied forces liberated Paris on 25 August 1944; just two days earlier, the German commander Von Choltitz had ignored Adolf Hitler's order to burn the city.

Top 10 Events in the French Revolution

1 14 July 1789
Storming of the Bastille prison, a symbol of repression, launches the Revolution.

2 4 August 1789
The abolition of feudalism, and the right of everyone to be a free citizen is declared.

3 26 August 1789
Formal declaration of the Rights of Man and the Citizen, which incorporated the ideals of equality and dignity, later incorporated into the 1791 Constitution.

4 October 1789
Citizens march on Versailles and the royal family returns to Paris as prisoners in the Tuileries Palace *(see p95)*.

5 20 June 1791
The royal family try to escape but are spotted in Varenne and return as captives.

6 10 August 1792
A mob storms the Tuileries and the royals are imprisoned in the Temple.

7 21 September 1792
The monarchy is formally abolished and the First Republic is proclaimed.

8 1792–4
"The Terror" reigns, under the radical Commune led by Robespierre, Danton and Marat. Thousands are executed by guillotine.

9 21 January 1793
Louis XVI is found guilty of treason and executed. His queen Marie-Antoinette follows him to the guillotine on 16 October.

10 28 July 1794
Robespierre is guillotined, ending the Terror, and the Revolution draws to a close.

Left **Plaque on Victor Hugo's house** Right **Film still from** *A Tale of Two Cities*

Historical Novels set in Paris

1 Les Misérables

The 1862 novel by Victor Hugo (1802–85) is an all-too-vivid portrayal of the poor and the dispossessed in early 19th-century Paris. At its centre is the tale of nobleman Jean Valjean, unfairly victimized by an unjust system. The younger character of Marius is based around Hugo's own experiences as an impoverished student.

2 The Hunchback of Notre-Dame

Better known by its English title, which inspired a film of the same name, Victor Hugo's Gothic novel was published in France in 1831 as *Notre-Dame de Paris*. Set in the Middle Ages, it tells the strange and moving story of a hunchback bell-ringer Quasimodo and his love for Esmeralda *(see p21)*.

3 A Tale of Two Cities

The finest chronicler of 19th-century London life, Charles Dickens (1812–70) chose to set his 1859 novel in London and Paris, against the background of the French Revolution *(see p45)*. His description of conditions in the Bastille prison makes for grim reading.

4 Le Père Goriot

Honoré de Balzac (1799–1850) chronicled Paris life masterfully in his 80-volume *La comédie humaine* series, and this 1853 novel is certainly among the finest. Balzac's house at 47 rue Raynouard in the 16th *arrondissement*, where he lived from 1840–47, is open to the public *(see p137)*.

5 Sentimental Education

Gustave Flaubert (1821–80) studied law in Paris but illness disrupted his chosen career and he devoted himself to literature. This work (*L'education sentimentale* in French), first published in 1870 in two volumes, stands alongside his greatest novel, *Madame Bovary* (1857), and marks the move from Romanticism to Realism in French literature.

6 Bel-Ami

Guy de Maupassant (1850–93) published this, one of his best novels, in 1885, criticizing the get-rich-quick Parisian business world of the *belle époque* (Beautiful Age). Maupassant is known as one of the world's greatest short-story writers, and he is buried in the cemetery at Montparnasse *(see p152)*.

Guy de Maupassant

Share your travel recommendations on traveldk.com

7 A la Recherche du Temps Perdu

The master work of Marcel Proust (1871–1922) was written in 13 volumes, the first novel appearing in 1913. Proust lived on boulevard Haussmann, and his epic tale is the fictionalized story of his own life, and of Paris during the *belle époque*. Proust is buried in Père Lachaise cemetery in eastern Paris *(see p153)*.

8 Nana

Perhaps the greatest Parisian chronicler of them all, Emile Zola (1840–1902) was born, lived and died in the city, although he spent part of his youth in Aix-en-Provence in southern France. *Nana* was published in 1880 and tells a shocking tale of sexual decadence, through the eyes of the central character, a dancer and prostitute.

9 L'Assommoir

Published in 1877, Zola's *Assommoir* (The Drunkard) shows a side of Paris that many at the time would have preferred to ignore – the alcoholism of the working classes. It is one of the author's series of 20 linked books known as the *Rougon-Macquart* sequence, which depict life in every quarter of society, through the eyes of two branches of the same family.

10 Thérèse Raquin

Here Zola focuses on the secret passions that lurk behind a single Paris shopfront, opening up to reveal a tale of obsessive lust that ultimately leads to a brutal murder. It was published in 1867 and, only his second novel, shows the author's astonishing maturity and unflinching examination of all aspects of 19th-century life.

Top 10 Foreign Writers who Lived in Paris

1 Ernest Hemingway
The US author (1899–1961) wrote *A Moveable Feast* as an affectionate portrait of his time in Paris from 1921–1926.

2 F. Scott Fitzgerald
Like Hemingway, US writer Fitzgerald (1896–1940) lived in Montparnasse and frequented the bar La Coupole *(see p125)*.

3 George Orwell
The English novelist (1903–50) tells of his shocking experiences living in poverty in *Down and Out in Paris and London* (1933).

4 Samuel Beckett
Born in Ireland in 1906, the playwright lived in Paris from 1928 until his death in 1989.

5 Anaïs Nin
US novelist Nin (1903–77) met her lover, fellow American Henry Miller, in Paris. Her *Diaries* tell of her time here.

6 Albert Camus
Algerian-born Camus (1913–60) moved to Paris in 1935 and lived here until his death.

7 Henry Miller
Miller (1891–1980) showed the seedier side of Paris in his novel *Tropic of Cancer* (1934).

8 Diana Mitford
Controversial fascist sympathiser and authoress, Mitford (1910–2003) spent her dotage in Paris.

9 James Joyce
Joyce (1882–1941) lived in Paris from 1920 to 1940. *Ulysses* was published here in 1922 by Shakespeare and Co.

10 Milan Kundera
Czech-born Kundera (b.1929) moved to Paris in 1978 where he wrote *The Unbearable Lightness of Being*.

 For literary haunts See p125

Left **Palais de Chaillot** Centre **Liberty Flame** Right **Pont Alexandre III**

🔟 Riverfront Sights

1 Eiffel Tower
Although the top of the Eiffel Tower can be seen above rooftops across the city, one of the best views of this Paris landmark is from the Seine. The Pont d'Iéna lies at the foot of the tower, bridging the river to link it to the Trocadéro Gardens. The tower, illuminated at night, is a highlight of a dinner cruise on the Seine *(see pp16–17).*

Eiffel Tower

2 Palais de Chaillot
The curved arms of the Palais de Chaillot encircling the Trocadéro Gardens can be seen from the Seine. In the centre of the gardens the magnificent fountains spout from the top of a long pool lined with statues, while two huge water cannons

spray their charges back towards the river and the Eiffel Tower on the opposite bank *(see p135).*

3 Liberty Flame
A replica of the Statue of Liberty's torch in New York was erected in 1987 by the *International Herald Tribune* to mark their centenary and honour the freedom fighters of the French Resistance during World War II. It is located on the right bank of the Pont de l'Alma, the bridge over the tunnel where Diana, Princess of Wales, was killed in an automobile crash in 1997. The Liberty Flame has now become her unofficial memorial and is often draped with notes and flowers laid in her honour. Map C3

4 Grand Palais and Petit Palais
Gracing either side of the Pont Alexandre III are these two splendid exhibition halls, built for the Universal Exhibition of 1900. The iron Art Nouveau skeleton of the Grand Palais is topped by an enormous glass roof, which is most impressive when illuminated at night. The Petit Palais is smaller but similar in style, with a dome and many Classical features *(see p103).*

5 Pont Alexandre III
The most beautiful bridge in Paris is the Pont Alexandre III, a riot of Art Nouveau decoration including cherubs, wreaths,

For Paris boat trips See p164

lamps and other elaborate statuary. Built for the Universal Exhibition of 1900, it leads to the Grand Palais and Petit Palais. There are wonderful views of the Invalides complex and the Champs-Elysées from the bridge (see p104).

Dôme Church

An impressive view of the Eglise de Dôme in the Hôtel des Invalides complex can be had from the Pont Alexandre III. The golden dome beckons visitors down the long parkway lined with streetlamps and statues (see pp32–3).

Musée du Louvre

This grand museum stretches along the river from the Pont Royal to the Pont des Arts. The Denon Wing, seen from the Seine, was largely built during the reigns of Henri IV and Louis XIII in the late 16th and early 17th centuries (see pp8–11).

Musée d'Orsay

The view of this modern art gallery from the Right Bank of the Seine is one of its finest angles, showing off the arched terminals and grand façade of this former railway station. Architect Victor Laloux

designed it specifically to harmonize with the Louvre and Tuileries Quarter across the river (see pp12–15).

Conciergerie

This huge and imposing building, which served as a notorious prison during the Revolution, commands the western end of the Ile de la Cité. The building retains some of the few medieval features on the island, including the torture chamber, clock and twin towers which rise above the quai de l'Horloge (see p69).

Notre-Dame

The great cathedral is never more majestic than when viewed from the Left Bank of the Seine. It rises at the eastern end of the Ile de la Cité above the remains of the ancient tribes who first settled Paris in the 3rd century BC (see pp18–21).

Notre-Dame

Left **Jardin des Tuileries** Right **Bois de Boulogne**

🔟 Walks in Paris

1 Jardin des Tuileries
A stroll through the beautiful Tuileries Gardens is one of the must-dos of Paris. Before the Revolution this was a prime spot for the aristocracy to show off their latest fashions. The gardens are now part of the Musée du Louvre (see p95).

2 The Left Bank
A very Parisian walk, particularly on a Sunday, is along the Left Bank (Rive Gauche) of the Seine. The riverside quays of the Latin Quarter have been lined with second-hand bookstalls (bouquinistes) for centuries. The books are mostly in French, but you'll also find stalls selling prints and postcards (see p122).

3 Montmartre
The steep streets of the Butte are a good place to get some exercise after indulging in the irresistible French cuisine. Although this famous artists' quarter is more touristy than Bohemian these days, its old charms can still be found in the winding back streets and small squares (see pp140–43).

4 The Marais
With inspiring art galleries, delectable delis, and shop after shop filled with contemporary fashions

Montmartre

and objets d'art, a walk in the Marais is great fun, even if you only window-shop. The beautiful mansions are a great backdrop for your stroll and there are plenty of cafés and bars for sustenance (see pp84–7).

5 Jardin des Plantes
In this historic botanical garden you can escape the bustle of the city and lose yourself on the shady tree-lined avenues, amid colourful flowerbeds, or the hothouses and exotic gardens. Or simply relax on the lawns (see p129).

6 Jardin du Luxembourg
Napoleon designated this the "garden of children", and whether or not you have little ones in tow you'll enjoy a walk through this favourite haunt of the Latin Quarter. After you've seen the octagonal pond and the Medicis Fountain, seek out the miniature Statue of Liberty and the statues of French queens (see p119).

7 The Passages
These covered arcades around the Grands Boulevards were built at the end of the 18th century to shelter elegant shoppers from bad weather. Now lined with speciality and antiques shops, they

For more on getting around Paris See p164

re wonderfully atmospheric places to explore. Most are in the 2nd *arrondissement*, and connecting passages Verdeau, Jouffroy and Panoramas together form the longest in Paris. ◈ *Map H5*

Ile St-Louis
Although you could walk end to end in about 10 minutes, the Seine's smaller island demands a more leisurely stroll. You'll discover superb little art galleries, trendy boutiques, and a village-like atmosphere within this up-market enclave *(see p68)*.

Bois de Boulogne
Come here at the weekend if you want to join the locals in the "great escape", and you'll have 8.65 sq km (3.34 sq miles) from which to choose your path. The Bagatelle Gardens are a fine place for a walk in spring and summer, when a stunning array of roses and other flowers are in bloom *(see p152)*.

Boulevard St-Germain

Boulevard St-Germain
There's no better way to enjoy the Latin Quarter than to do as the Parisians do – stroll the Boulevard St-Germain, preferably late on a Sunday morning. After your walk, honour the birthplace of café society with a coffee at either Les Deux Magots or Café le Flore, two of the city's most famous literary and intellectual haunts *(see p120)*.

Top 10 Outdoor Activities

Walking
Paris is a compact city so you can easily combine sightseeing with exercise.

Roller-blading
A fad which shows no sign of abating, skaters weave their way through traffic and pedestrians alike.

Cycling
Head for the Bois de Boulogne and Bois de Vincennes to escape the Paris traffic, or grab a Vélib' *(see p164)*.

Boating
Boating lakes in the Bois de Boulogne and Bois de Vincennes allow you to flex your rowing muscles.

Jogging
You can get your aerobic fix along the pathways of Paris's parks and gardens.

Table Tennis
Try your luck at the outdoor concrete tables found in several parks and squares.

Sunbathing
De rigueur on the *quais* beside the Seine, especially during "Paris Plages" in July and August *(see p57)*.

Swimming
There are 38 public pools in Paris, but hours are restricted during school terms. Or try the pool at the Forum des Halles.

Football
France's football team has many young imitators in parks, gardens and streets.

Posing
A sport indulged in mainly by young men and women, it is best done at outdoor cafés to be sure of the biggest audience.

Left **Café de Flore** Centre **La Closerie des Lilas** Right **Café Marly**

🔟 Cafés and Bars

1 Café de Flore
A hang-out for artists and intellectuals since the 1920s, its regulars have included Salvador Dali and Albert Camus. During World War II Jean-Paul Sartre and Simone de Beauvoir "more or less set up house in the Flore". Although its prices have skyrocketed, its Art Deco decor hasn't changed and it's still a favourite with French filmmakers and literati *(see p125)*.

2 Les Deux Magots
Rival to the neighbouring Flore as the rendezvous for the 20th-century intellectual élite. Hemingway, Oscar Wilde, Djuna Barnes, André Breton and Paul Verlaine were all regulars, and Picasso met his muse Dora Maar here in 1937. Similarly pricey, with outside tables facing the boulevard and the square *(see p125)*.

3 Le Petit Vendôme
The search for the best sandwiches in Paris stops here, with bread from the award-winning Julien bakery and just the right slathering of butter with cured ham or goat's cheese. Good hot dishes are served too. ◈ 8 rue des Capucines, 75002 • Map E3 • 01 42 61 05 88 • €

4 Café Marly
Superbly situated in the Richelieu wing of the Louvre *(see p9)*, the café offers simple but expertly prepared brasserie fare (steaks, salads, steak tartare, club sandwiches) as well as delicious desserts. The dining room has plush decor and velvet armchairs, but the best spot is under the arcade overlooking the glass pyramid and the cour Napoléon. ◈ 93 rue de Rivoli, 75001 • Map L2 • €€€

5 Café de la Paix
A grand Parisian café with prices to match, but it's worth a visit to enjoy the frescoed walls and sumptuous surroundings, designed by Charles Garnier, architect of the Opera House across the square *(see p97)*. This is another Paris landmark with a string of famous past patrons, and arguably the best *mille-feuille* cakes in town. ◈ 12 blvd de Capucines, 75008 • Map E3

6 La Closerie des Lilas
The main restaurant here is expensive, but the bar is a good spot to soak up the atmosphere of this historic site where artists and writers from Baudelaire to Archibald MacLeish have drunk since 1808. Look out for the famous names of visitors etched

Les Deux Magots

For more places to eat in Paris See pp64–5

on the tables in the bar. The busy brasserie also has live piano music in the evenings and attracts a chic crowd *(see p157)*.

7 Le Fumoir

There are many reasons to drop into this café-bar-restaurant next to the Louvre whether it be to people-watch from the terrace out front or hide out with a martini and game of backgammon in the comfy library at the back. The hot chocolate is heavenly, cocktails are expertly made and the bistro cooking shows Italian and Swedish influences.
 6 rue de l'Amiral de Coligny, 75001 • Map F4 • 01 42 92 00 24 • €€€€€

Café de la Paix

8 Chez Jeannette

Although the owners haven't touched the scruffy vintage decor, this café near Gare de l'Est has now become one of the hottest hang-outs in Paris with a crowd outside to prove it. Inside, the high ceilings, mirrors and old-fashioned booths, as well as reasonably priced food, create a lively atmosphere. 47 rue du Faubourg-Saint-Denis, 75010 • Map G2 • 01 47 70 30 89 • No disabled access • €€

9 Le Café de l'Industrie

Unpretentious but stylish, the Bastille café with three large rooms is decorated with everything from spears, to old film star publicity stills. The simple food, such as onion soup, is good value. Non-stop service from noon to midnight *(see p92)*.

10 Bistro Mélac

This friendly wine bar off the beaten track is full of character, with a rustic beamed ceiling hung with country hams and a vine growing around the walls. The owner is an enthusiastic wine lover and aims to please with his reasonably priced cellar. A fun harvest of the bar's vine is held on the second Saturday of September. 42 rue Léon-Frot, 75011 • Metro Charonne • 01 43 70 59 27 • Closed Sun, Mon, Easter, Aug and last week Dec

For price guides to Paris restaurants See p73

Left **Au Printemps** Right **Rue de Buci**

🔟 Shops and Markets

Flower and Bird Markets
Dating from 1808, the colourful Marché aux Fleurs (flower market) on the Ile de la Cité is the oldest and one of the largest flower markets in Paris. Its blooms brighten up the area between the stark walls of the Conciergerie and Hôtel Dieu from Monday to Saturday – everything from orchids to orange trees. On Sundays it is joined by the Marché aux Oiseaux (bird market) with equally colourful, caged species. ⊗ Pl Louis-Lépine, 75004 • Map P4

Au Printemps
One of Paris's two top department stores, Printemps opened in 1864. Its goods range from designer clothing and accessories, to middle-of-the-range labels and funky fashions, home decor and furniture. The sixth-floor brasserie is crowned with a lovely Art Nouveau stained-glass cupola. ⊗ 64 blvd Haussmann, 75009 • Map E2

Galeries Lafayette
Printemp's great rival store opened in 1894 and is a monument to Parisian style, topped by a glorious steel-and-glass dome. Along with designer clothes, there's a fabulous food hall. The seventh floor has great views. ⊗ 40 blvd Haussmann, 75009 • Map E2

Bastille Market
Every Thursday and Sunday morning, this market stretches along the tree-lined boulevard that separates the Marais from the Bastille. Sunday is the best day, when locals come to socialize as well as shop for foods such as fish, meat, bread and cheese. Some stalls sell North African and other international fare. ⊗ Blvd Richard-Lenoir, 75011 • Map H5

Marché aux Fleurs (flower market)

Place de la Madeleine
This is a gourmand's delight. Some of the most delectable speciality food shops in Paris are dotted around the edges of this square, including the famous Fauchon food hall and the smaller Hédiard. There's Maille for mustard, Kaspia for caviar, Marquise de Sévigné for chocolates and La Maison de la Truffe for truffles (see p98).

Rue de Buci
The artist Picasso reputedly did his shopping at this daily morning market in the heart of

t-Germain. The huge fruit and
vegetable stalls are of high
quality but of greater interest are
the food shops opening on to
the street, which sell specialist
and regional fare. You can also
buy prepared Italian dishes and
delicious pastries. ◈ Map L4

Rue Mouffetard
One of the oldest street
markets in Paris winds downhill
through the Latin Quarter every
Tuesday to Sunday morning.
Although this formerly cheap and
bohemian market has been
discovered as a tourist spot, it
retains its charm, the narrow
streets lined with food stalls and
speciality shops. There are also
good restaurants in the quieter
side streets. ◈ Map F6

Le Bon Marché
Paris's first department store
was founded on the Left Bank in
1852, its structure partially
designed by Gustave Eiffel (see
p17). Today it's even more hip
than its competitors, with an in-
store boutique featuring avant-
garde fashions. It also has
designer clothes, its own line of
menswear and the enormous La
Grande Epicerie food hall.
◈ 22 rue de Sèvres, 75007 • Map D5

Marché aux Puces du St-Ouen

Aligre Market
Away from the tourist bustle,
this Bastille market, dubbed the
"Notre-Dame of markets", retains
an authentic Parisian atmosphere.
Every morning from Tuesday to
Sunday North African traders
hawk inexpensive produce in the
open-air market, and there's an
adjacent flea market and a
covered market selling top-quality
fare. ◈ Pl d'Aligre, 75012 • Map H5

Marché aux Puces de St-Ouen
Every Saturday to Monday the
largest antiques market in the
world comes alive. There are
actually several markets here:
the oldest, Marché Vernaison, is
the most charming; Marché Malik
sells vintage clothing. Others
offer furniture, jewellery and
paintings. ◈ Porte de Clignancourt,
75018 • Metro Porte de Clignancourt

For more on shopping in Paris See p169

Left **Fête du Cinéma** Right **Tour de France**

🔟 Festivals and Events

1 Nuit Blanche
Paris held its first Nuit Blanche in 2002 and the all-night contemporary art event now attracts more than 1,500,000 people each year. Its goal is to give a fresh perspective on Paris with installations and exhibitions in several different neighbourhoods, and to make contemporary art more accessible to all. ◈ *First weekend Oct*

2 Fête du Cinéma
Film buffs should be sure to verify the exact dates of this annual event, held each June. For just three days, cinemagoers pay full price for the first film that they see, but can then see as many other films as they choose, for a few euros each. ◈ *www.feteducinema.com*

3 Paris Jazz Festival
Paris is home to jazz all year round *(see pp62–3)*, but every summer there is a major jazz festival in the city. Acts from all over the world come to play in the Parc Floral de Paris in the Bois de Vincennes *(see p151)*, but there are many lesser venues involved as well. ◈ *Jun–end Jul* • *www.parcfloraldeparis.com*

4 Grandes Eaux Nocturnes
A true midsummer night's dream with superb illuminations and installations in the gardens of Versailles, plus a spectacular firework display over the Grand Canal. ◈ *Dates in Jun, Jul and Aug*

5 Tour de France
Don't miss this summer highlight if you really want to understand the French passion for cycling. Towards the end of July each year, the world's greatest and most gruelling cycle race approaches Paris. On the final laps the riders pass the Louvre, race along the banks of the Seine, go down the rue de Rivoli and, of course, the Champs-Elysées. Thousands of fans pack the streets to cheer the riders home and see who will win the Yellow Jersey. ◈ *www.letour.fr*

6 Festival d'Automne à Paris
This major festival promotes contemporary arts across the board in Paris, encouraging all walks of life to see and enjoy performances of dance, music, film and drama. ◈ *mid-Sep–Dec* • *www.festival-automne.com*

Paris Jazz Festival

Fêtes des Vendanges

Paris used to be one of the country's major wine producers, but these days only the vineyards at Montmartre remain (see p142). These produce just under 800 litres (5 barrels) of wine each autumn, but great fun is had at the Fêtes des Vendanges with wine, food stalls and a street parade. ✪ Oct: first Fri (for three days)

Fête de la Musique

To celebrate the summer equinox, professional and amateur musicians take to the streets of Paris. Major shows are held in Place de la République and other concert venues, but the most fun is to be had wandering through residential neighbourhoods and dropping into locals' bars. ✪ 21 Jun

Paris Plages

Launched in 2002 by the mayor of Paris, Bertrand Delanoë, this hugely popular summer event transforms a stretch of the Seine quais and the Canal du l'Ourcq into a mini Cannes, with tons of soft sand, sunbeds, parasols and palm trees. There are also events and attractions for children.
✪ mid-Jul–mid-Aug • www.paris.fr

Mois de la Photo

Paris reveres the art of photography and every alternate November (in even-numbered years) it hosts the "Month of the Photo". Galleries, museums, shops, cultural centres and many other venues all give space to exhibitions, workshops and lectures on all aspects of the art. For anyone interested in photography, it is the most exciting time to visit Paris. ✪ Nov www.mep-fr.org

Top 10 Sports Events

1 Tour de France
This great cycle race reaches its climax in Paris.

2 Prix de l'Arc de Triomphe
This world-renowned horse race attracts the city's crème de la crème. ✪ Longchamp racecourse • Oct: first weekend

3 French Tennis Open
Paris's legendary clay-court tournament. ✪ Stade Roland Garros • end May–1st week Jun

4 Gucci Masters
Show-jumping fans and competitors descend on Paris. ✪ Paris Nord Villepinte • Dec

5 Six Nations Rugby
The French team plays against England, Scotland, Ireland, Wales and Italy in this Feb–Mar tournament. ✪ Stade de France

6 Paris Marathon
Runners start at the Champs-Elysées and end at avenue Foch. ✪ Apr

7 Football Cup Final
The biggest club event in French football. ✪ Stade de France • mid-May

8 Prix de Diane
Parisian high society flocks to this upmarket horse race ✪ Chantilly • Jun: second Sun

9 Top 14 Rugby Final
Some of the world's finest rugby players take part in the final for the French Rugby league. ✪ Stade de France • May/Jun

10 Ice-Skating Grand Prix
The Trophée Eric Bompard is the Parisian leg of the International Grand Prix. ✪ Palais Omnisports de Paris-Bercy • Nov

Left **The Lido** Centre **Le Crazy Horse Paris** Right **Théâtre de la Ville de Paris**

Entertainment Venues

1 Opéra National de Paris Garnier

Not just a night out, but a whole experience, opera has now returned to its original Paris base after the theatre had a spell as a dance-only venue. The vast stage can hold a cast of 450, and the building itself is an example of excessive opulence, complete with grand staircase, mirrors and marble (see p97).

2 Folies-Bergère

The epitome of Parisian cabaret, the Folies were, for a time, no more than a troupe of high-kicking, bare-breasted dancers. Today, the musical shows have largely returned to the nostalgic days when Maurice Chevalier and Josephine Baker (see p63) performed here. ◈ 32 rue Richer, 75009 • Map F2 • 08 92 68 16 50 • www.foliesbergere.com

Folies-Bergère

3 The Lido

Home to the world famous troupe of long-legged dancers, the Bluebell Girls, the fabulous special effects include aerial ballets and an on-stage skating rink. There are many who regard this dinner-cabaret as an essential Parisian experience. ◈ 116 bis ave des Champs-Elysées, 75008 • Map D3 • 01 40 76 56 10 • www.lido.fr

4 Moulin Rouge

The original home of the Can-Can, the theatre's dancers were immortalized on canvas by Toulouse-Lautrec during the belle époque and are on display in the Musée d'Orsay (see p13). The show still has all the razzamataz that has been dazzling audiences since 1889. The pre-show dinner is optional (see p142).

5 Le Crazy Horse Paris

More risqué than the other big-name cabaret shows, the Saloon has a reputation for putting on the most professional as well as the sexiest productions. Striptease features, along with glamorous dancing girls and other cabaret acts. The computer-controlled lighting effects are spectacular. ◈ 12 ave George 75008 • Map C3 • 01 4. 23 32 32 • www. lecrazyhorseparis.com

6 Le Cirque d'Hiver

Worth visiting for the façade alone, this whimsical listed building, dating from 1852, plays host to the traditional Cirque Bouglione, complete with acts such as trapeze artists, clowns, jugglers and tame tigers. ◈ 110 rue Amelot, 75011 • Map H3 • 01 47 00 28 81 • www.cirquedhiver.com

For more Paris cabarets and clubs See p146

Comédie Française

7 Paris's oldest theatre was founded in 1680 and is still the only one with its own repertory company, staging both classical and modern drama (in French). The current building dates from the 18th century. Around the corner from the main box office, a special window opens 45 minutes before curtain-up, selling reduced price tickets for under-27s and concessions. ◎ *1 pl Colette, 75001 • Map L1 • 08 25 10 16 80 (+33 1 44 58 15 15 from abroad) • www.comedie-francaise.fr*

Opéra National de Paris Bastille

8 Opened in 1992 as the largest opera house in the world, this modern building was heavily criticized, not least for its acoustics and poor facilities. However, this is still the best place to see opera in Paris. ◎ *Pl de la Bastille, 75012 • Map H5 • 08 92 89 90 90 (+33 1 71 25 24 23 from abroad) • www.operadeparis.fr*

Théâtre du Châtelet

9 The city's largest concert hall and fourth-largest auditorium was built in 1862. The repertoire covers classical music, ballet and opera, as well as popular Sunday morning chamber music concerts. ◎ *1 pl du Châtelet, 75001 • Map N2 • 01 40 28 28 00 • www.chatelet-theatre.com*

Théâtre de la Ville

10 Once known as the Sarah Bernhardt Theatre, in honour of the great Parisian actress who performed here and managed the theatre in the 19th century, today it puts on an eclectic range of modern dance, music shows and some classical theatre. ◎ *2 pl du Châtelet, 75004 • Map N2 • 01 42 74 22 77 • www.theatredelaville-paris.com*

Top 10 Films set in Paris

1 Les Enfants du Paradis
The city's underworld is shown in this 1944 classic.

2 Everyone Says I Love You
Woody Allen's 1996 movie included many scenes shot around Notre-Dame and the Left Bank.

3 A Bout de Souffle
French New Wave director Jean-Luc Godard's 1959 film stars Jean-Paul Belmondo as a car thief on the run.

4 French Can-Can
The Jean Renoir classic (1955) tells the story of how the famous dance was created in Montmartre clubs.

5 Last Tango in Paris
Controversial, erotic 1972 film starring Marlon Brando.

6 The Trial
Orson Welles used the then empty Gare d'Orsay (now the Musée d'Orsay) to create a convincingly huge and anonymous office for his 1962 version of Kafka's novel.

7 Subway
The metro was the star in this 1985 Luc Besson film about a man who seeks refuge at night in its stations.

8 Les 400 Coups
Gritty Paris streets feature in this 1959 François Truffaut film about a boy on the run.

9 Amélie
Jean-Pierre Jeunet's 2000 sensation about a girl's quest for love features numerous scenes in Montmartre.

10 Midnight in Paris
Woody Allen returns to Paris in this 2011 popular eulogy to 1920s bohemia.

Left **Grande Galerie de l'Evolution** Right **Jardin d'Acclimatation**

🔟 Children's Attractions

Disneyland Resort Paris
Formerly known as Euro-Disneyland, the French offspring of America's favourite theme park is a clone of its parent, and has now been joined by the Walt Disney Studios complex. Both have big queues, so arrive early. There are rides for children of all ages and most adults are equally enchanted (see p151).

Parc de la Villette
One of the city's top children's attractions, with activities for all ages. The Cité des Sciences et de l'Industrie, a high-tech hands-on science museum, gets star billing, while the Cité des Enfants is a science and nature attraction for younger children. Kids also love the Argonaute, a real submarine that voyaged

Parc de la Villette

around the world 10 times, the Géode with its IMAX screen and the futuristic outdoor playground (see p152).

Eiffel Tower
A trip to the top is one of the most memorable activities for children in Paris (see pp16–17).

Grande Galerie de l'Evolution
The most exciting and imaginatively designed section in the Natural History Museum is the Great Gallery of Evolution. Elephants, giraffes and other stuffed animals rise out of a re-created savannah, a huge whale skeleton hangs from the ceiling, while special displays help tell the story of the development of life on earth. Nature workshops are also held for children during school holidays (see p129).

Musée de la Magie et des Automates
Kids are enchanted by this museum of magic, located in the cellars of the former home of the Marquis de Sade. Magicians conjure up shows every half hour involving optical illusions, card tricks and lots of audience participation. Exhibits include working automata and memorabilia from master magicians such as Houdini (1874–1926). ◈ 11 rue St-Paul, 75004 • Map R4 • 01 42 72 13 26 • Open 2–7pm Wed, Sat, Sun (daily during school holidays, except Jul & Aug) • Admission charge • www.museedelamagie.com

Parc Astérix

Dozens of attractions including one of Europe's longest roller coasters, an adventure playground and a replica of Albert Uderzo's original comic book village. ⬡ Plailly, 60128 • RER B to Roissy CDG1, then shuttle from bus stop A3 • 08 26 30 10 40 (+33 3 44 62 31 31 from abroad) • Open Apr–Aug: 10am–6pm Mon–Fri, 9:30am–6pm Sat, Sun; Sep–Oct: 10am–6pm Sat, Sun • Admission charge • www.parcasterix.fr

Jardin d'Acclimatation

This amusement park at the north end of the Bois de Boulogne (see p152) has roller coasters, pony rides and puppet shows. An electric train, "le Petit Train," runs here from Porte Maillot. ⬡ Bois de Boulogne, 75016 • Map A2 • Open 10am–7pm daily (summer); 10am–6pm daily (winter) • Admission charge • www.jardindacclimatation.fr

Grévin

This waxworks museum was founded in 1882. Kids will have most fun seeing celebrities from the world of pop music and film, but there are also wonderful tableaux from French history. ⬡ 10 blvd Montmartre, 75009 • Map F2 • 01 47 70 85 05 • Open 10am–6:30pm Mon–Fri, 10am–7pm Sat, Sun & public hols (last admission 1 hour before closing) • Closed first week Jan • Admission charge • www.grevin.com

Jardin du Luxembourg

The park has tennis courts, puppet shows, donkey rides and a good playground (for a fee). But most fun of all is the Parisian pastime of sailing model boats in the fountain. ⬡ Jardin du Luxembourg • Map E5 • Open daylight–dusk

Parc des Buttes Chaumont

The highest park in Paris is great for a family picnic. Kids love the suspended bridges, waterfalls, donkey rides and puppet shows. ⬡ Parc des Buttes Chaumont, 75019 • Map H2 • Open 7am–10pm daily (9pm Oct–Apr) • Free

Lift, Eiffel Tower

For family-friendly hotels See p179

Left **Jazz Club Etoile** Centre **Au Duc des Lombards** Right **Le Baiser Salé**

🔟 Jazz Clubs

1 Sunset-Sunside
This club offers a double serving of late-night jazz – acoustic and modern at street level (Sunside) and electric, fusion and groove in the vaulted cellar room (Sunset). On Sunday afternoons there's a "jazz and tea" session for families.
🛇 *60 rue des Lombards, 75001 • Map N2*

2 Au Duc des Lombards
The Left Bank may be the traditional home of jazz clubs but this sleek, modern club is firmly on the Right Bank, in the Les Halles district *(see pp74–7)*. The memorabilia of the "greats" who played here may have disappeared during refurbishment but the club's policy is still to bring in the best overseas jazz artists to play alongside home-grown talent. Good food is served day and night. 🛇 *42 rue des Lombards, 75001 • Map N2*

3 Le Baiser Salé
Jazz, blues, Latin and African music are the mainstays at this tiny cellar club, which is low on space but high on volume. The Baiser was promoting World Music long before the phrase had been invented, and the eclectic approach has led to a relaxed

Caveau de la Huchette

and friendly atmosphere. It's also cheaper than many other clubs.
🛇 *58 rue des Lombards, 75001 • Map N2*

4 Caveau des Oubliettes
The ground floor is a pub, but the tiny jazz club in the vaulted basement below, which used to be a prison and dates back to the 12th century, is the main draw here. It's open until late and there's a concert on from 10pm every night except Mondays. There's no cover charge but drinks are expensive.
🛇 *52 rue Galande, 75005 • Map F5*

5 Autour de Midi et de Minuit
Halfway up La Butte, this atmospheric joint has added some welcome buzz to the slopes of Montmartre. It's jazz all the way, mostly swing but some modern jazz as well, performed in a vaulted cellar below the excellent bistro. 🛇 *11 rue Lepic, 75018 • Map E1*

6 Jazz Club Etoile
Formerly known as the Jazz Club Lionel Hampton, the Etoile serves up a wide range of sounds, including blues, rock and even gospel music. There's an emphasis on visiting African-American musicians

(Oscar Peterson and BB King have played here). Its Jazz Club Lounge offers a Jazzy Brunch on Sundays. ◈ Hôtel Le Méridien-Etoile, 81 blvd Gouvion-St-Cyr, 75017 • Map A2

New Morning
Seating up to 300 people, this large club's policy of embracing all kinds of music (jazz, blues, Latin, soul and the unclassifiable), not to mention inviting performers up from the floor, has led to a relaxed crowd of regulars. ◈ 7–9 rue des Petites-Ecuries, 75010 • Map F2

Le Petit Journal Montparnasse
This is the club that barely sleeps – the doors close at 2am, but open up again five hours later. You can just drink, or have a meal while listening to the live music, which is mainly big band jazz but on some nights takes in salsa, blues or rock. ◈ 13 rue du Commandant-Mouchotte, 75014 • Map D6

Le Petit Journal St-Michel
Older brother of the Montparnasse branch, this club opened in 1971 and concentrates on New Orleans-style swinging jazz. There's a fun atmosphere in this Latin Quarter cellar, together with a pleasant dining room in which to have a meal, just off the main stage area. ◈ 71 blvd St-Michel, 75005 • Map M5

Caveau de la Huchette
Don't be fooled by its tourist-trap setting in the heart of the Latin Quarter – this venue is worth every penny of the entrance price. The building was once home to the Knights Templar, and jazz has been played under the medieval vaults since 1947. ◈ 5 rue de la Huchette, 75005 • Map N4

Top 10 Musical Artistes in Paris

1 Edith Piaf
Discovered as a street singer in Paris, the diminutive Piaf (1915–63) became known as the "Little Sparrow".

2 Maurice Chevalier
The Parisian singer/actor (1888–1972) is, for many, the voice of France. In 1958 he won an Academy Award for his role in Gigi.

3 Django Reinhardt
Belgian gypsy guitarist Reinhardt (1910–53) first found fame in Paris in collaboration with Stephane Grappelli.

4 Lionel Hampton
US bandleader Hampton (b. 1909) regularly played in the Left Bank jazz clubs.

5 Sidney Bechet
US jazz virtuoso Bechet (1897–1959) settled in Paris in the 1940s and wrote his great tune "Les Oignons" in 1949.

6 Jacques Brel
Belgian singer/songwriter Brel (1929–78) moved to Paris in 1953, where audiences loved his melancholy songs.

7 Stephane Grappelli
Paris-born Grappelli (1908–97) studied classical violin, but later innovatively adapted the instrument to jazz.

8 Josephine Baker
The African-American dancer (1906–75) gained notoriety for dancing semi-nude at the Folies-Bergère.

9 Miles Davis
US trumpet-player Davis (1926–91) was a favourite in Paris for his "cool jazz" style.

10 Coleman Hawkins
US bebop saxophonist Hawkins (1904–69) played Paris many times in the 1930s.

Left **Guy Savoy** Centre **Le Jules Verne** Right **Taillevent**

🔟 Places to Eat

1 L'Astrance

There is probably no table in Paris that is more coveted than one in this sober 25-seat dining room, with its set menus at €70 (for lunch) or €310 (for dinner), orchestrated by young culinary genius Pascal Barbot. You'll need to book a month ahead for lunch, two months for dinner. ◈ *4 rue Beethoven, 75016 • Map B4 • 01 40 50 84 40 • Closed Sat–Mon, Feb, Aug, 1 week Oct (call to check) • No disabled access • €€€€€*

2 Guy Savoy

Artichoke and truffle soup is one of star chef Guy Savoy's signature dishes, in his chic and smart restaurant (jacket and ties required for male diners). One of the city's best dining

Brasserie Bofinger

experiences *(see p109)*. To sample Savoy's cooking at more affordable prices, try the bistro-style Les Bookinistes in the St-Germain quarter *(see p127)*.

3 Les Papilles

The setting – a wine shop lined with wooden tables – barely hints at this restaurant's remarkably sophisticated cooking, from a chef who once worked at Taillevent. Pick your wine straight off the shelves to accompany the bargain set menu *(see p127)*.

4 Taillevent

Taillevent's atmospheric oak-panelled dining room is frequented by a mix of businessmen and romantic couples. Dishes such as rex rabbit with Cremona mustard and black radish feature on the seasonal menu and there's an exceptional wine list. You need to book well ahead to dine here *(see p109)*.

5 Le Jules Verne

Now in the perfectionist hands of world-famous chef Alain Ducasse, this restaurant on the second floor of the Eiffel Tower has entered the 21st century. It has been revamped with a futuristic brown decor and there is a suitably luxurious menu, replete with truffles in winter. Service is excellent and the panoramic views are breathtaking, but book in advance *(see p117)*.

Brasserie Bofinger

6 One of Paris's oldest brasseries, dating from 1864, is worth a visit for the original wood and glass decor and leather banquette seating. Alsatian specialities include sauerkraut and paté. ◈ *5–7 rue de la Bastille, 75004 • Map H5 • 01 42 72 87 82 • No disabled access • €€€€€*

Le Chateaubriand

7 One of the best restaurant's in Paris, Le Chateaubriand provides a relaxed setting and offers affordable gastronomic cuisine. Basque chef Iñaki Aizpitarte creates innovative and award-winning dishes for a daily changing menu. Book in advance. ◈ *128 ave Parmentier, 75011 • Map H3 • 01 43 57 45 95 • €€€€€*

Pierre Gagnaire

8 Famous French chef Pierre Gagnaire creates culinary dishes at this formal diner. Try the foie gras, oysters and ginger served with tamarillo sorbet and Paris mushrooms. ◈ *6 rue Balzac, 75008 • Map B2 • 01 58 36 12 50 • No disabled access • Closed Sat, Sun L, Aug • €€€€€*

L'Arpege

9 Alain Passard's three-star restaurant is one of the most highly regarded in Paris. Dishes include turnip tatin with honey and roasted rapeseed. ◈ *84 rue de Varenne, 75007 • Map D4 • 01 47 05 09 06 • No disabled access • Closed Sat & Sun • €€€€€*

L'Atelier de Joël Robuchon

10 Take a seat at the lacquered bar to experience a top French chef's take on contemporary cuisine. Signature dishes are the merlan Colbert (fried whiting), and carbonara with Alsatian cream and bacon. ◈ *5 rue de Montalembert, 75007 • Map E4 • 01 42 22 56 56 • €€€€€*

L'Atelier de Joël Robuchon

For a price guide to Paris restaurants See p73

AROUND TOWN

PARIS TOP 10

Left **Notre-Dame** Right **Salle des Gens d'Armes, Conciergerie**

Ile de la Cité and Ile St-Louis

PARIS WAS BORN ON THE ILE DE LA CITÉ. *The first settlers came to this island on the Seine in 300 BC (see p44) and it has remained a focus of* church and state power through the centuries, with the great cathedral of Notre-Dame and the law courts of the Palais de Justice commanding the island. This tiny land mass also has the honour of being the geographical heart of the city – all distances from Paris are measured from Point Zéro, just outside Notre-Dame. While the Ile de la Cité seems overrun with tourists, the smaller Ile St-Louis, connected to its neighbour by a footbridge, has a village-like feel and has been an exclusive residential enclave since the 17th century. Its main street is lined with shops, galleries and restaurants and is a wonderful place for a stroll.

🔟 Sights

1. Notre-Dame
2. Sainte-Chapelle
3. Conciergerie
4. Marché aux Fleurs
5. Crypte Archéologique
6. Pont Neuf
7. Palais de Justice
8. Place Dauphine
9. St Louis-en-l'Ile
10. Square du Vert-Galant

Angel detail, Sainte-Chapelle

Sign up for DK's email newsletter on traveldk.com

Notre-Dame
See pp18–21.

Sainte-Chapelle
See pp30–31.

Conciergerie
This imposing Gothic palace, built by Philippe le Bel (the Fair) in 1301–15, has a rich history. Parts of it were turned into a prison, controlled by the concierge, or keeper of the king's mansion, hence the name. Ravaillac, assassin of Henri IV, was tortured here, but it was during the Revolution that the prison became a place of terror, when thousands were held here awaiting execution at the guillotine. Today you can see the Salle des Gardes and the magnificent vaulted Salle des Gens d'Armes (Hall of the Men-at Arms), the medieval kitchens, torture chamber, the Bonbec tower, and the prison. The cell where Marie-Antoinette was held and the history of other famous Revolution prisoners is on display. Outside, look for the square Tour de l'Horloge, erected in 1370, which houses the city's first public clock, still ticking away. ◎ 2 blvd du Palais, 75001 • Map N3 Open 9:30am–6pm daily Admission charge

Marché aux Fleurs
One of the last remaining flower markets in the city centre, the beautiful Marché aux Fleurs is also the oldest, dating from the early 19th century. It is held year-round, Monday to Saturday, in place Louis-

Sainte-Chapelle

Lépine, filling the north side of the Île de la Cité with dazzling blooms from 8am to 7pm. There is also a bird market here on Sundays, which sells some rare species (see p54). ◎ Map N3

Crypte Archéologique
Fascinating remnants of early Paris dating back to Gallo-Roman times were discovered in 1965 during an excavation of the square in front of Notre-Dame in order to build an underground car park. The archaeological crypt displays parts of 3rd-century Roman walls, rooms heated by hypocaust, as well as remains of medieval streets and foundations. The scale models showing the evolution of the city from its origins as a Celtic settlement are particularly interesting. ◎ Place du Parvis-Notre-Dame, 75004 • Map P4 • Open 10am–6pm Tue–Sun • Admission charge

Crypte Archéologique

The Guillotine

Dr Joseph Guillotine invented his "humane" beheading machine at his home near the Odéon and it was first used in April 1792. During the Revolution some 2,600 prisoners were executed on the places du Carrousel, de la Concorde, de la Bastille and de la Nation, after awaiting their fate in the Conciergerie prison.

Pont Neuf

An incongruous name (New Bridge) for the oldest surviving bridge in Paris. Following its completion in 1607, Henri IV christened it by charging across on his steed; the bronze equestrian statue of the king was melted down during the Revolution but replaced in 1818. Decorated with striking carved heads, the bridge was unique for its time in that it had no houses built upon it. It has 12 arches and a span of 275 m (912 ft) extending both sides of the island. ◈ Map M3

Palais de Justice

Stretching across the west end of the Ile de la Cité from north to south, the Palais de Justice, along with the

Conciergerie, was once part of the Palais de la Cité, seat of Roman rule and the home of the French kings until 1358. It took its present name during the Revolution and the buildings now contain the city's law courts. You can watch the courts in session from Monday to Friday and wander through the public areas with their many ornate features. The Cour du Mai (May Courtyard) is the area through which prisoners passed during the Revolution on their way to execution.
◈ 4 blvd du Palais, 75001 • Map M3 • Open 8:30am–6pm Mon–Fri, 9:30am–6pm Sat • Free

Place Dauphine

In 1607 Henri IV transformed this former royal garden into a triangular square and named it after his son, the Dauphin and future King Louis XIII. Surrounding the square were uniformly built houses of brick and white stone. No. 14 is one of the few that retains its original features. One side was destroyed to make way for the expansion of the Palais de Justice. Today this quiet, charming spot is a good place to relax over a drink or meal *(see p73)*. ◈ Map M3

Pont Neuf and Square du Vert-Galant

Sculptured relief, Palais de Justice

9 St-Louis-en-l'Ile

This lovely Baroque church on Ile St-Louis was designed between 1664 and 1726 by the royal architect Louis Le Vau. The exterior features an iron clock (1741) at the entrance and an iron spire, while the interior, richly decorated with gilding and marble, has a statue of St Louis holding his Crusader's sword.
Ⓢ 19 bis rue St-Louis-en-l'Ile, 75004 • Map Q5 • Open 9am–1pm, 2–7:30pm Tue–Sun

10 Square du Vert-Galant

The tranquil western tip of the Ile de la Cité, with its verdant chestnut trees, lies beneath the Pont Neuf – take the steps behind Henri IV's statue. This king had a notoriously amorous nature and the name of this peaceful square recalls his nickname, meaning "old flirt". From here there is a wonderful view of the Louvre (see pp8–11) and the Right Bank. It is also the departure point for cruises on the Seine on Les Vedettes du Pont-Neuf (see p165). Ⓢ Map M3

A Day on the Islands

Morning

🕐 Arrive at **Notre-Dame** (see pp18–21) by 8am to beat the crowds and appreciate its magnificence, then head for the fragrant Marché aux Fleurs. As well as flowers, you can buy all kinds of garden accessories and seeds. Return to Notre-Dame if you want to ascend the towers, which open at 10am. Take a coffee break at **Le Flore en l'Ile** (see p73), with its views of the cathedral.

The fascinating Crypte Archéologique is worth a half-hour visit, then spend the late morning at **Sainte-Chapelle** (see pp30–31), when the sun beams through the stained-glass windows.

🍴 There are plenty of places for lunch, but on a sunny day try **La Rose de France** (see p73), which has terrace seating.

Afternoon

📍 Spend a leisurely afternoon strolling the narrow streets of the Ile St-Louis, which are filled with characterful shops and galleries (see p72).

☕ Wind up with an afternoon treat by visiting **Berthillon,** considered the best ice-cream purveyor in all of France (see p73). With at least 70 delicious varieties of ice cream on offer, ranging from plain vanilla to whisky, and including virtually any fruit you can think of, the hardest part will be choosing. There will be plenty of time to make your choice however, as there will inevitably be a long queue, especially in summer.

Left **Pylones Boutique** Centre **Librairie Ulysse** Right **Boulangerie des Deux Ponts**

🔟 Shopping

1 L'Épicerie du Terroir
A comprehensive and mouth-watering range of French regional gourmet delights, including mustards, preserves, olive oils, wines and sweets, all sourced from small producers and at prices to suit most budgets.
🔘 *10 rue Jean de Bellay, 75004 • Map P4*

2 La Petite Scierie
This friendly, old-fashioned shop sells all types of foie gras and other duck preserves, straight from the owner's farm. 🔘 *60 rue St-Louis-en-l'Ile, 75004 • Map G5 • 01 55 42 14 88 • Closed Tue, Wed*

3 Librairie Ulysse
Today Paris, tomorrow the world. This eccentric travel book-shop will take you anywhere you want with thousands of titles in French and English – including many on Paris itself. 🔘 *26 rue St-Louis-en-l'Ile, 75004 • Map Q5 • Closed Sat–Mon*

4 Calixte
The place to stock up for a picnic or the day's treats, Calixte sells superb croissants for the morning, and pâtés, terrines and irresistible desserts for lunch.
🔘 *64 rue St-Louis-en-l'Ile, 75004 • Map Q5*

5 Clair de Rêve
This interesting boutique sells curiosities such as puppets, robots and miniature theatres making it an ideal shop if you're looking for a present with a difference. 🔘 *35 rue St-Louis-en-l'Ile, 75004 • Map Q5*

6 Alain Carion
A wealth of meteorites, fossils and minerals. Some are made into imaginative jewellery. 🔘 *92 rue St-Louis-en-l'Ile, 75004 • Map Q5 • Closed Sun, Mon*

7 Pylones Boutique
Rubber and painted metal are used to create the whimsical jewellery and accessories here, along with novelty gifts. 🔘 *57 rue St-Louis-en-l'Ile, 75004 • Map Q5*

8 Boulangerie des Deux Ponts
You won't be able to resist the freshly baked bread at this old-fashioned bakery. 🔘 *35 rue des Deux-Ponts, 75004 • Map Q5 • Closed Wed, Thu, Aug*

9 Arche de Noé
Translated as Noah's Ark, this is a treasure trove for children's gifts, with a good selection of old-fashioned toys.
🔘 *70 rue St-Louis-en-l'Ile, 75004 • Map Q5*

10 La Ferme Saint Aubin
Cheese in all shapes and sizes from all over France. An aromatic delight. 🔘 *76 rue St-Louis-en-l'Ile, 75004 • Map Q5 • Closed Mon*

For more on shopping in Paris **See p169**

Price Categories

For a three-course	**€** under €30
meal for one with half	**€€** €30–€40
a bottle of wine (or	**€€€** €40–€50
equivalent meal, taxes	**€€€€** €50–€60
and extra charges	**€€€€€** over €60

Left **La Rose de France** Right **Taverne Henry IV**

Places to Eat

1 Isami
One of the best Japanese restaurants in the city, but tiny so book ahead. Good choice of sushi. ◈ 4 quai d'Orléans, 75004 • Map P5 • 01 40 46 06 97 • Closed Sun, Mon, Aug (3 wks), 2 weeks Christmas • No disabled access • €€€€

2 Kitchen Galerie Bis
KGB serves inspired and innovative cuisine in a sleek setting. The menu offers a mix of traditional French dishes with modern global influences. ◈ 25 rue des Grands Augustins, 75006 • Map Q5 • 01 46 33 00 85 • Closed Sun, Mon and 4 weeks Jul–Aug • €€€

3 Les Fous de L'Ile
This modern Parisian bistro serves French classics such as entrecôte or steak tartare. It also hosts exhibitions and live concerts. ◈ 33 rue des Deux Ponts, 75004 • Map Q4 • 01 43 25 76 67 • Closed Tue L, Sat, Sun, end Feb, Aug • €€

4 Le Petit Plateau
This tea room is a great lunch spot, as it serves delicious home-made salads, quiches and cakes. ◈ 1 quai aux Fleurs, 75004 • Map G5 • 01 44 07 61 86 • Closed D, Sat in winter • No disabled access • €

5 Brasserie de l'Ile St-Louis
Wooden tables and a rustic look complement hearty Alsace fare such as Tripe in Riesling wine. ◈ 55 quai de Bourbon, 75004 • Map P4 • 01 43 54 02 59 • Closed Wed, Aug • No disabled access • €€€

6 La Rose de France
Lovely terrace and a cosy dining room. ◈ 24 pl Dauphine, 75001 • Map M3 • 01 43 54 10 12 • €€

7 Taverne Henri IV
A fine wine list and simple plates of *charcuterie* or cheese. ◈ 13 pl du Pont-Neuf, 75001 • Map M3 • 01 43 54 27 90 • Closed Sat, Sun, Aug • €€

8 Mon Vieil Ami
A chic interior is the backdrop for dishes such as foie gras. ◈ 69 rue St-Louis-en-l'Ile, 75004 • Map Q5 • 01 40 46 01 35 • Closed Mon, Tue, Jan, Aug • No disabled access • €€€€

9 Le Flore en l'Ile
Go for the views as well as the food in this bistro and tea room, open from breakfast until 1am. ◈ 42 quai d'Orléans, 75004 • Map P5 • 01 43 29 88 27 • No disabled access • €€

10 Berthillon
There is always a queue outside this legendary ice cream shop and tea room. ◈ 31 rue St-Louis-en-l'Ile, 75004 • Map G5 • 01 43 54 31 61 • Closed Mon, Tue, 1 week Feb, 1 week Easter, Aug • No credit cards • €

> **Note:** Unless otherwise stated, all restaurants accept credit cards and serve vegetarian meals

Left **Stravinsky fountains** Centre **Fashion in Les Halles** Right **One of the cinemas in Forum des Halles**

Beaubourg and Les Halles

THE SMALL BUT LIVELY BEAUBOURG QUARTER, *brimming with art galleries and cafés, has become a major tourist attraction since the construction of the Centre Georges Pompidou. This inside-out hulk of modern architecture has become the focus of the area and is France's third most visited site after the Musée du Louvre and the Eiffel Tower. Les Halles was the marketplace of Paris for 800 years, its glass-covered pavilions packed with butchers, fishmongers and fruit and vegetable stalls; novelist Emile Zola called it "the belly of Paris". In 1969, the market was demolished and moved to the suburbs to alleviate traffic congestion. The soulless underground shopping mall, Forum des Halles, which replaced it is currently undergoing a large-scale renovation, however some bistros and speciality shops can still be visited.*

Le Défenseur du Temps

Sights

1 Centre Georges Pompidou
2 Forum des Halles
3 St-Eustache
4 Bourse du Commerce
5 Le Défenseur du Temps
6 Fontaine des Innocents
7 Eglise St-Merri
8 St-Germain l'Auxerrois
9 Musée de la Poupée
10 Tour St-Jacques

74

1 Centre Georges Pompidou
See pp26–7.

2 Forum des Halles
Ten years after the original market was demolished, the so-called "largest urban hole in Europe" was filled with this controversial shopping complex. This largely underground maze caters to the young, with music shops and boutiques. Outside, buskers, young people and tourists throng the steps and gardens (not a place to linger at night). Today, it's more of a sore spot than a hotspot and French architect David Mangin has been commissioned to oversee its renovation, which will include a revamped shopping centre, gardens, metro and RER station. This is due to be completed by 2016/2017. ◈ *Map N2*

3 St-Eustache
With its majestic arches and pillars, St-Eustache is one of the most beautiful churches in Paris. Although Gothic in design, it took 105 years to build (1532–1637) and its interior decoration reflects the Renaissance style of this time. The church was modelled on Notre-Dame *(see pp18–21)*, with double side aisles and a ring of side chapels. The stained-glass windows made from sketches by Philippe de Champaigne (1631) and the ornate tomb of politician Jean-Baptiste Colbert (1619–83) are highlights. Don't miss the naive sculpture in Chapelle St-Joseph which recalls Les Halles' market days. ◈ *2 impasse St-Eustache, 75001 • Map M1 • Open 9:30am–7pm Mon–Fri, 10am–7pm Sat, Sun • Free*

4 Bourse du Commerce
The circular building which houses the Commodities Exchange was erected as a grain market in 1767 and remodelled in the 19th century. It was first covered with a wooden dome, then by subsequent structures of iron and copper. Under today's glass dome, activity in the world commodities market proceeds at a leisurely pace compared to the way other financial centres operate. ◈ *2 rue de Viarmes, 75001 • Map M1 • Open 8:30am–6pm Mon–Fri (identification papers are required to visit)*

St-Eustache

Georges Pompidou

Georges Pompidou (1911–74) had the unenviable task of following General de Gaulle as President of France, from 1969 until his death. During his tenure he initiated many architectural developments in Paris, including the controversial but ultimately successful Pompidou Centre, and the less popular scheme to demolish the Les Halles market.

Le Défenseur du Temps

The "Defender of Time", Paris's modern public clock, stands in the grim Quartier de l'Horloge (Clock Quarter) shopping area. This fantasy mechanical sculpture of brass and steel by Jacques Monastier is 4 m (13 ft) high and weighs 1 tonne. When the clock strikes the hour, the warrior fends off a savage cockerel, crab or dragon (representing air, water and earth) with his sword, with accompanying sound effects. At noon, 6pm and 10pm he vanquishes all three (when the clock is working). ◈ *Rue Bernard-de-Clairvaux, 75003 • Map P2*

Fontaine des Innocents

The Square des Innocents is a Les Halles crossroads and a hangout for street performers and young people. It was built atop a cemetery in the 18th century, and two million human remains were transferred to the Catacombs at Denfert-Rochereau. The Renaissance fountain, the last of its era built in the city, was designed by Pierre Lescot and carved by sculptor Jean Goujon in 1547. It originally stood against a wall on rue St-Denis, and was moved to the new square, when the fourth side was added *(see p39)*. ◈ *Rues St-Denis & Berger, 75001 • Map N2*

Eglise St-Merri

Formerly the parish church of the Lombard moneylenders, St-Merri was built between 1520 and 1612, and reflects the Flamboyant Gothic style. Its name is a corruption of St-Médéric, who was buried on this site in the early 8th century. The bell in the church's northwest turret, thought to be the oldest in Paris, dates from 1331 and hung in a chapel that once stood on the site. Other highlights include the decorative west front, the 17th-century organ loft, beautiful stained glass and carved wood panelling. ◈ *76 rue de la Verrerie, 75004 • Map P2 • Open noon–6:45pm daily • Free*

St-Germain l'Auxerrois

When the Valois kings moved to the Louvre palace in the 14th century *(see p8)*, this became the church of the royal family. On 24

St-Germain l'Auxerrois

ugust 1572, the tolling of its bell
was used as the signal for the
t Bartholomew's Day Massacre,
when thousands of Huguenots
who had come to Paris for the
wedding of Henri of Navarre to
Marguerite of Valois were
murdered *(see p20)*. The church
features a range of architectural
styles, from its flamboyant Gothic
façade to its Renaissance choir.
Try and visit on Sunday afternoon
when there are organ recitals.
⊛ *2 pl du Louvre, 75001* • *Map M2* • *Open*
am–7pm Mon–Sat, 9am–8pm Sun • *Free*

Musée de la Poupée
This delightful museum has
superb collection of 300 rare
French dolls, including unglazed
and-painted porcelain dolls which
were manufactured between
800 and 1945. The museum
explores the function of dolls and
their construction. It also features
the main doll makers of Germany
nd France. The museum runs a
oll hospital where doll doctor
Véronique Derez works miracles
n dolls of all ages. ⊛ *Impasse*
erthaud, 75003 • *Map P2* • *Open*
Oam–6pm Tue–Sun • *Closed public hols*
Admission charge

Tour St-Jacques
The late Gothic tower, dating
rom 1523, is all that remains of
he church of St-Jacques-la-
Boucherie, once the largest
medieval church in Paris and a
tarting point for pilgrims on
heir journey to Santiago de
Compostela in Spain. In the 17th
century the physicist Blaise Pascal
sed the tower for barometrical
xperiments. The church was
ulled down after the Revolution.
Visitors can explore the lower
oors of the tower and visit the
ardens around the base.
⊛ *39 rue de Rivoli, 75004*
Map N3

A Day in Les Halles

Morning

Start your day with
breakfast at the **Le Zimmer
Café** *(1 pl du Châtelet, 01
42 36 74 03)* before admiring
some of Picasso's paintings
at the **Centre Georges
Pompidou** *(see pp26–7)*
where the temporary
exhibits are also well worth
a look. If you need refresh-
ment after all that art, it
has to be **Georges**, the
chic brasserie at the top of
the centre with good views
and a choice of drinks,
snacks or main meals.

On leaving the centre turn
right into the Quartier de
l'Horloge to catch the noon
battle of the **Défenseur du
Temps** clock.

Providing you have booked
ahead, lunch at the 1912
bistro **Benoit** *(see p81)*,
whose lunchtime menu is
far cheaper than in the
evening. After lunch visit
the **Eglise St-Merri**.

Afternoon

Pass the **Fontaine des
Innocents** as you head for
Les Halles, but first go
into the church of **St-
Eustache** *(see p75)*, which
was the place of worship
of the market workers at
the old Les Halles. You
could then spend the rest
of the afternoon shopping
at the vast, if somewhat
unprepossessing **Forum
des Halles** *(see p75)*.

Stop for a drink at Tour
de Montlhéry, more
commonly known as **Chez
Denise** *(see p81)*. It's
packed at mealtimes, but
by late afternoon you
might be lucky enough to
get a seat and be ready to
try their famous Gâteau
Marguerite with straw-
berries and cream.

Left **Le Cochon à l'Oreille** Right **Sculpture outside St-Eustache church**

10 Memories of Les Halles

1 Le Cochon à l'Oreille
Dating back to the early 20th century, this ornate former working men's café/bar, decorated with historic tiles and murals, has only a small dining room so book in advance. *15 rue Montmartre, 75001 • Map F3*

2 Au Pied de Cochon
This 24-hour brasserie still serves dishes that used to appeal to the earthy tastes of market workers, including pigs' trotters *(see p81)*.

3 St-Eustache Sculpture
The naive sculpture by Raymond Mason in the church's Chapelle St-Joseph is a tribute to the beloved market. Its colourful figures depict *The Departure of Fruit and Vegetables from the Heart of Paris, 28 February 1969*.

4 Rue Montorgueil
The colourful market (Tuesday to Sunday) along this cobbled street is a reminder of the old Les Halles and is frequented by many Paris chefs. *Map N1*

5 Stöhrer
One of the loveliest old-fashioned patisseries in the city, founded in 1730 by a pastry chef who had worked for Louis XV. *51 rue Montorgueil, 75002 • Map N1*

6 Bistrot d'Eustache
A visit here is like stepping back into the jazz spots of Paris in the 1930–40s. It offers good, reasonably priced brasserie fare and live music on Friday and Saturday. *37 rue Berger, 75001 • Map N*

7 La Fresque
This wonderful restaurant used to be a fishmongers. An original fresco of a fishing scene still decorates the back room. *100 rue Rambuteau, 75001 • Map N1*

8 Dehillerin
Since 1820, everyone from army cooks to gourmet chefs has come here for copper pots, cast-iron pans and cooking utensils. *18 rue Coquillière, 75001 • Map N*

9 Duthilleul et Minart
For more than 100 years this shop has sold French work clothes and uniforms such as chef's hats and watchmaker's smocks. *14 rue de Turbigo, 75001 • Map P1*

10 A La Cloche des Halles
This wine bar literally rings with history. The "cloche" is the bronze bell whose peal once signalled the beginning and end of the market day. *28 rue Coquillière, 75001 • Map M1*

Left **Typical Paris beer bar** Centre **Le Sous-Bock** Right **Au Trappiste**

🔟 Beer Bars

1 Le Sous-Bock
A good place for *moules* (mussels), with 200 types of beer to wash them down with. There are also 40 whiskies.
49 rue St-Honoré, 75001 • Map M2

2 Quigley's Point
Right in front of Eglise St-Eustache, this friendly Irish pub serves beer from Holland, Germany, Ireland and Britain.
5 rue du Jour, 75001 • Map M1

3 Hall's Beer Tavern
Although situated in a fairly touristy street, this is a relaxed and friendly place with a good selection of draught beers, including La Chouffe and Duvel.
68 rue St-Denis, 75001 • Map N2

4 Le Bogman
Formerly the Goblet d'Argent, this bar may have changed name and location, but it retains an Irish pub feel, with a dartboard and live music on Tuesdays. *2 rue de la Petite Truanderie, 75001 • Map N1*

5 The Frog and Rosbif
For homesick English or Anglophiles, this is the place to find real ale (brewed downstairs) and fish and chips, play pub quizzes, read English newspapers and watch live football and rugby matches.
116 rue St-Denis, 75002 • Map F3

6 McBrides
A popular place to watch football, this friendly Irish sports bar attracts homesick expats with its fried breakfasts. Enjoy live music on Sunday nights.
54 rue St-Denis, 75001 • Map F4 • 01 40 26 46 70

7 Au Trappiste
Among the many beers on tap, sample Jenlain, a French brew, and the Belgian Hoegaarden. Food is also served. *4 rue St-Denis, 75001 • Map F3*

8 Guinness Tavern
Fourteen beers are on tap in this Irish bar with live music every night and a bigger Irish concert once a month. The party really kicks off after 10pm. *31 bis rue des Lombards, 75004 • Map N2*

9 Café Oz
A range of Australian beers and wines combined with archetypal Outback decor makes this rowdy bar popular with antipodean expatriates and French patrons alike. *18 rue St-Denis, 75001 • Map F3*

🔟 La Taverne de Maître Kanter
Part of a chain of Alsatian-style taverns, this is a good place to relax over a pint of French beer. Food is also served. *16 rue Coquillière, 75001 • Map F3 • 01 42 36 74 24*

⟹ *For more cafés and bars* See pp52–3

79

Left **View of Les Halles c.1870-80**

🔟 Historical Events in Les Halles

1 Roman Era
A marketplace was first established on the Right Bank of the Seine in a place then called Les Champeaux.

2 10th Century
A larger market for meat, fruit and vegetables is known to have existed in the part of Paris which is now Les Halles.

3 1183
The market is enlarged by King Philippe Auguste, who built shelters for the market traders near St-Eustache church *(see p75)*. This date is generally accepted as the founding of Les Halles as the city's market.

4 1850s
Twelve huge iron and glass market halls are built. Napoleon III declares that Les Halles is essential to Paris life.

5 1965
Work begins on a modern wholesale market south of Paris, at Rungis.

6 1969
The central Paris market is closed and moved to Rungis, partly to ease the traffic congestion that was by now too much for the centre of the city.

7 1971
The old buildings are demolished and digging begins, to create for a time what is

known as the *trou des Halles* (the hole of Les Halles).

8 Mid-1970s
As well as the shopping malls, gardens are created and buildings next to the cleared space can be seen properly for the first time, including the church of St-Eustache.

9 1977
The Forum des Halles opens and ensures that the area remains as busy as ever, although the goods for sale (high fashion, CDs, fast food) have changed considerably since the market's early days.

10 2010
Massive renovation and restructuring begins; the renovation is scheduled to be completed by 2016/2017 and the area is expected to undergo a complete face-lift.

St-Eustache

 For more on shopping in Paris **See p169**

Price Categories

For a three-course meal for one with half a bottle of wine (or equivalent meal), taxes and extra charges

€ under €30
€€ €30–€40
€€€ €40–€50
€€€€ €50–€60
€€€€€ over €60

Above **Au Pied de Cochon**

🔟 Places to Eat

1 Dans le Noir
For brave souls only, this pitch-black restaurant provides a unique dining experience. ◎ 51 rue Quincampoix, 75004 • Map F4 • 01 42 77 98 04 • Closed lunch Sun–Wed • No disabled access • €€€€

2 Au Pied de Cochon
Long-time Les Halles favourite. If your taste is not for offal, there are options such as oysters and steak. Open 24 hours a day. ◎ 6 rue Coquillière, 75001 • Map M1 • 01 40 13 77 00 • €€€

3 Benoit
Super-chef Alain Ducasse's smart bistro in Paris, which has one Michelin star but erratic service. ◎ 20 rue St-Martin, 75004 • Map P1 • 01 42 72 25 76 • Closed Aug • No disabled access • €€€€€

4 L'Ambassade d'Auvergne
Auvergne cooking, with lots of pork and cabbage dishes. Shared tables; good for solo diners. ◎ 22 rue du Grenier-St-Lazare, 75003 • Map P1 • 01 42 72 31 22 • Closed Sun, Mon, mid-Jul–mid-Aug • No disabled access • €€

5 Tour de Montlhéry, Chez Denise
A Les Halles legend for its huge portions. Book in advance. ◎ 5 rue des Prouvaires, 75001 • Map N2 • 01 42 36 21 82 • Closed Sat, Sun, mid-Jul–mid-Aug • €€€

6 Le Tambour
This 24-hour bistro draws a lively crowd with its friendly service and hearty French fare. ◎ 41 rue Montmartre, 75002 • Map N1 • 01 42 33 06 90 • Closed Mon • €€

7 Café Beaubourg
The terrace here overlooks the Pompidou Centre. Steak tartare is a house special. ◎ 43 rue St-Merri, 75004 • Map P2 • 01 48 87 63 96 • No disabled access • €€

8 Spring
American chef Daniel Rose offers a fixed menu, which includes dishes made with fresh ingredients from the market. Book in advance. ◎ 6 rue Bailleul, 75001 • Map M2 • 01 45 96 05 72 • €€€€€

9 Restaurant Georges
Sleek design and a great view make this museum restaurant a great choice for a glamorous night out. ◎ Centre Georges Pompidou, 19 rue Beaubourg, 75004 • Map G4 • 01 44 78 47 99 • Closed Tue • €€€€

10 Le Hangar
Hidden down a street near the Pompidou, this small, friendly bistro is no secret to locals, who keep returning for the fabulous food, such as steak tartare, foie gras and moelleux au chocolat. ◎ 12 Impasse Berthaud, 75003 • Map G4 • 01 42 74 55 44 • Closed Sun, Mon • €€€

Left **Place des Vosges street sign** Centre **Place de la Bastille** Right **Maison de Victor Hugo**

Marais and the Bastille

FOR MANY, THE MARAIS IS THE MOST ENJOYABLE quarter of Paris, with its mansions, museums and medieval lanes, but the district was little more than a muddy swamp until Henri IV built the place Royale (now place des Vosges) in 1605. Following its notoriety as the birthplace of the Revolution, the Bastille district sank into oblivion, until artists and designers arrived in the 1990s. Its streets are now home to the city's liveliest nightspots.

🔟 Sights

1	Musée Picasso	**6**	Marché d'Aligre
2	Musée Cognacq-Jay	**7**	The Passages
3	Place des Vosges	**8**	Rue de Lappe
4	Musée Carnavalet	**9**	Maison Européenne de la Photographie
5	Place de la Bastille	**10**	Maison de Victor Hugo

Bastille passage

Preceding pages **Notre-Dame seen from the Seine**

Musée Picasso

When the Spanish-born artist Pablo Picasso died in 1973, his family donated thousands of his works to the French state in lieu of estate taxes. Thus Paris enjoys the largest collection of Picassos in the world. Housed in the Hôtel Salé *(see p90)*, the museum displays the range of his artistic development, from his Blue and Pink Periods to Cubism, and reveals his proficiency in an astonishing range of techniques and materials *(see p36)*. The museum is due to reopen in mid-2013 after extensive renovations.

◈ *5 rue de Thorigny, 75003* • *Map R2*
• *Closed for refurbishment* • *Admission charge (free first Sun of month)*
• *www.musee-picasso.fr*

Musée Cognacq-Jay

This small but excellent museum portrays the sophisticated French lifestyle in the so-called Age of Enlightenment, which centred around Paris. The 18th-century art and furniture on display were once the private collection of Ernest Cognacq and his wife, Louise Jay, founders of the Samaritaine department store. It is superbly displayed in the Hôtel Donon, an elegant late 16th-century town mansion *(see p35)*. ◈ *8 rue Elzévir, 75003* • *Map Q3*
• *Open 10am–6pm Tue–Sun* • *www. cognacq-jay.paris.fr*

Place des Vosges

Paris's oldest square is also one of the most beautiful in the world. The square was commissioned by Henri IV. Its 36 houses with red-gold brick and stone façades, slate roofs and dormer windows were laid out with striking symmetry in 1612. Originally built for silk workers, the likes of Cardinal Richelieu (1585–1642) and playwright Molière (1622–73) quickly moved in and it remains an upper-class residential address. But everyone can enjoy a stroll around the area and the art galleries under the arcades. ◈ *Map R3*

Musée Carnavalet

Devoted to the history of Paris, this museum sprawls through two mansions, the 16th-century Carnavalet and 17th-century Le Peletier de Saint-Fargeau. The former was the home of Madame de Sévigné, the famous letter-writer, from 1677 to 1696 and a gallery here portrays her life. The extensive museum contains period rooms filled with art and portraits. Revolutionary artifacts and memorabilia of 18th-century philosophers Rousseau and Voltaire can be found *(see p34)*.
◈ *23 rue de Sévigné, 75003* • *Map R3*
• *Open 10am–6pm Tue–Sun* • *www. carnavalet.paris.fr*

Place de la Bastille

Today this notorious square has become a busy traffic circle. Originally, the Bastille was a fortress built by Charles V to

Musée Cognacq-Jay

The Jewish Quarter

The Jewish Quarter, centred around rues des Rosiers and des Écouffes, was established in the 13th century and has attracted immigrants since the Revolution. Many Jews fled here to escape persecution in Eastern Europe, but were arrested during the Nazi Occupation. Since World War II, Sephardic Jews from North Africa have found new homes here.

defend the eastern edge of the city, but it soon became a jail for political prisoners. Angry citizens, rising up against the excesses of the monarchy, stormed the Bastille on 14 July 1789 *(see p45)*, setting off the French Revolution, and destroyed this hated symbol of oppression. In its place is the bronze Colonne de Juillet (July Column), 52 m (171 ft) high and crowned by the Angel of Liberty, which commemorates those who died in the revolutions of 1830 and 1848. Looming behind it is the Opéra Bastille, once the largest opera house in the world, which opened on the bicentennial of the Revolution in 1989. 🅜 Map H5

6 **Marché d'Aligre**
Set around an old guardhouse and clock-tower, the wonderful Aligre market is a melting pot of Parisians from all walks of life. It dates back to 1643 and was once as important as the more famous Les Halles *(see p75)*. In the gourmet covered market you'll see everything from rows of pheasants to a whole wild boar hanging from the stalls. North African traders give the outdoor produce market an ethnic flare. The flea market dates back to the days when nuns distributed second-hand clothing to the poor *(see p55)*. 🅜 place d'Aligre • Map H5 • Open until 1am Tue–Sat, to 2am Sun

7 **The Passages**
The Bastille has been a quarter of working-class artisans and craft guilds since the 17th century and many furniture makers are still located in these small alleyways, called *passages*. The rue du Faubourg-St-Antoine is lined with shops displaying a striking array of both traditional period furniture and modern designs, but don't neglect to visit the narrow *passages*, such as the Passage de l'Homme, running off this and other streets

Rue de Lappe

the Bastille. Many artists and craftspeople have their ateliers (workshops) in these atmospheric alleys. ◈ Map H5

Rue de Lappe
Once famous for its 1930s dance halls (bals musettes), rue de Lappe is still the Bastille's after-dark hotspot. This short, narrow street is filled with bars, clubs, restaurants and cafés, and positively throbs with music. Crowds of hip night-owls trawl the cobblestones looking for action, and spill into the adjoining rue de la Roquette and rue de Charonne where there are even more trendy bars and restaurants. ◈ Map H5

Maison Européenne de la Photographie
This excellent gallery showcasing contemporary European photography opened in 1996 in an early 18th-century mansion, Hôtel Hénault de Cantorbre. The restoration is a mix of historic features and modern spaces that show off its permanent collection and changing exhibitions of items from its archives.
◈ 5–7 rue de Fourcy, 75004 • Map Q3 • Open 11am–8pm Wed–Sun • Admission charge (free Wed after 5pm & for under 8s) • www.mep-fr.org

Maison de Victor Hugo
French author Victor Hugo (1802–85) lived on the second floor of the Hôtel de Rohan-Guéménée, the largest house on the place des Vosges, from 1832 to 1848. He wrote most of Les Misérables here (see p46) and many other works. In 1903 the house became a museum of his life. ◈ 6 pl des Vosges, 75004 • Map R4 • Open 10am–6pm Tue–Sun • Closed public holidays • Admission charge for exhibitions • www.musee-hugo.paris.fr

A Day in the Marais

Morning

Begin the morning at the **Musée Carnavalet** (see p85), to beat the crowds and allow enough time to view the impressive collections. There is also a lovely garden courtyard. Afterwards, walk to the place des Vosges. Stand in the centre near the fountains to take in the whole square.

Have a coffee at Ma Bourgogne (19 pl des Vosges • 01 42 78 44 64), right on the square. Afterwards, tour the **Maison de Victor Hugo**, then go to the southwest corner of the square, through a wooden door to the pretty garden of the **Hôtel de Béthune-Sully** (see p90). Then walk to place de la Bastille.

A good lunch choice is **Brasserie Bofinger** (see p65), with its ornate decor and true Parisian feel.

Afternoon

The **place de la Bastille** (see p85) is something of a traffic nightmare, but take time to admire the column in the centre and contemplate the events that happened here when this was the site of the city's dreaded prison. Walk around the square and along rue Faubourg-St-Antoine, a now fashionable shopping street. Turn off down some of the passageways to see the furniture-makers and craft workshops that have a long history in the area.

From here it's not far to the **Gare de Lyon** and dinner in style beneath the chandeliers and frescoes of **Le Train Bleu** (20 blvd Diderot • 01 43 43 09 06).

Left **Isabel Marant** Right **Antoine et Lili**

TOP 10 Shops

1 Izraël
Also called the "World of Spices", this is a treasure trove of the world's best food and drink. Tiny but packed with meat, cheese, wine, rum, dates, honey, mustard...it has to be seen. ◈ 30 rue François-Miron, 75004 • Map P3

2 BHV
The Bazar de l'Hôtel de Ville is an upmarket all-round shopper's paradise at which you can track down everything from DIY products to stylish underwear. ◈ 52–64 rue de Rivoli, 75004 • Map F4

3 Antoine et Lili
Vibrant and eclectic clothes for women inspired by tzigane and Oriental styles using colourful natural fabrics. ◈ 51 rue des Francs-Bourgeois, 75004 • Map Q3

4 Autour du Monde
Stylish clothes and objects for the home from French designer Bensimon. The canvas sneakers in pastel colours for kids and adults are a classic. ◈ 8, 12 rue des Francs Bourgeois, 75003 • Map G4 • 01 42 77 16 18

5 Florence Kahn
This shop offers a range of cakes with freshly baked rye bread and a deli. ◈ 24 rue des Ecouffes, 75004 • Map Q3

6 Fleux
This concept store is dedicated to contemporary Parisian interior design, with furniture and innovative home accessories. ◈ 39 rue Sainte Croix de Bretonnerie, 75004 • Map P2

7 Isabel Marant
A designer starting to get a lot of recognition outside Paris, her work is hip but elegant. ◈ 16 rue de Charonne, 75011 • Map H5

8 Sessùn
This is the flagship store of the young French womenswear label, which produces chic, edgy clothes and accessories. ◈ 34 rue de Charonne, 75011 • Map H5

9 Merci
This trendy, three-storey concept store stocks clothes, homeware and stationery. It is also home to three cafés. ◈ 111 blvd Beaumarchais, 75003 • Map H4 • 01 42 77 00 33

10 Emery & Cie
Stylish, coloured ceramics, tiles, lamps and other goods, run by an interior decorator. ◈ 18 passage de la Main d'Or, 75011 • Map H5

For more on shopping in Paris **See p169**

Left **The Red Wheelbarrow** Centre **A la Petite Fabrique** Right **L'Arbre à Lettres**

TOP 10 Specialist Shops

1 The Red Wheelbarrow Bookstore
An English-language bookshop where you can pick up that translated French classic you may have been inspired to read. ◈ 22 rue St-Paul, 75004 • Map R4

2 Mariage Frères
This famous tea house was founded in 1854 and sells all kinds of blends, as well as tea-making paraphernalia. ◈ 6 rue du Bourg-Tibourg, 75004 • Map Q3

3 Goumanyat
Paris's top chefs stock up on herbs, spices and teas here. This is a great place to find an interesting food gift or souvenir. ◈ 3 rue Dupuis, 75003 • Map R1 • 01 44 78 96 74

4 Pasta Linea
Visit for fresh pasta dishes all made in-house from organic flour. Not much seating, but the leafy place des Vosges is nearby. ◈ 9 rue de Turenne, 75004 • Map G4 • Closed Sun, Mon, Aug

5 Village Saint-Paul
This wonderful maze of art galleries, fine antiques and design shops is located behind Eglise Saint-Paul. ◈ Between rue St-Paul and rue des Jardins St-Paul, 75004 • Map R4

6 L'Art du Bureau
If your desk is your altar, you'll find everything you could possibly need here, and it's all in the most modern designs. In fact, this shop is worth visiting for the design aspects alone. ◈ 47 rue des Francs-Bourgeois, 75004 • Map R3

7 L'Arbre à Lettres
A beautiful bookshop; its content is on the serious side, focusing on fine arts, literature and human sciences. ◈ 56 rue du Faubourg-St-Antoine, 75012 • Map H5

8 A l'Olivier
Since 1822, this shop has specialized in all kinds of oil, from the finest olive oil to other Provençal specialities. ◈ 23 rue de Rivoli, 75004 • Map H5

9 Papeterie Saint Sabin
Parisian stationery shops are a class apart, and here you will find stylish notebooks, pens, pads and other tasteful items. ◈ 16 rue St-Sabin, 75011 • Map H4

10 A la Petite Fabrique
This shop doesn't just sell chocolate, you can watch it being made. More than 40 flavours and novelty chocolates in all shapes. ◈ 12 rue St-Sabin, 75011 • Map H4

Left **Hôtel de Sens** Centre **Hôtel de Soubise** Right **Hôtel de Lamoignon**

Mansions

Hôtel de Coulanges
1 This mansion boasts beautiful early 18th-century architecture, although the right wing dates from the early 1600s. ◎ 35 rue des Francs-Bourgeois, 75004 • Map Q2 • Open only for concerts

Hôtel Salé
2 Built in 1656–9 for Aubert de Fontenay, a salt-tax collector, this mansion is now the home of the Musée Picasso (see p85).

Hôtel Guénégaud
3 Designed by the architect François Mansart in the mid-17th century, this splendid mansion houses a Hunting Museum. ◎ 60 rue des Archives, 75003 • Map P3 • Open 11am–6pm Tue–Sun • Admission charge

Hôtel de Beauvais
4 The young Mozart performed at this 17th-century mansion. Notice the balcony decorated with goats' heads. ◎ 68 rue François-Miron, 75004 • Map P3 • Closed to the public

Hôtel de Béthune-Sully
5 This 17th-century mansion was home to the Duc de Sully, chief minister to Henri IV. It now houses the French National Monuments administration. ◎ 62 rue St-Antoine, 75004 • Map R4 • Closed to the public except gardens

Hôtel de Sens
6 One of Paris's few medieval mansions. Henri IV's wife Marguerite de Valois (see p20) lived here after their divorce. It is now home to a fine arts library. ◎ 1 rue Figuier, 75004 • Map Q4 • Closed to the public

Hôtel de St-Aignan
7 The plain exterior hides an enormous mansion within. It is now the Museum of Jewish Art and History. ◎ 71 rue du Temple, 75003 • Map P2 • Open 11am–6pm Mon–Fri, 10am–6pm Sun • Admission charge • www.mahj.org

Hôtel de Soubise
8 Along with the adjacent Hôtel de Rohan, this mansion houses the national archives. ◎ 60 rue des Francs-Bourgeois, 75003 • Map Q2 • Open 10am–12:30pm, 2–5:30pm Wed–Fri, 2–5:30pm Sat & Sun • Admission charge

Hôtel de Lamoignon
9 Built in 1584 for the daughter of Henri II. ◎ 24 rue Pavée, 75004 • Map Q3 • Closed to the public

Hôtel de Marle
10 The Swedish Institute is located here. ◎ 11 rue Payenne, 75003 • Map G4 • Open noon–6pm Tue–Sun • Closed mid-Jul–end Aug

For more historic buildings in Paris **See pp42–3**

eft **Galerie Patrick Seguin** Centre **Galerie Lavignes-Bastille** Right **Galerie Nikki Diana Marquardt**

Galleries

1 Galerie Marian Goodman
Housed in a 17th-century mansion, this gallery is a slice of New York. Artists include Jeff Wall and video-maker Steve McQueen. ⊗ *79 rue du Temple, 75003 • Map P2 • Open 11am–7pm Tue–Sat • Closed Aug*

2 Galerie Akié Arichi
Eclectic exhibitions covering photography, sculpture and paint, often with an Asian influence. ⊗ *26 rue Keller, 75011 • Map H5 • Open 2:30–7pm Tue–Sat • www.galeriearichi.com*

3 Galerie Alain Gutharc
Alain Gutharc devotes his space to the work of young, contemporary artists. ⊗ *7 rue St Claude, 75003 • Map H4 • Open 11am–1pm, 2–7pm Tue–Sat • www.alaingutharc.com*

4 Galerie Daniel Templon
A favourite among the French contemporary art establishment, exhibiting big, international names as well as talented newcomers. ⊗ *30 rue Beaubourg, 75003 • Map P2 • Open 10am–7pm Mon–Sat • www.danieltemplon.com*

5 Galerie Karsten Greve
A leading international gallery with top names in modern and contemporary art and photography. ⊗ *5 rue Debelleyme, 75003 • Map R2 • Open 10am–7pm Tue–Sat*

6 Galerie Patrick Seguin
This gallery features stylish 20th-century furniture and architecture. ⊗ *5 rue des Taillandiers, 75011 • Map H4 • Open 10am–7pm Tue–Sat*

7 Galerie Lavignes-Bastille
Narrative figuration, Op Art and new artists are featured here. ⊗ *27 rue de Charonne, 75011 • Map H5 • Open 2–7pm Tue–Sat • www.lavignesbastille.com*

8 Galerie Thaddeus Ropac
A major contemporary gallery showcasing new, international artists. ⊗ *7 rue Debelleyme, 75003 • Map Q1 • Open 10am–7pm Tue–Sat • www.ropac.net*

9 Galerie Yvon Lambert
One of the stalwarts of contemporary art in Paris, this gallery hosts changing exhibitions and photography. ⊗ *108 rue Vieille du Temple, 75003 • Map Q1 • Open 10am–7pm Tue–Sat • www.yvon-lambert.com*

10 Galerie Nikki Diana Marquardt
This gallery contains politically motivated artworks executed in all types of art media. ⊗ *9 pl des Vosges, 75004 • Map R3 • Open 1–6pm Mon–Fri • www.galerienikkidiana marquardt.com*

Left **Le Square Trousseau** Right **Pop In**

Sidebar text (rotated): Around Town – Marais & the Bastille

TOP10 Fashionable Hang-outs

1 Zéro Zéro
It doesn't get much cooler than this den-like bar with wood panelling and flowered wallpaper. Though not listed on the menu, cocktails are a speciality. ✆ *89 rue Amelot, 75011* • Map H4

2 Andy Wahloo
Located in one of Henri IV's former mansions, pop art and Oriental decor form a backdrop for some of the city's most fashionable soirées. ✆ *69 rue des Gravilliers, 75003* • Map Q1

3 La Perle
This popular bistro is one of the capital's most famous hang-outs, drawing a fashionable crowd in the evening. ✆ *78 rue Vieille du Temple, 75003* • Map Q2 • 01 42 72 69 93

4 Bataclan
This venerable concert hall attracts international artists as well as household French names. The adjoining bar provides beer and meals. ✆ *50 boulevard Voltaire, 75011* • Map H4

5 Pop In
This shabby-chic bar cum nightclub has cheap drinks, friendly staff, a cool crowd and funky DJs. It is open on Sundays. ✆ *105 rue Amelot, 75011* • Map H4

6 Café de l'Industrie
This fashionable and sizeable café has three rooms where the walls are lined with paintings and old-fashioned artifacts. The food is cheap but pretty good, and the later it gets the better the buzz *(see p53)*. ✆ *16 rue St-Sabin, 75011* • Map H4

7 Grazie
This Italian pizzeria with an industrial loft-style decor attracts a hip crowd. ✆ *91 blvd Beaumarchais, 75003* • Map H4 • 01 42 78 11 96

8 Le Panic Room
Top Parisian DJs set the tone at this quirky bar offering fancy cocktails, a smoking room and cellar dance floor. ✆ *101 rue Amelot, 75011* • Map H4

9 Le Square Trousseau
This media haunt in the Bastille district serves breakfast, lunch and dinner and has a lovely heated terrace. ✆ *1 rue Antoine-Vollon, 75012* • Map H5

10 Le Progrès
The pavement terrace of this corner café in the trendy Northern Marais fills up during Paris Fashion Week. ✆ *1 rue de Bretagne, 75003* • Map R2 • 01 42 72 01 44

*For more bars in Paris **See pp52–3***

Price Categories

For a three-course **€** under €30
meal for one with half **€€** €30–€50
a bottle of wine (or **€€€** €40–€50
equivalent meal), taxes **€€€€** €50–€60
and extra charges **€€€€€** over €60

Left **La Gazzetta**

10 Places to Eat

1 L'Ambroisie
The finest service matches the finest of food. The wine list is renowned and the chocolate tart is out of this world. Reserve in advance. ❀ *9 pl des Vosges, 75004 • Map R3 • 01 42 78 51 45 • Closed Sun, Mon • €€€€€*

2 Café des Musées
A traditional bistro, which serves classic French dishes such as steak tartare and *crème brûlée*. ❀ *49 rue de Turenne, 75003 • Map R2 • 01 42 72 96 17 • No disabled access • €€*

3 Patisserie Carette
Salads and sandwiches, as well as delicious cakes, feature at this patisserie and tea room on the picturesque place des Vosges. ❀ *25 pl des Vosges, 75003 • Map G4 • 01 48 87 94 07 • €*

4 Au Vieux Chêne
Hidden down a side street, this atmospheric bistro is a treat. Expect updated French classics such as duck *pot-au-feu* with foie gras. ❀ *7 rue Dahomey, 75011 • 01 43 71 67 69 • Closed Sat, Sun, Aug • €€€*

5 La Gazzetta
Inventive, contemporary dishes, such as venison, polenta, dried figs and dandelion leaves are served in a relaxing Neo-Art Deco setting. ❀ *29 rue de Cotte, 75012 • Map H5 • 01 43 47 47 05 • Open Tue–Sat • €€€*

6 Breizh Café
An award-winning crêperie with a contemporary take on both savoury and sweet Breton pancakes. ❀ *109 rue Vieille du Temple, 75003 • Map G4 • 01 42 72 13 77 • Closed Mon, Tue • €€*

7 Le Baron Rouge
Cold meats and cheese platters are served in an authentic setting by the Aligre Market. ❀ *1 rue Théophile-Roussel, 75012 • Map H5 • 01 43 43 14 32 • Closed Mon, Sun D • €*

8 Chez Paul
This old bistro has a fairly simple but delicious menu. Book ahead. ❀ *13 rue de Charonne, 75011 • Map H5 • 01 47 00 34 57 • €€*

9 Septime
This modern restaurant serves dishes such as cress and sorrel risotto and veal tartare. ❀ *80 rue de Charonne, 75011 • Map H5 • 01 43 67 38 29 • €€*

10 L'As du Fallafel
This is the best falafel joint in the city. The "special" with aubergine and spicy sauce is a must. ❀ *34 rue des Rosiers, 75004 • Map Q3 • 01 48 87 63 60 • Closed Fri D, Sat • €*

Note: *Unless otherwise stated, all restaurants accept credit cards and serve vegetarian meals*

Left **Musée du Louvre** Centre **Café Marly, Louvre** Right **Musée Nationale de la Mode et du Textile**

Tuileries and Opéra Quarters

THESE TWO QUARTERS were once the province of the rich and the royal. Adjoining the Tuileries Gardens is the largest museum in the world, the Louvre, while the grand opera house gives the second quarter its name. The place de la Concorde is one of the most historic sites in the city.

Sights

1. Musée du Louvre
2. Rue de Rivoli
3. Place de la Concorde
4. Jardin des Tuileries
5. Musée des Arts Décoratifs
6. Art Nouveau Museum
7. Palais-Royal
8. Place Vendôme
9. Opéra National de Paris Garnier
10. Place de la Madeleine

Opéra de Paris Garnier

Share your travel recommendations on traveldk.com

1 Musée du Louvre
See pp8–10.

2 Rue de Rivoli
Commissioned by Napoleon and named after his victory over the Austrians at Rivoli in 1797, his grand street links the Louvre with the Champs-Elysées (see p103). It was intended as a backdrop for victory marches but was not finished until the 1850s, long after the emperor's death. Along one side, railings replaced the old Tuileries walls, opening up the view, while opposite, Neo-Classical apartments sit atop the long arcades. These are now filled with a mix of shops, selling luxury goods or tourist souvenirs. ◈ Map M2

3 Place de la Concorde
This historic octagonal square, covering more than 8 ha (20 acres), is bounded by the Tuileries Gardens on one side and marks the starting point of the Champs-Elysées on the other. It was built between 1755–75 to designs by architect Jacques-Ange Gabriel as the grand setting for a statue of Louis XV, but by 1792 it had become the place de la Révolution and its central monument was the guillotine. Louis XVI, Marie-Antoinette and more than 1,000 others were executed here (see p70). In 1795, in the spirit of reconciliation, it received its present name. The central obelisk, 23 m (75 ft) tall and covered in hieroglyphics, is from a 3,300-year-old Luxor temple, and was a gift from Egypt, erected in 1833. Two fountains and eight statues representing French cities were also added. On the north side of the square are the mansions Hôtel de la Marine and Hôtel Crillon, also by Gabriel. ◈ Map D3

Arcades on rue de Rivoli

4 Jardin des Tuileries
These gardens (see p38) were first laid out as part of the old Tuileries Palace, which was built for Catherine de Médici in 1564 but burned down in 1871. André Le Nôtre redesigned them into formal French gardens in 1664. At the Louvre end is the Arc de Triomphe du Carrousel, erected by Napoleon in 1808. Here is also the entrance to the underground shopping centre, the Carrousel du Louvre. Nearby, sensuous nude sculptures by Aristide Maillol (1861–1944) adorn the ornamental pools and walkways. At the far end is the hexagonal pool, the Jeu de Paume gallery (see p36) and the Musée de l'Orangerie (see p37), famous for its giant canvases of Monet waterlilies. ◈ Map J2

5 Musée des Arts Décoratifs
This huge collection covers the decorative arts from the Middle Ages to the 20th century. With over 100 rooms, the many highlights include the Medieval and Renaissance rooms, the Art Deco rooms and a superb jewellery collection. Also in the same building is the Musée Nationale de la Mode et du Textile with displays of fashion, textiles, posters and advertising ephemera in changing temporary exhibitions. ◈ 107 rue de Rivoli, 75001 • Map M2 • Open 11am–6pm Tue–Sun (until 9pm Thu) • Admission charge • www.lesartsdecoratifs.fr

Storming of the Tuileries

Looking at the Tuileries Gardens now, where children play and lovers stroll, it is hard to imagine the scenes that took place here on 20 June 1792. The palace and gardens were invaded by French citizens seeking to overthrow the monarchy. This was finally achieved on 10 August, when the Tuileries Palace was sacked and Louis XVI overthrown.

Art Nouveau Museum

This small museum (which is part of the famous Maxim's restaurant) houses Pierre Cardin's impressive Art Nouveau collection. The 750 works of art, designed by big names such as Tiffany, Toulouse-Lautrec, Galle Massier and Marjorelle, are set in a re-created 1900s apartment. A guided visit can be combined with dinner in the glamorous restaurant. ◎ 3 rue Royale, 75008 • Map D3 • Open 2–5:30pm Wed–Sun, guided tours 2pm (in English), 3:15pm, 4:30pm • Adm • www.maxims-musee-artnouveau.com

Palais-Royal

In the late 18th century extensive changes were made under the dukes of Orléans. The architect Victor Louis was commissioned to build 60 uniformly styled houses around three sides of the square and the adjacent theatre, which now houses the Comédie Française (see p59). Today the arcades house specialist shops, galleries and restaurants, and the courtyard and gardens contain modern works of art (see p43). ◎ Pl du Palais-Royal, 75001 • Map L1 • Open Oct–Mar: 7am–8:30pm daily; Apr–May: 7:30am–10:15pm daily; Sep: 7am–9:30pm daily • Public access to gardens and arcades only

Place Vendôme

Jules Hardouin-Mansart, the architect of Versailles (see p151), designed the façades of this elegant royal square for Louis XIV in 1698. Originally intended for foreign embassies, bankers soon moved in and built lavish dwellings. It remains home to jewellers and financiers today.

Palais Royal courtyard

Opéra de Paris Garnier façade

the world-famous Ritz hotel was established here at the turn of the 20th century. It is currently closed for renovations until 2016. The central column, topped by a statue of Napoleon, is a replica of the one destroyed by the Commune in 1871. ◈ Map E3

9 Opéra National de Paris Garnier

Designed by Charles Garnier for Napoleon III in 1862, Paris' opulent opera house took 13 years to complete. A range of styles from Classical to Baroque incorporates stone friezes and columns, statues and a green, copper cupola. The ornate interior has a Grand Staircase, mosaic domed ceiling over the Grand Foyer and an auditorium with a ceiling by Marc Chagall. There's even an underground lake – the inspiration for Gaston Leroux's Phantom of the Opera – sadly closed to visitors (see p58). ◈ Pl de l'Opéra, 75009 • Map E2 • 01 71 25 24 23 • Open 10am–5pm daily (closes at 1pm on day of matinee performances; closed public hols) • Admission charge • www.operadeparis.fr

10 Place de la Madeleine

Surrounded by 52 Corinthian columns, the huge Classical-style La Madeleine church (see p40) commands this elegant square. On the east side a colourful flower market is held Tuesday to Saturday. The square is surrounded by some of the most upmarket épiceries (food stores) and speciality shops in the city (see p98). ◈ Map D3

A Day in the Tuileries

Morning

⏱ Visiting the **Louvre** (see pp8–11) takes planning, and you should get there at least 15 minutes before opening (unless you've already bought your ticket). Spend the whole morning and pick up a map as you enter so that you can be sure to see the main highlights. Have a morning coffee in the elegant Richelieu, Denon or Mollien cafés within the museum.

From the Louvre, either visit the Carrousel du Louvre's underground shops or walk along **rue de Rivoli** towards **place de la Concorde** (see p95). This end of the street is filled with souvenir shops but avoid the overpriced cafés and turn right to rue Mondovi for a good lunch at Lescure, a little rustic bistro (7 rue de Mondovi • 01 42 60 18 91 • Closed Sat, Sun).

Afternoon

After being indoors all morning, get some fresh air in the **Jardin des Tuileries** (see p95) then walk down to **place de la Madeleine** to spend the afternoon shopping in its many food stores, or visit the **Art Nouveau Museum** and admire its decorative arts collection. Later, take tea in the restaurant of one of the best shops, **Hédiard** (see p98).

Spend the evening attending a classical music concert at **L'Eglise de la Madeline** (see p40) or watching a performance at **L'Opera Garnier**. Finish the day with a delicious gastronomic dinner at Michelin-starred **Senderens** (see p99).

Left **Fauchon biscuits** Right **La Maison du Miel honey**

Food Shops

Hédiard
1 Founded in 1854, this world food emporium features a cornucopia of fruits and vegetables, exotic spices and oils and a host of other gourmet delights. ✆ *21 pl de la Madeleine, 75008 • Map D3*

Fauchon
2 The king of Parisian *épiceries* (grocers). The mouth-watering window displays are works of art and tempt you inside for pastries, exotic fruits and some 3,500 other items. ✆ *26–30 pl de la Madeleine, 75008 • Map D3*

Au Verger de la Madeleine
3 Rare vintage wines are the speciality at this store. The owner will help you find a wine to match the year of any special occasion. ✆ *4 blvd Malesherbes, 75008 • Map D3*

Caviar Kaspia
4 The peak of indulgence. Caviars from around the world, plus smoked eels, salmon and other fishy fare. ✆ *17 pl de la Madeleine, 75008 • Map D3*

La Maison de la Truffe
5 France's finest black truffles are sold here during the winter truffle season. Preserved truffles and other delicacies can be savoured in the shop or at home. ✆ *19 pl de la Madeleine, 75008 • Map D3*

La Maison du Miel
6 The "house of honey", family-owned since 1908, is the place to try speciality honeys, to spread on your toast or your body in the form of soaps and oils. ✆ *24 rue Vignon, 75009 • Map D3*

Boutique Maille
7 The retail outlet for one of France's finest mustard-makers. Fresh mustard served in lovely ceramic jars and seasonal limited edition mustards are available. ✆ *6 pl de la Madeleine, 75008 • Map D3*

La Maison du Chocolat
8 A superb chocolate shop, which offers fine chocolates and pastries including eclairs, tarts and macaroons. ✆ *8 blvd Madeleine, 75009 • Map E3 • 01 47 42 86 52*

Betjeman and Barton
9 This tea shop offers some 200 varieties from all over the world, as well as wacky teapots ✆ *23 blvd Malesherbes, 75008 • Map D3*

Ladurée
10 A splendid *belle époque* tea salon that has been serving the best macaroons in Paris since 1862. ✆ *16 rue Royale, 75008 • Map D3*

For more on shopping in Paris **See p169**

Price Categories

For a three-course	**€** under €30
meal for one with half	**€€** €30–€40
a bottle of wine (or	**€€€** €40–€50
equivalent meal), taxes	**€€€€** €50–€60
and extra charges	**€€€€€** over €60

10 Places to Eat

Le Soufflé
A wide choice of soufflés, from savoury leek to sweet passionfruit, are on offer here. 🕲 *36 rue du Mont Thabor, 75001 • Map E3 • 01 42 60 27 19 • Closed Sun • No disabled access • €€€*

Le Meurice
Try the herbed lamb and semolina roasted with lemon and capers at this three-starred Michelin establishment. 🕲 *228 rue de Rivoli, 75001 • Map E3 • 01 44 58 10 55 • Closed Sat & Sun • €€€€€€*

Le Grand Véfour
This beautiful 18th-century restaurant with two Michelin stars is a gourmet treat. 🕲 *17 rue Beaujolais, 75001 • Map E3 • 01 42 96 56 27 • Closed Fri D, Sat, Sun, Aug, some Dec • No disabled access • €€€€€*

Senderens
Chef Alain Senderens maintains a two Michelin star status and superb quality food. 🕲 *9 pl de la Madeleine, 75008 • Map D3 • 01 42 65 22 90 • Closed Aug & public hols • No disabled access • €€€€€*

Le Zinc d'Honoré
Join the lunchtime business crowds and the evening theatre-goers for well-priced bistro cuisine. 🕲 *36 pl du Marché St-Honoré, 75001 • Map E3 • Open daily • €€*

Higuma
This no-frills Japanese noodle house serves great value food. 🕲 *32 bis rue Sainte-Anne, 75001 • Map E3 • 01 47 03 38 59 • €*

A Casaluna
Traditional Corsican specialities such as baked aubergines with goat's cheese are served at this charming restaurant. 🕲 *6 rue Beaujolais, 75001 • Map E3 • 01 42 60 05 11 • No disabled access • €€€*

Willi's Wine Bar
This cosy bar and dining room is a popular haunt for lovers of modern French food and wines from small producers. 🕲 *13 rue des Petits-Champs, 75001 • Map E3 • 01 42 61 05 09 • Closed Sun, 10 days Aug • €€€*

Restaurant du Palais Royal
Contemporary French cooking is served in the bucolic Palais Royal gardens *(see p39)*. 🕲 *110 galerie de Valois, 75001 • Map E3 • 01 40 20 00 27 • Closed Sun • No disabled access • €€€€*

Chartier
Waiters race about serving simple soups, meat and fish dishes. No bookings are taken, but the inevitable queues move quickly. 🕲 *7 rue du Faubourg-Montmartre, 75009 • Map E3 • 01 47 70 86 29 • €*

Note: *Unless otherwise stated, all restaurants accept credit cards and serve vegetarian meals*

Left **Arc de Triomphe** Right **Palais de L'Elysée**

Champs-Elysées Quarter

THE CHAMPS-ELYSEES IS UNDOUBTEDLY *the most famous street in Paris and the quarter that lies around it is brimming with wealth and power. It is home to the president of France, great haute couture fashion houses, embassies and consulates, and the five-star hotels and fine restaurants frequented by the French and foreign élite. The Champs-Elysées itself runs from the place de la Concorde to the place Charles de Gaulle, which is known as L'Etoile (the star) because of the 12 busy avenues that radiate out from it. It is the most stately stretch of the so-called Triumphal Way, built by Napoleon, where Parisians celebrate national events with parades or mourn at the funeral cortèges of the great and good.*

🔟 Sights

1. Arc de Triomphe
2. Avenue des Champs-Elysées
3. Grand Palais
4. Petit Palais
5. Pont Alexandre III
6. Palais de la Découverte
7. Rue du Faubourg-St-Honoré
8. Avenue Montaigne
9. Palais de l'Elysée
10. Musée Jacquemart-André

Home of La Marseillaise

Preceding pages **French patisseries**

Arc de Triomphe
See pp24–5.

Avenue des Champs-Elysées
One of the most famous avenues in the world came into being when the royal gardener André Le Nôtre planted an arbour of trees beyond the border of the Jardin des Tuileries in 1667 *(see p95)*. First called the Grand Cours (Great Way), it was later renamed the Champs-Elysées (Elysian Fields). In the mid-19th century the avenue acquired pedestrian paths, fountains, gas lights and cafés, and became the fashionable place for socialising and entertainment. Since the funeral of Napoleon in 1840, this wide thoroughfare has also been the route for state processions, victory parades and other city events. The Rond Point des Champs-Elysées is the prettiest part, with chestnut trees and flower beds. In recent years, formerly touristy parts have been revamped and flagship stores of international brands have been welcomed back. A walk along the avenue is still an essential Paris experience. ◈ *Map C3*

Grand Palais
This immense *belle époque* exhibition hall was built for the Universal Exhibition in 1900. Its splendid glass roof is a landmark of the Champs-Elysées. The façade, the work of three architects, is a mix of Art Nouveau ironwork, Classical stone columns and a mosaic frieze, with bronze horses and chariots at the four corners of the roof. The Galleries du Grand Palais host temporary art exhibitions. ◈ *3 ave du Général-Eisenhower, 75008 • Map D3 • 01 44 13 17 17 • Opening hours vary according to exhibition • Closed 1 May • Admission charge depending on exhibition • www.grandpalais.fr*

Petit Palais
The "little palace" echoes its neighbour in style. Set around a semi-circular courtyard, with Ionic columns and a dome, the building now houses the Musée des Beaux-Arts de la Ville de Paris. This includes medieval and Renaissance art, 18th-century furniture and a collection of 19th-century paintings. ◈ *Ave Winston Churchill, 75008 • Map D3 • 01 53 43 40 00 • Open 10am–6pm Tue–Sun (to 8pm Thu for temporary exhibitions) • www.petitpalais.paris.fr*

Avenue des Champs-Elysées

La Marseillaise

The stirring French national anthem was written in 1792 by a French army engineer named Claude Joseph Rouget de Lisle. He lived for a time in this district, at 15 rue du Faubourg-St-Honoré. The rousing song got its name from the troops from Marseille who were prominent in the storming of the Tuileries during the Revolution *(see p45)*.

Pont Alexandre III

Built for the 1900 Universal Exhibition to carry visitors over the Seine to the Grand and Petit Palais, this bridge is a superb example of the steel architecture and ornate Art Nouveau style popular at the time. Named after Alexander III of Russia, who laid the foundation stone, its decoration displays both Russian and French heraldry. The bridge creates a splendid thoroughfare from the Champs-Elysées to the Invalides *(see p48)*. ◉ *Map D3*

Palais de la Découverte

Set in a wing of the Grand Palais, this museum showcasing scientific discovery was created by a Nobel Prize-winning physicist for the World's Fair of 1937. The exhibits focus on invention and innovation in the sciences, from biology to chemistry, to astronomy and physics, with interactive exhibits and demonstrations (the magnetism show is especially spectacular). There is also a planetarium, while the Planète Terre (Planet Earth) rooms examine global warming. ◉ *Ave Franklin-D.-Roosevelt, 75008 • Map D3 • Open 9:30am–6pm Tue–Sat, 10am–7pm Sun • Closed 1 Jan, 1 May, 14 Jul, 15 Aug, 25 Dec • Admission charge*

Rue du Faubourg-St-Honoré

Running roughly parallel to the Champs-Elysées, this is Paris's equivalent of Fifth Avenue, Bond Street or Rodeo Drive. From Christian Lacroix and Versace to Gucci and Hermès, the shopfronts read like a *Who's Who* of fashion. Even if the prices may be out of reach, window-shopping is fun. There are also elegant antiques and art galleries. Look out for swallows that nest on many of the 19th-century façades. ◉ *Map D3*

Avenue Montaigne

In the 19th century the Avenue Montaigne was a nightlife hotspot. Parisians danced the night away at the Mabille Dance Hall until it closed in 1870 and Adolphe Sax made music with his newly invented saxophone in the Winter Garden. Today this chic avenue is a rival to the rue Faubourg-St-Honoré as the home to more *haute couture* houses such as Christian Dior and Valentino. There are also luxury hotels, top restaurants, popular cafés, and the Comédie des Champs-Elysées and Théâtre des Champs-Elysées. ◉ *Map C3*

Pont Alexandre III

Rue du Faubourg-St-Honoré

9 Palais de l'Elysée

Built in 1718, after the Revolution this elegant palace was turned into a dance hall, then, in the 19th century, became the residence of Napoleon's sister Caroline Murat, followed by his wife Empress Josephine. His nephew, Napoleon III, also lived here while plotting his 1851 coup. Since 1873 it has been home to the president of France. For this reason, it is worth noting that the palace guards don't like people getting too close to the building (see p42). ◈ 55 rue du Faubourg-St-Honoré, 75008 • Map D3 • Closed to the public

10 Musée Jacquemart-André

This fine display of art and furniture, once belonging to avid art collectors Edouard André and his wife Nélie Jacquemart, is housed in a late 19th-century mansion. It is best known for its Italian Renaissance art, including frescoes by Tiepolo and Paolo Uccello's *St George and the Dragon* (c.1435). The reception rooms feature the art of the 18th-century "Ecole française", with paintings by François Boucher and Jean-Honoré Fragonard. Flemish masters are in the library. ◈ 158 blvd Haussmann, 75008 • Map C2 • 01 45 62 11 59 • Open 10am–6pm daily (to 9pm Mon & Sat for temporary exhibits) • Adm • www.musee-jacquemart-andre.com

A Day of Shopping

Morning

🕒 The **Champs-Elysées** (see p103) is an area for leisurely strolls. Begin by window-shopping along one side of the **avenue Montaigne**, where Prada, Nina Ricci, Dior and many more have their flagship stores – the area oozes money. Have a break in the Bar des Théâtres, where fashion names and the theatre crowd from the Comédie des Champs-Élysées across the street sometimes hang out (6 ave Montaigne • 01 47 23 34 63).

Return up the other side of avenue Montaigne to the Champs-Elysées, for the stroll to the Arc de Triomphe. Here you will find many flagship shops of world-famous brands. Break for lunch at **Spoon Paris** but get there early to get a table (see p109).

Afternoon

Continuing up the Champs-Elysées, look past the showrooms and fast food outlets to note the many interesting buildings that house them.

Take the underpass to the **Arc de Triomphe** (see pp24–5) and climb to the top for the views, which are superb at dusk when the avenues light up. Walk or take the metro to the **rue du Faubourg-St-Honoré**, for more designer shops.

For tea and cakes, **Ladurée**, located a short walk away at 75 Avenue des Champs-Eleseés, is a wonderfully elegant experience.

Left **Avenue de Marigny** Centre **Avenue Franklin-D.-Roosevelt** Right **25 Avenue Montaigne**

International Connections

1 Avenue de Marigny
American author John Steinbeck lived here for five months in 1954 and described Parisians as "the luckiest people in the world". ⊙ Map C3

2 8 Rue Artois
Here, in September 2001, the legendary Belgian mobster François Vanverbergh – godfather of the French Connection gang – fell victim to a drive-by assassin as he took his afternoon mineral water. ⊙ Map C2

3 37 Avenue Montaigne
Having wowed Paris with her comeback performances, iconic German actress and singer Marlene Dietrich spent her reclusive final years in a luxury apartment here. ⊙ Map C3

4 Pont de l'Alma
Diana, Princess of Wales, was killed in a tragic accident in the underpass here in 1997. Her unofficial monument nearby attracts thousands of visitors each year *(see p48).* ⊙ Map C3

5 31 Avenue George V, Hôtel George V
A roll-call of rockers – from the Rolling Stones and Jim Morrison to J-Lo and Ricky Martin – have made this their regular Paris home-from-home. ⊙ Map C3

6 Hôtel d'Elysée-Palace
Mata Hari, the Dutch spy and exotic dancer, set up her lair in Room 113 before finally being arrested outside 25 Avenue Montaigne. ⊙ Map C3

7 37 Avenue George V
Franklin D. Roosevelt and his new bride visited his aunt's apartment here in 1905. He was later commemorated in the name of a nearby avenue. ⊙ Map C3

8 49 Avenue des Champs-Elysées
Author Charles Dickens may well have had "the best of times and the worst of times" when he resided here from 1855–6. Ten years earlier he had also lived at 38 Rue de Courcelles. ⊙ Map C3

9 114 Avenue des Champs-Elysées
Brazilian aviation pioneer Alberto Santos-Dumont planned many of his amazing aeronautical feats – notably that of circling the Eiffel Tower in an airship in 1901 – from this address. ⊙ Map C2

10 102 Boulevard Haussmann
Hypochondriac author Marcel Proust lived in a soundproofed room here, turning memories into a masterwork. ⊙ Map D2

Left **Student riots, 1968** Right **Bastille Day celebrations**

10 Events on the Champs-Elysées

1616
Paris's grand avenue was first laid out when Marie de Médici, wife of Henri IV, had a carriage route, the Cours-la-Reine (Queen's Way), constructed through the marshland along the Seine.

1667
Landscape gardener Le Nôtre lengthened the Jardin des Tuileries to meet the Cours-la-Reine, and opened up the view with a double row of chestnut trees, creating the Grand Cours.

1709
The avenue was re-named the Champs-Elysées (Elysian Fields). In Greek mythology, the Elysian Fields were the "place of ideal happiness", the abode of the blessed after death.

1724
The Duke of Antin, overseer of the royal gardens, extended the avenue to the heights of Chaillot, the present site of the Arc de Triomphe *(see pp24–5)*.

1774
Architect Jacques-Germain Soufflot lowered the hill of the Champs-Elysées by 5 m (16 ft) to reduce the steep gradient, therefore making an easier and safer passage for residents' horses and carriages.

26 August 1944
Parisians celebrated the liberation of the city from the German Nazi Occupation of World War II with triumphant processions and festivities.

30 May 1968
The infamous student demonstrations of May 1968, when student protests against state authority spilled over into riots and massive gatherings. De Gaulle and his supporters held a huge counter-demonstration here, marking a turning point in the uprising.

12 November 1970
The death of President Charles de Gaulle was an immense event in France, as he had been the single most dominant French political figure for 30 years. He was honoured by a silent march along the Champs-Elysées.

14 July 1989
The parade on Bastille Day marking the bicentennial of the Revolution, was a dazzling display of folk culture and avant-garde theatre. It was a distinct change from the usual military events, and was organized by Mitterand's Culture Minister, Jack Lang.

12 July 1998
Huge, ecstatic crowds packed the Champs-Elysées to celebrate France's football team winning the World Cup. People came from all over Paris to join in the festivities that captured the nation's imagination.

Left **Christian Dior bag** Centre **Chanel** Right **Boutique Prada**

ᵀᴼᴾ10 Designer Shops

Christian Dior
1 The grey and white decor, with silk bows on chairs, makes a chic backdrop for fashions from lingerie to evening wear. ◈ *30 ave Montaigne, 75008 • Map C3*

Chanel
2 Chanel classics, from the braided tweed jackets to two-toned shoes as well as Lagerfeld's more daring designs, are displayed in this branch of the main rue Cambon store. ◈ *42 ave Montaigne, 75008 • Map C3*

Givenchy
3 This fashion house has been synonymous with Parisian style since the 1930s. Shop for women's and men's ready-to-wear outfits here. ◈ *3 ave George V, 75008 • Map C3 • 01 44 31 50 00*

Balenciaga
4 This world-famous label is known for its modern creations, which are now designed by Nicolas Ghesquière. ◈ *10 ave George V, 75008 • Map C3 • 01 47 20 21 11*

Boutique Prada
5 A stylish boutique offering clothes and accessories from the latest collection. ◈ *10 ave Montaigne, 75008 • Map C3*

Joseph
6 Renovated by the leading architect Raed Abilama, this shop stocks the Joseph brand and a selection of other designer labels. ◈ *14 ave Montaigne, 75008 • Map C3*

Jil Sander
7 A minimal and modern store, just like the clothes it sells. Sander's trouser suits, cashmere dresses and overcoats in neutral colours are displayed on two floors. ◈ *56 ave Montaigne, 75008 • Map C3*

Chloé
8 Simple, classy, ready-to-wear designer womens' clothes and accessories are sold in this minimalist temple of feminine chic. ◈ *44 ave Montaigne, 75008 • Map C3*

Eres
9 A range of luxury swimwear and lingerie in subtle colours and with a certain Parisian sensuality, are beautifully displayed in this elegant boutique. ◈ *40 ave Montaigne, 75008 • Map C3 • 01 47 23 07 26*

Barbara Bui
10 High-end Parisian fashion designer Barbara Bui has been creating elegant womenswear since the 1980s. Lovely neutral colours and luxury fabrics are available here. ◈ *50 ave Montaigne, 75008 • Map C3 • 01 42 25 05 25*

Price Categories

For a three-course	€ under €30
meal for one with half	€€ €30–€40
a bottle of wine (or	€€€ €40–€50
equivalent meal), taxes	€€€€ €50–€60
and extra charges	€€€€€ over €60

Above **Au Plaza Athénée**

🔟 Places to Eat

1 Alain Ducasse au Plaza Athénée

Superchef Alain Ducasse's flagship restaurant. Langoustines with caviar is just one mouthwatering bite. ◎ *Hôtel Plaza Athénée, 25 ave Montaigne, 75008 • Map C3 • 01 53 67 65 00 • Closed Mon–Wed L, Sat, Sun, Aug, some of Dec • €€€€€*

2 Le Mini Palais

A modern French restaurant with a beautiful terrace. Try the duck fillet and foie gras burger, with truffle sauce. ◎ *Grand Palais, ave Winston Churchill, 75008 • Map D3 • 01 70 98 74 00 • €€€€€*

3 Les Ambassadeurs

Jacket and tie are required at this grandiose restaurant, which serves modern French cuisine. ◎ *Hôtel de Crillon, 10 pl de la Concorde, 75008 • Map D3 • 01 44 71 16 16 • €€€€€*

4 Spoon Paris

Alain Ducasse's hip and innovative offshoot. ◎ *14 rue de Marignan, 75008 • Map C3 • 01 40 76 34 44 • Closed Sat, Sun, Aug • €€€€€*

5 Taillevent

One of the city's best dining experiences. Langoustine with citrus and green tea marmalade is a signature dish *(see p64).* ◎ *15 rue Lamennais, 75008 • Map C3 • 01 44 95 15 01 • Closed Sat, Sun, Aug • €€€€€*

6 Gagnaire

Chef Pierre Gagnaire is legendary for his artistry for blending flavours, such as lamb cutlets with truffles. ◎ *6 rue Balzac, 75008 • Map C3 • 01 58 36 12 50 • Closed Sat, Sun L, Aug, 1 week Dec–Jan • No disabled access • €€€€€*

7 Tokyo Eat

This trendy restaurant, housed in a contemporary art museum, serves fruity smoothies and fusion food. ◎ *Palais de Tokyo, 13 ave du Président-Wilson, 75016 • Map B3 • 01 47 20 00 29 • €€€*

8 Bread and Roses

A fabulous tea salon and bakery. Great for breakfast or lunch. ◎ *25 rue Boissy d'Anglas, 75008 • Map D3 • 01 47 42 40 00 • Closed Sun • €€€*

9 L'Atelier des Chefs

This cooking school offers a range of classes in French, from €15 for a 30-minute lunchtime session, after which you get to eat the meal you've made. ◎ *10 rue de Penthièvre, 75008 • Map D2 • 01 53 30 05 82 • www.atelierdeschefs.fr*

10 Le Cinq

The George V's *(see p106)* two Michelin-starred restaurant serves French cuisine with a fresh twist. ◎ *31 ave George V, 75008 • Map C3 • 01 49 52 70 00 • €€€€€*

Left **Dôme church** Centre **Pont Alexandre III** Right **Champs-de-Mars**

Invalides and Eiffel Tower Quarters

TWO OF PARIS'S BEST-KNOWN LANDMARKS, the golden-domed Hôtel des Invalides and the Eiffel Tower, are found in these quarters. Large parts of the area were created in the 19th century, when there was still room to construct wide avenues and grassy esplanades. To the east of the Invalides are numerous stately mansions now converted into embassies, and the French parliament. Jean Nouvel's musée du quai Branly is a striking feature beside the Seine.

🔟 Sights

1 Hôtel des Invalides	6 musée du quai Branly
2 Eiffel Tower	7 Rue Cler
3 Les Egouts	8 Ecole Militaire
4 Musée de l'Armée	9 UNESCO
5 Musée Rodin	10 Assemblée Nationale

The Thinker, Musée Rodin

Sign up for DK's email newsletter on traveldk.com

1 Hôtel des Invalides
See pp32–3.

2 Eiffel Tower
See pp16–17.

3 Les Egouts
In a city of glamour and grandeur, the sewers *(égouts)* of Paris are an incongruously popular attraction. They date from the Second Empire (1851–70), when Baron Haussmann was transforming the city *(see p45)*. The sewers, which helped to sanitize and ventilate Paris, are considered one of his finest achievements. Most of the work was done by an engineer named Belgrand. The 2,100-km (1,300-mile) network covers the area from Les Halles to La Villette – if laid end-to-end the sewers would stretch from Paris to Istanbul. An hour-long tour includes a walk through some of the tunnels, where you'll see water pipes and various cables. The Paris Sewers Museum, which is situated in the sewers beneath the Quai d'Orsay on the Left Bank, tells the story of the city's water and sewers,

from their beginnings to the present day. There is also an audio-visual show. ✺ *Opposite 93, quai d'Orsay, 75007 • Map C4 • Open May–Sep: 11am–5pm Sat–Wed; Oct–Apr: 11am–4pm Sat–Wed • Closed 1 Jan, two weeks mid-Jan, 25 Dec • Admission charge*

4 Musée de l'Armée
The Army Museum contains one of the largest and most comprehensive collections of arms, armour and displays on military history in the world. There are weapons ranging from pre-historic times to the end of World War II, representing countries around the world. Housed in the Hôtel des Invalides, the galleries occupy the old refectories in two wings on either side of the court-yard. The museum ticket includes entry to the Musée des Plans-Reliefs, the Historial Charles de Gaulle, the Musée de L'Ordre de la Libération and Napoleon's Tomb *(see p114)*. ✺ *Hôtel des Invalides, 75007 • Map C4 • Open 10am–6pm Wed–Mon, (until 9pm Tue & 5pm in winter) • Closed 1st Mon of month (except Jul–Sep), public hols • Admission charge*

5 Musée Rodin
An impressive collection of works by the sculptor and artist Auguste Rodin (1840–1917) is housed in a splendid 18th-century mansion, the Hôtel Biron *(see p116)*, where he spent the last nine years of his life. The rooms display his works roughly chronologically, including his sketches and watercolours. Masterpieces such as *The Kiss* and *Eve* are displayed in the airy rotundas. One room is devoted to works by his talented model and muse, Camille Claudel, and Rodin's personal collection of paintings by Van Gogh, Monet and other masters hang on the walls. The museum's other

General Foch, Musée de l'Armée

Young Napoleon

The most famous alumnus of the Ecole Militaire was Napoleon Bonaparte, who was admitted as a cadet, aged 15, in 1784 and deemed "fit to be an excellent sailor". He graduated as a lieutenant in the artillery, and his passing-out report stated that "he could go far if the circumstances are right". The rest, as they say, is history.

highlight is the gardens, the third-largest private gardens in Paris, where famous works such as *The Thinker*, *Balzac* and *The Gates of Hell* stand among the lime trees and rose bushes. ✆ *79 rue de Varenne, 75007 • Map C4 • Open 10am–5:45pm Tue–Sun • Admission charge • www.musee-rodin.fr*

musée du quai Branly

The aim of this museum is to showcase the arts of Africa, Asia, Oceania and the Americas. The collection boasts nearly 300,000 artifacts, of which 3,500 are on display, including a fantastic array of African instruments, Gabonese masks, Aztec statues and 17th-century painted animal hides from North America (once the pride of the French royal family). Designed by Jean Nouvel, the building is an exhibit in itself: glass is ingeniously used to allow the surrounding greenery to act as a natural backdrop to the collection. ✆ *37 quai Branly, 75007 • Map B4 • Open 11am–7pm Tue–Sun (until 9pm Thu–Sat) • Admission charge*

Rue Cler

The cobblestone pedestrianized road that stretches south of rue de Grenelle to avenue de La Motte-Picquet is the most exclusive street market in Paris. Here greengrocers, fishmongers, butchers, and wine merchants sell top-quality produce to the well-heeled residents of the area. Tear yourself away from the mouth-watering cheeses and pastries, however, to feast your eyes on the Art Nouveau buildings at Nos. 33 and 151. ✆ *Map C*

Ecole Militaire

At the urging of his mistress Madame Pompadour, Louis XV approved the building of the Royal Military Academy in 1751. Although its purpose was to educate the sons of impoverished officers, a grand edifice was designed by Jacques-Ange

musée du quai Branly

Gabriel, architect of the place de la Concorde *(see p95)* and the Petit Trianon at Versailles, and completed in 1773. The central pavilion with its quadrangular dome and Corinthian pillars is a splendid example of the French classical style. ◈ *1 pl Joffre, 75007 • Map C5 • Open to the public by special permission only (apply in writing)*

9 UNESCO
The headquarters of the United Nations Educational, Scientific and Cultural Organization (UNESCO) were built in 1958 by an international team of architects from France (Zehrfuss), Italy (Nervi) and the United States (Breuer). Their Y-shaped building of concrete and glass may be unremarkable, but inside, the showcase of 20th-century art by renowned international artists is well worth a visit. There is a huge mural by Picasso, ceramics by Joan Miró, and a 2nd-century mosaic from El Djem in Tunisia. Outside is a giant mobile by Alexander Calder and a peaceful Japanese garden. ◈ *7 pl de Fontenoy, 75007 • Map C5 • 01 45 68 10 00 • By appointment only • Free*

10 Assemblée Nationale
Built for the daughter of Louis XIV in 1722, the Palais Bourbon has housed the lower house of the French parliament since 1827. The Council of the Five Hundred met here during the Revolution, and it was the headquarters of the German occupation during World War II. Napoleon added the Classical riverfront façade in 1806 to complement La Madeleine *(see p97)* across the river. ◈ *33 quai d'Orsay, 75007 • Map D4 • Open for tours only (identity papers compulsory); advance reservation required, see www. assemblee-nationale.fr • Free*

A Day Around the Invalides Quarter

Morning

Begin the day with an early morning visit to the **Musée Rodin** *(see p111)*. A magnificent collection of Rodin's works are displayed both indoors and outside in the attractive garden. There are also excellent temporary exhibitions. Stop for a coffee at the garden café with its leafy terrace.

Move on to the **Hôtel des Invalides** *(see pp32–3)* next door to see Napoleon's Tomb and the **Musée de l'Armée** *(see p111)*. From here, walk along the esplanade towards the Seine and the **Pont Alexandre III** *(see p104)*, turning left before the river on to rue Saint-Dominique. Stop here for lunch at **Les Cocottes de Constant** *(see p117)*, which serves good, fresh meals.

Afternoon

After lunch, follow the rue de l'Université to the **musée du quai Branly** where you can enjoy the fascinating collections of tribal art and superb modern architecture. The Café Branly, located in the museum's restful gardens, is the perfect place to stop and enjoy a cup of tea.

Make sure you book ahead, by phone or online, for a late-afternoon visit to the **Eiffel Tower** *(see pp16–17)*. The views are spectacular at dusk. Splash out on dinner at the world-famous **Le Jules Verne** restaurant on level 2, or head back to the Branly museum, and its rooftop restaurant **Les Ombres** *(see p117)*.

Left *The Abdication of Napoleon* (1814), François Pigeot Right **Suit of armour**

1 Modern Department (1648–1792)

The modern royal army, from its birth under Louis XIV to the training of Revolutionary soldiers, is related through objects such as some fine early rifles.

2 Modern Department (1792–1871)

Displays here cover the beginnings of the Revolution to the Paris Commune, including the personal belongings of Napoleon I.

3 Ancient Armoury Department

The third-largest collection of armoury in the world is on show in the northeast refectory. Assembled over a 40-year period since the 1960s, these items had been lost since the Revolution.

4 17th-Century Murals

In the Ancient Armoury Department, restored 17th-century murals by Joseph Parrocel celebrate Louis XIV's military conquests.

5 The World Wars

Two rooms on the second floor are devoted to World War I and World War II. Documents, uniforms, maps, photographs and other memorabilia bring the conflicts of both wars to life, often to disturbing effect.

6 Banners and Trophies

A small collection of 17th–20th-century military banners is displayed in the east wing.

7 Historial of Charles de Gaulle

This state-of-the-art display on the life of the former wartime president is in the Cour d'Honneur, Orient wing.

8 Musée des Plans Reliefs

On the fourth floor of the east wing is a collection of relief models of French towns showing the development of fortifications from the 17th century onwards.

9 Artillery

Over 800 cannons are displayed inside and in front of the museum.

10 Salle Orientale

This collection of arms and armour reflects the military styles of different nations.

Verdun (1917), Felix Vallotton, **Two World Wars**

For the Musée de l'Armée **See p111**

Left **View from the Eiffel Tower** Right **Pont Alexandre III and Hôtel des Invalides**

10 Views

Top of the Eiffel Tower
There is nowhere in Paris to match the view from the top of the tower, so hope for good weather. With the cityscape and the sparkling waters of the Seine below, it is the highlight of any visit *(see pp16–17)*. ◉ *Map B4*

Pont d'Iéna
There is no bad approach to the Eiffel Tower, but the best is from the Trocadéro direction, walking straight to the tower across the Pont d'Iéna. ◉ *Map B4*

Base of the Eiffel Tower
Everybody wants to race to the top, but don't neglect the view from the ground. Looking directly up at the magnificent structure makes one appreciate the feat of engineering all the more *(see pp16–17)*. ◉ *Map B4*

Eiffel Tower at Night
To usher in the Millennium the tower was "robed" in lights and since then there have been a variety of lighting displays. For five minutes every hour, from dusk to midnight, the whole edifice twinkles. ◉ *Map B4*

Saxe-Breteuil Market
This old street market in avenue de Saxe is a little off the usual tourist track, but the view of the Eiffel Tower above the fruit and vegetable stalls is totally Parisian and will especially appeal to photographers. ◉ *Map C5 • 7am–2:30pm Thu, 7am–3pm Sat*

Pont Alexandre III
Flanked by impressive gilded statues, superb views can be enjoyed from this magnificent bridge *(see p48)*. ◉ *Map D4*

Musée Rodin Gardens
The golden Dôme church gleams through the trees that line these delightful gardens. ◉ *Map D5*

Hôtel des Invalides
The majestic gilded dome above Napoleon's tomb dominates the skyline. It is a particularly superb sight when seen from the river on a sunny morning *(see pp32–3)*. ◉ *Map D4*

Pont de la Concorde
The Egyptian obelisk at the centre of place de la Concorde *(see p95)* is at its most impressive from the bridge. ◉ *Map D4*

musée du quai Branly
Jean Nouvel's bold, colourful building is best seen from the riverside. Note the striking "Green Wall" at the west end *(see p112)*. ◉ *Map B4*

Left **Hôtel de Biron** Right **Hôtel de Villeroy**

TOP 10 Mansions

1 Hôtel Biron
Built in 1730, from 1904 this elegant mansion was transformed into state-owned artists' studios. Among its residents was Auguste Rodin (1840–1917). After the sculptor's death the house became the Musée Rodin *(see p111)*.

2 Hôtel de Villeroy
Built in 1724 for Charlotte Desmarnes, an actress, it is now the Ministry of Agriculture. Ⓢ *78–80 rue de Varenne, 75007 • Map D4 • Closed to the public*

3 Hôtel Matignon
One of the most beautiful mansions in the area is now the official residence of the French prime minister. Ⓢ *57 rue de Varenne, 75007 • Map D4 • Closed to the public*

4 Hôtel de Boisgelin
Built in 1732 by Jean Sylvain Cartaud, this mansion has housed the Italian Embassy since 1938. Ⓢ *47 rue de Varenne, 75007 • Map D4 • Call 01 49 54 03 00 for appointment*

5 Hôtel de Gallifet
This attractive mansion was built between 1776 and 1792 with Classical styling. It is now the Italian Institute. Ⓢ *50 rue de Varenne, 75007 • Map D4 • Open 10am–1pm, 3–6pm Mon–Fri.*

6 Hôtel d'Estrées
Three floors of pilasters feature on this 1713 mansion. Formerly the Russian embassy, Czar Nicolas II lived here in 1896. It is now a government building. Ⓢ *79 rue de Grenelle, 75007 • Map B5 • Closed to the public*

7 Hôtel d'Avaray
Dating from 1728, this mansion belonged to the Avaray family for nearly 200 years. It became the Dutch Embassy in 1920. Ⓢ *85 rue de Grenelle, 75007 • Map B5 • Closed to the public*

8 Hôtel de Brienne
This mansion houses the Ministry of Defence. Napoleon's mother lived here from 1806–17. Ⓢ *14–16 rue St Dominique, 75007 • Map D4 • Closed to the public*

9 Hôtel de Noirmoutiers
Built in 1724, this was once the army staff headquarters. It now houses ministerial offices. Ⓢ *138–140 rue de Grenelle, 75007 • Map B5 • Closed to the public*

10 Hôtel de Monaco de Sagan
Now the Polish Embassy, this 1784 mansion served as the British Embassy until 1825. Ⓢ *57 rue St-Dominique, 75007 • Map D4 • Closed to the public*

For more historic buildings in Paris **See pp42–3**

Above **Le Jules Verne**

Price Categories
For a three-course meal for one with half a bottle of wine (or equivalent meal), taxes and extra charges €€€€ €50–€60 €€€€€ over €60

Around Town – Invalides & Eiffel Tower Quarters

Places to Eat

1 Le Jules Verne
Book a window table for the view and then sit back and enjoy the fine food from Alain Ducasse. A reservation is required for dinner. ® 2nd Level, Eiffel Tower, Champ-de-Mars, 75007 • Map B4 • 01 45 55 61 44 • No disabled access • €€€€€

2 Le Casse-Noix
A charming restaurant serving desserts such as *île flottante* (meringue floating on vanilla custard). ® 107 rue de la Fédération, 75015 • Map B5 • 01 45 66 09 01 • Closed Sat & Sun • No disabled access • €€€

3 L'Arpège
Among the best restaurants in the city. Chef Alain Passard produces exquisite food.
® 84 rue de Varenne, 75007 • Map D4 • 01 47 05 09 06 • Closed Sat, Sun • No disabled access • €€€€€

4 Le Violin d'Ingres
Chef Stéphane Schmidt is another shining star. The seasonal menu offers classic French cuisine with a modern twist.
® 135 rue Saint-Dominique, 75007 • Map C4 • 01 45 55 15 05 • €€€€€

5 Café Constant
Chef Christian Constant serves modern French fare that changes seasonally. ® 139 rue Saint-Dominique, 75007 • Map C4 • 01 47 53 73 34 • Closed Mon • No disabled access • €€

6 Thoumieux
Inventive cuisine by former Crillon chef Jean-François Piège,

in an historical setting.
® 79 rue Saint-Dominique, 75007 • Map C4 • 01 47 05 49 75 • €€€€

7 L'Ami Jean
Inventive dishes such as marinated scallops with ewe's milk cheese. ® 27 rue Malar, 75007 • Map C4 • 01 47 05 86 89 • Closed Sun, Mon • No disabled access • €€€€

8 Les Cocottes de Constant
Star chef Christian Constant's French take on a diner, with bar seating and delicious food. ® 135 rue Saint-Dominique, 75007 • Map C4 • 01 45 50 10 31 • Closed Sun • €€

9 Les Ombres
Fine food from rising star Sébastien Tasset. Ask for a table with a view of the famous Eiffel Tower. ® 27 quai Branly, 75007 • Map B4 • 01 47 53 68 00 • €€€€€

10 La Fontaine de Mars
Sumptuous classic dishes such as foie gras are served at this archetypal French restaurant. ® 129 rue Saint-Dominique, 75007 • Map C4 • 01 47 05 46 44 • €€€€€

Note: Unless otherwise stated, all restaurants accept credit cards and serve vegetarian meals

Left **Musée d'Orsay** Centre **Panthéon** Right **St-Sulpice**

St-Germain, Latin and Luxembourg Quarters

THIS AREA OF THE LEFT BANK IS *possibly the most stimulating in Paris. St-Germain-des-Prés, centred around the city's oldest church, is a synonym* for Paris's café society, made famous by the writers and intellectuals who held court here in the first half of the 20th century. Although it's more touristy today, a stroll around the back streets reveals lovely old houses plastered with plaques noting famous residents. The Latin Quarter takes its name from the Latin spoken by students of the Sorbonne until the Revolution. The scholastic centre of Paris for more than 700 years, it continues to buzz with student bookshops, cafés and jazz clubs. It was also the site of a Roman settlement and remains from that era can be seen in the Musée du Moyen-Age. The area's western boundary is the bustling boulevard Saint-Michel and to the south is the tranquil greenery of the Luxembourg Quarter.

Jardin du Luxembourg

🔟 Sights

1. Musée d'Orsay
2. Panthéon
3. Jardin du Luxembourg
4. St-Sulpice
5. La Sorbonne
6. Musée du Moyen Age
7. Boulevard St-Germain
8. Boulevard St-Michel
9. Quai de la Tournelle
10. Musée Maillol

Sign up for DK's email newsletter on traveldk.com

Musée d'Orsay
See pp12–15.

Panthéon
See pp28–9.

Jardin du Luxembourg
This 25-ha (60-acre) park is a swathe of green paradise on the very urban Left Bank. The formal gardens are set around the Palais du Luxembourg *(see p43)*, with broad terraces circling the central octagonal pool. A highlight of the garden is the beautiful Medici Fountain *(see p39)*. Many of the garden's statues were erected during the 19th century, among them the monument to the painter Eugène Delacroix and the statue of Ste Geneviève, patron saint of Paris. There is also a children's playground, open-air café, a bandstand, tennis courts, a puppet theatre and even a bee-keeping school *(see p38)*. ✪ *Map L6*

St-Sulpice
Begun in 1646, this enormous church unsurprisingly took 134 years to build. Its Classical façade by the Florentine architect Giovanni Servandoni features a two-tiered colonnade and two incongruously matched towers. Notice the two holy water fonts by the front door, made from huge shells given to François I by the Venetian Republic. *Jacob*

Medici Fountain, Jardin du Luxembourg

Clock, La Sorbonne

Wrestling with the Angel and other splendid murals by Delacroix (1798–1863) are in the chapel to the right of the main door. ✪ *2 rue Palatine, pl St-Sulpice, 75006 • Map L5 • Open 7:30am–7:30pm daily • Free*

La Sorbonne
Paris's world-famous university *(see p43)* was founded in 1253 and was originally intended as a theology college for poor students. It soon became the country's main centre for theological studies. It was named after Robert de Sorbon, confessor to Louis IX. Philosophers Thomas Aquinas (c.1226–74) and Roger Bacon (1214–92) taught here; Italian poet Dante (1265–1321), St Ignatius Loyola (1491–1556), the founder of the Jesuits, and church reformer John Calvin (1509–64) are among its list of alumni. Its tradition for conservatism led to its closure during the Revolution (it was reopened by Napoleon in 1806) and to the student riots of 1968 *(see p45)*. ✪ *47 rue des Ecoles, 75005 • Map M5 • 01 40 46 21 11 • Group tours only, Mon–Fri and one Sat each month (advance booking) • Admission charge*

Jazz on the Left Bank

Jazz has been played in Paris, especially on the Left Bank, since the 1920s. Numbers of black musicians moved here from the US as they found France less racially prejudiced, and Paris became a second home for many jazz musicians such as Sidney Bechet *(see p63)*. The city has never lost its love of jazz, nor jazz its love for the city.

6 Musée National du Moyen Age

This impressive mansion was built by the abbots of Cluny at the end of the 15th century and now houses a magnificent collection of art, from Gallo-Roman antiquity to the 15th century. It adjoins the ruins of 2nd-century Roman baths *(thermes)* with their huge vaulted *frigidarium* (cold bath). Nearby are the 21 carved stone heads of the kings of Judea from Notre-Dame, decapitated during the Revolution. The museum's highlight is the exquisite *Lady and the Unicorn* tapestry series, representing the five senses *(see p34)*. ✪ 6 pl Paul-Painlevé, 75005 • Map N5 • Open 9:15am–5:45pm Wed–Mon • Closed 1 Jan, 1 May, 25 Dec • Admission charge • www.musee-moyenage.fr

7 Boulevard St-Germain

This famous Left Bank boulevard runs for more than 3 km (2 miles) anchored by the bridges of the Seine at either end. At its heart is the church of St-Germain-des-Prés, established in 542, although the present church dates from the 11th century. Beyond the famous cafés, Flore and Les Deux Magots *(see p125)*, the boulevard runs west past art galleries, bookshops and designer boutiques to the Pont de la Concorde. To the east, it cuts across the Latin Quarter through the pleasant street market in the place Maubert, to join the Pont de Sully which connects to the Ile St-Louis *(see p69)*. ✪ Map J3

8 Boulevard St-Michel

The main drag of the Latin Quarter was created in the late 1860s as part of Baron Haussmann's city-wide makeover *(see p45)*, and named after a chapel that once stood near its northern end. It's now lined with a lively mix of cafés, clothes shops and cheap restaurants. Branching off to the east are rues de la Harpe and de la Huchette, which date back to medieval times. The

Boulevard St-Germain

Quai de la Tournelle

...tter is an enclave of the city's Greek community, with many souvlaki stands and Greek restaurants. In the place St-Michel is a huge bronze fountain that depicts St Michael killing a dragon. ◈ Map M4

Quai de la Tournelle
From this riverbank, just before the Pont de l'Archevêché here are lovely views across to Notre-Dame. The main attraction of this and the adjacent Quai de Montebello, however, are the dark-green stalls of the *bouquinistes (see p122)*. The Pont de la Tournelle also offers splendid views up and down the Seine. ◈ Map P5

Musée Maillol
Dina Vierny, who modelled for the artist Aristide Maillol (1861–1944) from the ages of 15 to 25, went on to set up this foundation dedicated largely to his works. Set in an 18th-century mansion, it features his sculpture, paintings, drawings, engravings and terracotta works. The museum puts on two temporary exhibitions per year, and there are also drawings by masters of French Naive art, including Degas, Matisse and Picasso. ◈ 59–61 rue de Grenelle, 75007 • Map J4 • Open 10:30am–7pm daily; to 9:30pm Fri • Admission charge • www.museemaillol.com

A Day on the Left Bank

Morning

🕐 This area is as much about atmosphere as sightseeing, so take time to soak up some of that Left Bank feeling. Begin on the **quai de la Tournelle**, strolling by the booksellers here and on the adjacent quai de Montebello, which runs parallel to rue de la Bûcherie, home to **Shakespeare and Company** (see p122).

From here head south down any street away from the river to the busy **boulevard St-Germain**. Turn right for two famous cafés, the **Flore** and **Les Deux Magots**, and stop for a break (see p125) among the locals talking the morning away.

Cut your way south to the rue de Grenelle and the **Musée Maillol**, a delightful lesser-known museum. Then enjoy lunch at **L'Épi Dupin** (see p127), a popular bistro, which attracts a mix of locals and travellers.

Afternoon

The later you reach the **Musée d'Orsay** (see pp12–15) the less crowded it will be. Spend an hour or two exploring the collection. The most popular displays are the Impressionists on the upper level.

After the museum visit, enjoy tea and a cake at **Christian Constant** (see p123), one of the best chocolate-makers in Paris. Or if it's dinner time, stay at the Musée d'Orsay and indulge in their set menu (Thu only).

Left **Bouquinistes** Right **The Village Voice**

Booksellers

1 Shakespeare and Company

Bibliophiles spend hours in the rambling rooms of Paris's renowned English-language bookshop. There are regular readings in English and French. ◈ *37 rue de la Bûcherie, 75005 • Map N5*

2 Bouquinistes

The green stalls of the book-sellers *(bouquinistes)* on the quays of the Left Bank are a Parisian landmark. Pore over the posters, old postcards, magazines, hardbacks, paperbacks, comics and sheet music. ◈ *Map N5*

3 Musée d'Orsay Bookshop

As well as its wonderful collections, the museum has a bewilderingly large and busy art bookshop *(see pp12–15)*.

4 La Hune

Renowned literary hangout. Good collections on art, photo-graphy and literature. ◈ *170 boulevard St-Germain, 75006 • Map K4*

5 Gibert Jeune

A cluster of bookshops that sell everything from travel guides and French literature to cookery books and children's stories. ◈ *3 and 5 place St-Michel, 27 quai St-Michel, 30–34 blvd St-Michel, 75006*

6 Album

Specialist in comic books, which are big sellers in France, from Tintin to erotica. ◈ *8 rue Dante, 75005 • Map L4*

7 Librairie Présence Africair

Specialist on books on Africa, as the name suggests. Good information point, too, if you want to eat African food or hear African music. ◈ *25 bis rue d' Écoles, 75005 • Map P6 • Closed Aug*

8 Tea & Tattered Pages

An excellent venue for a relaxed afternoon's browsing among thousands of English-language books; you can have a cuppa, too. ◈ *24 rue Mayet, 75006 • Map D5/D6*

9 Librairie Maeght

Specialist in books on art adjoining the Maeght art gallery with a good collection of posters, postcards and other items. ◈ *42 rue du Bac, 75007 • Map N5*

10 The Village Voice

North American bias, but works by writers from around the world as well. ◈ *6 rue Princess, 75006 • Map L4*

t Paris chocolatier Right Patisserie

10 Specialist Food Shops

1 Patrick Roger
One of a new generation of *chocolatiers*, Patrick Roger already has legions of fans thanks to his lifelike sculptures and ganache-filled chocolates. ✆ 108 boulevard St Germain, 75006 • Map F5 • Closed Sun

2 Christian Constant
Famous French chef Christian Constant's chocolate shop offers ganache, truffles and filled chocolates of all different flavours. ✆ 37 rue d'Assas, 75006 • Map E5 • 01 53 63 15 15

3 Jean-Paul Hévin
Another very distiguished *chocolatier*. Elegant, minimalist presentation and superb flavour combinations. ✆ 3 rue Vavin, 75006 • Map E6 • Closed Sun, Mon, Aug

4 Poilâne
Founded in the 1930s, this tiny bakery produces rustic, naturally leavened loaves in a wood-fired oven. ✆ 8 rue du Cherche-Midi, 75006 • Map E5 • Closed Sun

5 La Dernière Goutte
The owners of this English-speaking wine shop, which specializes in bottles from small producers, also run the nearby wine bar Fish. ✆ 6 rue Bourbon Le Château, 75006 • Map E5

6 Debauve & Gallais
This shop dates from 1800 when chocolate was sold for medicinal purposes. ✆ 30 rue des Sts-Pères, 75007 • Map K4 • Closed Sun

7 Pierre Hermé Paris
Here are some of the city's very finest cakes and pastries, including innovative flavoured macaroons. ✆ 72 rue Bonaparte, 75006 • Map L5

8 Ryst Dupeyron
Wine shop specializing in fine Bordeaux, rare spirits and champagne. ✆ 79 rue du Bac, 75007 • Map N5 • Closed Sun, Mon am

9 Sadaharu Aoki
Aoki cleverly incorporates Japanese flavours such as yuzu, green tea and black sesame into intoxicating classic French pastries that taste as good as they look. ✆ 35 rue de Vaugirard 75006 • Map E5 • Closed Mon

10 Gérard Mulot
Here you'll find some of the finest pastries in Paris, along with some truly miraculous macaroons. ✆ 76 rue de Seine, 75006 • Map L4 • Closed Wed

Left **Le 10 Bar** Right **Pub Saint Germain**

Late-Night Bars

Le 10 Bar
Incredibly lively bar, aimed at people who like to talk and drink. Happy hour 6–8pm. ⊗ *10 rue de l'Odéon, 75006 • Map L5*

Café de la Mairie
An old-fashioned Parisian café, which offers great views of St-Sulpice Church from its pavement terrace. Open until 2am daily except Sunday. ⊗ *8 pl St-Sulpice, 75006 • Map K5 • 01 43 26 67 82*

Prescription Cocktail Club
The expertly-mixed drinks are the main attraction at this chic and hip cocktail bar. ⊗ *23 rue Mazarine, 75006 • Map L4*

Pub Saint Germain
Sip drinks until dawn at this pub *à la français*. It has tables and lounge areas on three floors. ⊗ *17 rue Ancienne Comédie, 75006 • Map L4 • 01 56 81 13 13*

L'Assignat
Pleasant, bright family-run L'Assignat is full of regulars propping up the bar with a beer or a glass of wine. ⊗ *7 rue Guénégaud, 75006 • Map L3 • Closed Sun*

Mezzanine
The lounge bar of the legendary Alcazar *(see p127)* is the place to be seen. Drinks are not expensive given the buzz and the wonderful location. ⊗ *Alcazar, 62 rue Mazarine, 75006 • Map L3*

Curio Parlor
Cosy private alcoves and low lighting make this the perfect place to relax. ⊗ *16 rue des Bernardins, 750[0] • Map P5 • 01 44 07 12 47 • Closed M[o]*

Le Bob Cool
Close to St-Michel, this shabby-chic bar plays host to thirsty local nighthawks as well as trendier partygoers on late-night cocktails. ⊗ *15 rue des Grands Augustins, 75006 • Map M4 • Closed S[*

Coolin
An Irish bar that appeals to drinkers, talkers and listeners of all ages, who like their draught Guinness with a blarney chaser. ⊗ *15 rue Clément, 75006 • Map L4*

L'Urgence Bar
Hit this hospital-themed ba[r] for cocktails with names like "Laxative" and "Liposuction", served in a test-tube or baby's bottle. ⊗ *45 rue Monsieur le Prince, 75006 • Map M5 • Closed Sun, Mon*

Left **Café de Flore** Right **Shakespeare and Company**

10 Literary Haunts

1 La Palette
This café has been patronised by the likes of Henry Miller, Apollinaire and Jacques Prévert. *43 rue de Seine, 75006 • Map L4 • Open 8am–2am daily*

2 Les Deux Magots
This was home to the literary and artistic élite of Paris as well as a regular haunt of Surrealists such as François Mauriac *(see p52)*. ✪ *6 pl St-Germain-des-Prés, 75006 • Map K4 • Open 7:30am–1am daily*

3 Café de Flore
Guillaume Apollinaire founded his literary magazine, *Les Soirées de Paris*, here in 1913 *(see p52)*. *172 blvd St-Germain, 75006 • Map K4 • Open 7am–1:30am daily*

4 Le Procope
The oldest café in Paris, this was a meeting place for writers such as Voltaire, Balzac and Zola. *13 rue de l' Ancienne-Comédie, 75006 • Map L4 • Open 10:30am–1am daily*

5 Brasserie Lipp
Ernest Hemingway pays homage to this café in *A Moveable Feast*. It was also visited by Symbolist novelist André Gide. *151 blvd St-Germain, 75006 • Map L4 • Open 9:30am–12:45am daily*

6 Hotel Pont Royal
Henry Miller drank here at the time of writing his *Tropic of Capricorn* and *Tropic of Cancer*. *5–7 rue de Montalembert, 75007 • Map J3 • Open 8am–midnight daily*

7 Shakespeare and Company
This renowned bookshop was once described by novelist Henry Miller as a "wonderland of books" *(see p122)*.

8 Le Sélect
F. Scott Fitzgerald and Truman Capote were among many American writers who drank in this café. ✪ *99 blvd du Montparnasse, 75006 • Map E6 • Open 7am–2am Mon–Fri (to 4am Sat & Sun)*

9 La Coupole
Opened in 1927, this former coal depot was transformed by artists into a lavish Art Deco brasserie. It attracted such luminaries as Louis Aragon and Françoise Sagan *(see p157)*.

10 Le Petit St-Benoît
Camus, de Beauvoir and James Joyce once took their daily coffee here. ✪ *4 rue St Benoît, 75006 • Map K3 • Open noon–2:30pm, 7–10:30pm Mon–Sat*

For more on writers in Paris **See p47**

Left **Rue de Buci market** Right **Parisian patisserie**

🔟 Picnic Providers

1 Rue de Buci Market
Head for this chic daily market where you'll find the very best regional produce, wine and pastries *(see p54)*. 🔍 *Map L4*

2 Poilâne
Get the best bread for your picnic, made from the recipe of the late king of bread-makers, Lionel Poilâne. 🔍 *8 rue du Cherche-Midi, 75006 • Map J5*

3 Maubert Market
A small market specializing in organic produce every Tuesday, Thursday and Saturday morning. A good place to pick up olives, cheese, tomatoes and fruit. 🔍 *Pl Maubert, 75006 • Map N5*

4 Fromagerie Androuet
One of the oldest cheese shops in Paris, where the cheese is aged onsite. 🔍 *134 rue Mouffetard, 75005 • Map D5 • Closed Sun pm & Mon*

5 Naturalia
For a fully organic picnic, look no further: excellent breads, wines, cheeses, hams, fruits, desserts and much more. 🔍 *36 rue Monge, 75005 • Map N6 • Closed Sun*

6 Marché Raspail
An organic market held on Tuesday, Friday and Sunday mornings. Superb produce but pricey. 🔍 *Blvd Raspail, 75006 • Map J4*

7 Bon
Wonderful patisserie and chocolatier, with a good line in small fruit tarts, such as lemon and strawberry, and chocolates in the shape of the Eiffel Tower. 🔍 *159 rue St-Jacques, 75005 • Map N*

8 La Grande Epicerie de Paris
Hunt for treasures such as Breton seaweed butter and *coucou de Rennes* at the food hall in Le Bon Marché *(see p55* 🔍 *Le Bon Marché, 38 rue de Sèvres, 75007 • Map D5*

9 Le Pirée
Delicious, freshly prepared Greek and Armenian specialitie such as stuffed vegetables and honey-soaked cakes, are sold he 🔍 *47 blvd St-Germain, 75005 • Map N*

10 Kayser
If you don't want to make your own picnic then try a read made sandwich from the baker Mouthwatering combinations include goat's cheese with pea 🔍 *14 rue Monge, 75005 • Map P6*

Above **Alcazar**

Price Categories

For a three-course	**€** under €30
meal for one with half	**€€** €30–€40
a bottle of wine (or	**€€€** €40–€50
equivalent meal), taxes	**€€€€** €50–€60
and extra charges	**€€€€€** over €60

🔟 Places to Eat

1 L'Épi Dupin
The dishes, such as scallop risotto, are sublime but be sure to reserve a table in advance. ◎ 11 rue Dupin, 75006 • Map J5 • 01 42 22 64 56 • Closed Sat, Sun, Mon L, Aug • €€€

2 La Tour d'Argent
This historic restaurant with fine views of Notre-Dame serves duckling as the speciality. ◎ 15 quai de la Tournelle, 75005 • Map P5 • 01 43 54 23 31 • Closed Sun, Aug • €€€€€

3 Les Bouquinistes
Creative cooking is served at this bistro, owned by Guy Savoy, on the banks of the Seine. ◎ 53 quai des Grands-Augustins, 75006 • Map N4 • 01 43 25 45 94 • Closed Sat L, Sun, Aug • No disabled access • €€€€

4 Alcazar
A stylish brasserie with a mix of French, Asian and British food. ◎ 62 rue Mazarine, 75006 • Map L3 • 01 53 10 19 99 • €€€€

5 Lapérouse
Classic French cuisine served in a setting unchanged since 1766. ◎ 51 quai des Grands-Augustins, 75006 • Map M4 • 01 43 26 68 04 • Closed Sat L, Sun, Aug • €€€€€

6 L'Atelier Maître Albert
Spit-roasted meats and signature dishes by top chef Guy Savoy. Aim for a table in front of the giant fireplace. ◎ 1 rue Maître Albert, 75005 • Map F5 • 01 56 81 30 01 • Closed Sat L, Sun L over Christmas • €€€€

7 La Bastide Odéon
A taste of Provence in an elegant setting. Try the risotto with scallops. ◎ 7 rue Corneille, 75006 • Map L5 • 01 43 26 03 65 • Closed Sun, Mon, Aug • No disabled access • €€€

8 Le Pré Verre
Dine on classic French cooking with Asian flourishes. ◎ 8 rue Thénard, 75005 • Map F5 • 01 43 54 59 47 • Closed Sun, Mon, Aug, 25 Dec–1 Jan • €€

9 Les Papilles
Pick your wine straight off the shelves to accompany the stunning menu (see p64). ◎ 30 rue Gay Lussac, 75005 • Map F6 • 01 43 25 20 79 • Closed Sun, Mon, Aug, 25 Dec–1 Jan • No disabled access • €€€

10 Au Moulin à Vent
One of the best bistros in Paris, with frogs' legs on the menu. ◎ 20 rue des Fossés-St-Bernard, 75005 • Map P6 • 01 43 54 99 37 • Closed Sat L, Sun, Mon, Aug • €€€€

Note: Unless otherwise stated, all restaurants accept credit cards and serve vegetarian meals

Left **Jardin des Plantes** Centre **Natural History Museum** Right **Institut du Monde Arabe**

Jardin des Plantes Quarter

TRADITIONALLY ONE OF THE MOST PEACEFUL areas of Paris, the medicinal herb gardens which give the quarter its name were established here in 1626. It retained a rural atmosphere until the 19th century, when the city's population expanded and the surrounding streets were built up. Near the gardens is the Arènes de Lutèce, a well-preserved Roman amphitheatre. The rue Mouffetard, winding down the hill from the bustling place de la Contrescarpe, dates from medieval times and has one of the best markets in the city. The area is also home to a sizeable Muslim community, focused on the Institut du Monde Arabe cultural centre and the Paris Mosque. In contrast to the striking Islamic architecture are the grey slab 1960s buildings of Paris University's Jussieu Campus.

Riding a stone hippopotamus at the Ménagerie

🔟 Sights

1. Jardin des Plantes
2. Muséum National d'Histoire Naturelle
3. Ménagerie
4. Institut du Monde Arabe
5. Mosquée de Paris
6. Rue Mouffetard
7. Arènes de Lutèce
8. Place de la Contrescarpe
9. St-Médard
10. Manufacture des Gobelins

Sign up for DK's email newsletter on traveldk.com

1 Jardin des Plantes

The 17th-century royal medicinal herb garden was planted by Jean Hérouard and Guy de la Brosse, physicians to Louis XIII. Opened to the public in 1640, it flourished under the curatorship of Comte de Buffon. It contains some 6,500 species, and 10,000 plants. There is also a Cedar of Lebanon that was planted in 1734, a hillside maze, and Alpine and rose gardens (see p132). ✪ 57 rue Cuvier, 75005 • Map G6 • 01 40 79 30 00 • Open 8am–5:30pm daily, 7:30am–8pm summer

2 Muséum National d'Histoire Naturelle

Separate pavilions in the Jardin des Plantes house exhibits on anatomy, fossils, geology, mineralogy and insects. The Grande Galerie de l'Evolution (see p60) has a magnificent collection of stuffed African mammals, a giant whale skeleton and an endangered species exhibit (see p34). ✪ 57 rue Cuvier, 75005 • Map G6 • Pavilions: open 10am–5pm Wed–Mon; Evolution Gallery: open 10am–6pm Wed–Mon • Closed 1 May • Admission charge • www.mnhn.fr

3 Ménagerie

The country's oldest public zoo was founded during the Revolution to house the surviving animals from the royal menagerie at Versailles. Other animals were donated from circuses and abroad, but during the Siege of Paris in 1870–71 (see p45) the unfortunate creatures were eaten by hungry citizens. A favourite with children (see p60), the zoo has since been restocked. ✪ Jardin des Plantes, 75005 • Map G6 • Open 9am–5pm daily • Admission charge

4 Institut du Monde Arabe

This institute was founded in 1980 to promote cultural relations between France and the Arab world. The stunning building (1987) designed by architect Jean Nouvel (see musée du quai Branly p112) features a southern wall of 240 photo-sensitive metal screens that open and close like camera apertures to regulate light entering the building. The design is based on the latticed wooden screens of Islamic architecture. Inside is a redesigned museum featuring Islamic artworks, from 9th-century ceramics to contemporary art, and a fine tea salon and restaurant. ✪ 1 rue des Fossés-St-Bernard, pl Mohammed V, 75005 • Map G5 • 01 40 51 38 38 • Open 10am–6pm Tue–Sun • Admission charge • www.imarabe.org

5 Mosquée de Paris

Built in 1922–6, the mosque complex is the spiritual centre for Parisian Muslims (see p41). The beautiful Hispano-Moorish decoration, particularly the grand patio, was inspired by the Alhambra in Spain. The minaret soars nearly 33 m (100 ft). There is also an Islamic school, tea room and Turkish baths, open to men and women on separate days. ✪ 2 bis pl du Puits-de-l'Ermité, 75005 • Map G6 • Tours: 9am–noon, 2–6pm Sat–Thu; closed Islamic hols • Admission charge

Minaret, Mosquée de Paris

French North Africa

France has always had close connections with North Africa, though not always harmonious. Its annexation of Algeria in 1834 led to the long and bloody Algerian War of Liberation (1954–62). Relations with Tunisia, which it governed from 1883 to 1956, and Morocco, also granted independence in 1956, were better. Many North Africans now live in Paris.

Rue Mouffetard

Although the rue Mouffetard is famous today for its lively street market held every Tuesday to Sunday (see p55), it has an equally colourful past. In Roman times this was the main road from Paris to Rome. Some say its name comes from the French word *mouffette* (skunk), as a reference to the odorous River Bièvre (now covered over) here waste was dumped by tanners and weavers from the nearby Gobelins tapestry factory. Though no longer poor or Bohemian, the neighbourhood still has lots of character, with its 17th-century mansard roofs, old-fashioned painted shop signs and affordable restaurants. In the market you can buy everything from Auvergne sausage to horse meat and ripe cheeses. ◊ Map F6

Arènes de Lutèce

The remains of the 2nd-century Roman amphitheatre from the settlement of Lutetia (see p44) lay buried for centuries and were only discovered in 1869 during construction of the rue Monge. The novelist Victor Hugo, concerned with the preservation of his city's historic buildings, including Notre-Dame (see p21), led the campaign for the restoration. The original arena would have had 35 tiers and could seat 15,000 spectators for theatrical performances and gladiator fights. ◊ 47 rue Monge, 75005 • Map G6 • Open 9am–9:30pm daily (summer); 8am–5:30pm daily (winter) • Free

Place de la Contrescarpe

This bustling square has a village community feel, with busy cafés and restaurants and groups of students from the nearby university hanging out here after dark. In medieval times it lay outside the city walls, a remnant of which still

Arènes de Lutèce

ands. Notice the memorial
aque above the butcher's at
p. 1, which marks the site of
e old Pine Cone Club, a café
here François Rabelais and
her writers gathered in the
5th century. ◈ Map F5

St-Médard

The church at the bottom of
e Mouffetard dates back to the
th century, when it was a parish
urch dedicated to St Médard,
unsellor to the Merovingian
ngs. The present church,
ompleted in 1655, is a mixture
Flamboyant Gothic and
enaissance styles. Among the
e paintings inside is the 17th-
entury *St Joseph Walking with
e Christ Child* by Francisco de
urbarán. The churchyard was
e scene of hysterical fits in the
8th century, when a cult of
convulsionnaires" sought
iracle cures at the grave of a
nsenist deacon. ◈ 141 rue
ouffetard, 75005 • Map G6 • Open
m–noon, 2:30–7pm Tue–Sat, 9am–noon
un • Free

Manufacture des Gobelins

This internationally renowned
pestry factory was originally a
yeing workshop, founded by
e Gobelin brothers in the mid-
5th century. In 1662, Louis
IV's minister Colbert set up a
yal factory here and gathered
e greatest craftsmen of the
ay to make furnishings for the
alace at Versailles *(see p151)*.
ou can see the traditional
eaving process on a guided
ur. ◈ 42 ave des Gobelins, 75013
Metro Gobelins • Tours: 1pm and 3pm
e–Thu (arrive 30 minutes prior), open
r temporary exhibitions only 11am–6pm
e–Sun • Tickets must be bought prior to
e visit at a branch of FNAC

A Day in the Gardens

Morning

If it's a fine morning get an early start and enjoy a stroll in the **Jardin des Plantes** *(see p129)* before the city gets truly busy. The **Muséum National d'Histoire Naturelle** *(see p129)* doesn't open until 10am, but the garden is close enough to **rue Mouffetard** to enable you to enjoy the fabulous market, which gets going by about 8am. Don't forget to take your eyes off the stalls every now and then to see the splendid old buildings on this medieval street. Then return to the museum and its Evolution Gallery.

From the gardens it is a short walk to the **place de la Contrescarpe**. Enjoy this friendly square before walking down the rue Mouffetard for a coffee at one of its many cafés. Once revived, walk down to the bottom of the road to see the church of **St-Médard** on your left.

Turn left along rue Monge to the **Arènes de Lutèce**. A couple of minutes away is a little bistro, **Le Buisson Ardent** *(see p133)*, which is ideal for lunch.

Afternoon

You can spend part of the afternoon at the **Institut du Monde Arabe** *(see p129)*, exploring its beautiful Islamic artworks, before walking down to admire the Moorish architecture of the **Mosquée de Paris** *(see p129)*. Finish the day with a mint tea at the Café de la Mosquée *(pl du Puits-de-l'Ermité • 01 43 31 18 14)*.

Left **Flowers in the Jardin des Plantes** Right **Dinosaur model**

🔟 Jardin des Plantes Sights

1 Dinosaur Tree
One of the trees in the Botanical Gardens is a *Ginkgo biloba*, which was planted in 1795, but the species is known to have existed in exactly the same form in the days of the dinosaurs, 125 million years ago.

2 Cedar of Lebanon
This magnificent tree was planted in 1734, and came from London's Botanic Gardens in Kew, although a story grew up that its seed was brought here all the way from Syria in the hat of a scientist.

3 Rose Garden
Although only a fairly recent addition, being planted in 1990, the beautiful *roseraie* has some 170 species of roses and 180 rose bushes on display. Spectacular when they are in full bloom in spring and summer.

4 Rock Gardens
One of the stars of the Botanical Gardens, with more than 3,000 plants from the world's many diverse Alpine regions. There are samples from Corsica to the Caucasus, Morocco and the Himalayas.

5 Sophora of Japan
Sent to Paris under the label "unknown seeds from China" by a Jesuit naturalist living in the Orient, this tree was planted in 1747, first flowered in 1777, and still flowers today.

6 Iris Garden
An unusual feature is this designated garden which brings together more than 400 different varieties of iris.

7 Dinosaur Model
Outside the Palaeontology Gallery, which is crammed with precious dinosaur skeletons, is a huge dinosaur model of a stegosaurus *(see p60)*.

8 Nile Crocodile
The crocodile in the Reptile House now has a better home than he once did. This creature was found in 1998, when he was six months old, in the bathtub of a Paris hotel room, left behind as an unwanted pet!

9 Greenhouses
Otherwise known as *Les Grandes Serres*, these 19th-century greenhouses were at one time the largest in the world. Today, they house a prickly Mexican cacti garden and a tropical winter garden kept at a constant 22°C (74°F) and 80 per cent humidity.

10 Young Animal House
One of the zoo's most popular features for children is this house where young creatures, which for one reason or another cannot be looked after by their natural parents, are raised. Once they reach adulthood they are returned to their natural habitat.

Above **L'Avant-Goût**

Price Categories

For a three-course meal for one with half a bottle of wine (or equivalent meal), taxes and extra charges

€ under €30
€€ €30–€40
€€€ €40–€50
€€€€ €50–€60
€€€€€ over €60

Places to Eat

1 Le Petit Pascal
This family-run, provincial-style bistro, popular with locals at dinner, has a menu of regional dishes that changes daily. ◈ 33 rue Pascal, 75013 • Metro Gobelins • 01 45 35 33 87 • Closed Sat, Sun, Aug • €€

2 Léna et Mimile
Those in the know avoid the touristy restaurants around rue Mouffetard to savour a meal at this ambitious bistro with a peaceful terrace. ◈ 32 rue Tournefort, 75005 • 01 47 07 72 47 • €€€

3 Au Petit Marguery
One for meat lovers, with plenty of steak, veal and game on the menu. Boisterous atmosphere. ◈ 9 blvd de Port-Royal, 75013 • Map F6 • 01 43 31 58 59 • €€€€

4 Le Buisson Ardent
This creative bistro is a romantic night-time destination serving classic French dishes with a twist. Set menus offer good value. ◈ 25 rue Jussieu, 75005 • Map G6 • 01 43 54 93 02 • Closed Sun, Sat L, Aug, 24 Dec • €€€

5 La Truffière
A 17th-century building, a wood fire and welcoming staff all make for a great little bistro. Naturally, the menu features truffles. ◈ 4 rue Blainville, 75005 • Map F6 • 01 46 33 29 82 • Closed Sun, Mon • €€€€€

6 L'Agrume
This restaurant is popular for its affordable five-course fixed-price menu. ◈ 15 rue des Fossés Saint-Marcel, 75005 • Map G6 • 01 43 31 86 48 • No disabled access • Closed Sun, Mon • €€€€

7 Chez Paul
Not the best place for vegetarians, with pot au feu, tongue and other meaty delights, but there is also fish. ◈ 22 rue de la Butte-aux-Cailles, 75013 • Metro Place d'Italie • 01 45 89 22 11 • €€€

8 Au Coco de Mer
Spicy Seychelles cuisine, plus a "beach hut" terrace with soft sand. Vegetarians should book ahead. ◈ 34 blvd St-Marcel, 75005 • Map G6 • 06 81 57 29 29 • Closed Sun, Mon L, Aug • €€

9 L'Avant-Goût
Small and noisy with tables crammed together. Try the pot au feu or apple flan, if available, though the menu changes daily. ◈ 26 rue Bobillot, 75013 • Metro Place d'Italie • 01 53 80 24 00 • Closed Sun, Mon • €€€

10 Chez Gladine
A lively place with waiters running around serving huge portions of Basque cuisine. Arrive early to get a table. ◈ 30 rue des Cinq Diamants, 75013 • 01 45 80 70 10 • Closed Jul • No credit cards • €

Left **Jardins du Trocadéro** Center **Cinéaqua** Right **Café Carette**

Chaillot Quarter

CHAILLOT WAS A SEPARATE VILLAGE *until the 19th century, when it was swallowed up by the growing city and bestowed with wide avenues and lavish mansions during the Second Empire building spree* (see p45). *Its centrepiece is the glorious Palais de Chaillot which stands on top of the small Chaillot hill, its wide white-stone wings embracing the Trocadéro Gardens and its terrace gazing across the Seine to the Eiffel Tower. Behind the palace is the place du Trocadéro, laid out in 1858 and originally called the place du Roi-de-Rome (King of Rome), the title of Napoleon's son. The square is ringed with smart cafés, overlooking the central equestrian statue of World War I hero Marshal Ferdinand Foch. Many of the elegant mansions in this area now house embassies, and there are numerous fine dining spots. To the west are the exclusive residential neighbourhoods of the Parisian bourgeoisie.*

Sights

1. Palais de Chaillot
2. Cinéaqua
3. Musée de la Marine
4. Cité de l'Architecture et du Patrimoine
5. Musée d'Art Moderne de la Ville de Paris
6. Cimetière de Passy
7. Jardins du Trocadéro
8. Musée du Vin
9. Maison de Balzac
10. Musée National des Arts Asiatiques-Guimet

Exhibit at the Musée du Vin

Palais de Chaillot

The fall of his empire scuppered Napoleon's plans for an opulent palace for his son on Chaillot hill, but the site was later used for the Trocadéro palace, built for the Universal Exhibition of 1878. It was replaced by the present Neo-Classical building with its huge colonnaded wings for the prewar exhibition of 1937. The two pavilions house three museums, including the Musée de la Marine *(see below)*. The broad terrace is the domain of souvenir sellers and skateboarders by day, while at night it is crowded with tourists admiring the splendid view of the Eiffel Tower across the Seine. Two bronzes, *Apollo* by Henri Bouchard and *Hercules* by Pommier, stand to the front of the terrace. Beneath the terrace is the 1,200-seat Théâtre National de Chaillot. *17 pl du Trocadéro, 75016 • Map B4*

Palais de Chaillot

Cinéaqua

Originally built in 1878 for the Universal Exhibition, Paris's fascinating aquarium is home to over 10,000 species, including seahorses, stonefish and some spectacular sharks and rays. Built into a former quarry, the site has been designed to blend in with the Chaillot hillside. There is also a futuristic cinema complex. *Ave Albert de Mun, 75016 • Map B4 • Open 10am–7pm daily Oct–Mar: to 6pm) • Closed 1 Jan, 1 May, 4 Jul, 25 Dec • Admission charge www.cineaqua.com*

Musée de la Marine

Three hundred years of French naval history is the focus of this museum, whether in war, trade and commerce, or industries such as fishing. The displays range from naval art to science to maritime adventure and popular legends and traditions. Among the highlights is an outstanding collection of model ships, from the feluccas of ancient Egypt, to medieval galleys and nuclear submarines. You can also watch craftsmen at work on the models. Napoleon's royal barge is also on show *(see p35).* *Palais de Chaillot, 17 pl du Trocadéro, 75016 • Map B4 • Open 11am–6pm Wed–Mon (to 7pm Sat & Sun) • Closed 1 Jan, 1 May, 25 Dec • Admission charge • www.musee-marine.fr*

Cité de l'Architecture et du Patrimoine

Occupying the east wing of the Palais Chaillot, this museum is a veritable ode to French architect-ural heritage, showcasing its development through the ages as well as contemporary architecture. The Galerie des Moulages (Medieval to Renaissance) contains moulded portions of churches and great French cathedrals such as Chartres. The Galerie Moderne et Contemporain includes a reconstruction of an apartment designed by Le Corbusier, and architectural

General Foch

General Ferdinand Foch (1851–1929), whose statue stands in the centre of place du Trocadéro, was the commander-in-chief of the Allied armies by the end of World War I. His masterful command ultimately led to victory over the Germans in 1918, whereupon he was made a Marshal of France and elected to the French Academy.

designs from 1990 onwards. The wall-painting gallery in the Pavillon de Tête has a stunning collection of murals copied from medieval frescoes. ◈ *Palais de Chaillot, 75116* • *Map B4* • *Open 11am–7pm Wed–Mon (until 9pm Thu)* • *01 58 51 52 00* • *Admission charge* • *www.citechaillot.fr*

Musée d'Art Moderne de la Ville de Paris

This modern art museum is housed in the east wing of the Palais de Tokyo, built for the 1937 World Fair. Its permanent collection includes such masters as Chagall, Picasso, Modigliani and Léger; further highlights include Raoul Dufy's enormous mural *The Spirit of Electricity* (1937), and Picabia's *Lovers (After the Rain)* (1925). The museum also promotes up-and-coming artists by showcasing their work in the west wing. ◈ *11 ave du Président-Wilson, 75016* • *Map B4* • *Open 10am–6pm Tue–Sun (until 10pm Thu during temporary exhibitions)* • *01 53 67 40 00* • *Permanent collection free; temporary exhibitions admission charge* • *www.mam.paris.fr*

Cimetière de Passy

This small cemetery covers only 1 ha (2.5 acres), yet many famous people have been laid to rest here with the Eiffel Tower as their eternal view *(see p138)*. It is worth a visit just to admire the striking sculptures on the tombs. ◈ *Pl du Trocadéro (entrance rue du Commandant Schloessing) 75016* • *Map A4*

Jardins du Trocadéro

Designed in 1937, the tiered Trocadéro Gardens descend gently down Chaillot hill from the palace to the Seine and the Pont d'Iéna. The centrepiece of this 10-ha (25-acre) park is the long rectangular pool lined with stone and bronze statues, including *Woman* by Georges Braque (1882–1963). Its illuminated fountains are spectacular at night. With flowering trees, walkways and bridges over small streams, the gardens are a romantic place for a stroll *(see p39)*. ◈ *Map B4*

Cimetière de Passy

Musée du Vin

The vaulted 14th-century cellars where the monks of Passy once made wine are an atmospheric setting for this wine museum. Waxwork figures depict the history of the wine-making process, and there are displays of wine paraphernalia. There are tasting sessions, wine for sale and a restaurant. ◉ *5 square Charles-Dickens, rue des Eaux, 75016 • Map A4 • Open 10am–6pm Tue–Sun • Admission charge • www. museeduvinparis.com*

Maison de Balzac

The writer Honoré de Balzac (see p46) rented an apartment here from 1840–44, and assumed a false name to avoid his many creditors. He worked on several of his famous novels here, including *La cousine Bette* and *La comédie humaine*. The house is now a museum displaying first editions and manuscripts, personal mementoes and letters, and paintings and drawings of his friends and family as well as housing temporary exhibitions. ◉ *47 rue Raynouard, 75016 • Map A4 • Open 10am–6pm Tue–Sun • Closed public hols • Admission charge for temporary exhibitions • www.balzac.paris.fr*

Musée National des Arts Asiatiques-Guimet

One of the world's foremost museums of Asiatic and Oriental art, founded in 1889. The Khmer Buddhist temple sculptures from Angkor Wat are the highlight of a fine collection of Cambodian art. Guimet's original collection tracing Chinese and Japanese religion from the 4th to 19th centuries is also on display, as are artifacts from India, Indonesia and Vietnam. ◉ *6 pl d'Iéna, 75016 • Map B3 • Open 10am–6pm Wed–Mon • Admission charge • www.guimet.fr*

A Day in Chaillot

Morning

It would be hard to imagine a better start to a day in Paris than going to the **Palais de Chaillot** (see p135) and seeing the perfect view it has across the Seine to the **Eiffel Tower** (see pp16–17). Then tour the fascinating collections of the **Cité de l'Architecture** (see pp135–6) and, if marine history is your thing, the **Musée de la Marine** (see p135), both in the palace. Outside the palace, take a break in the Café du Trocadéro (8 pl du Trocadéro • 01 44 05 37 00) and watch the comings and goings in the square.

Afterwards, head along rue Benjamin Franklin and rue Raynouard, where you will find first the **Musée du Vin** and the **Maison de Balzac**. Walk to the far side of the Maison de Radio France building for a brunch or lunch at **Zebra Square** (see p139).

Afternoon

Revived, walk back along the Seine towards the Palais de Chaillot, and head up to the place d'Iéna to the refurbished and much improved **Musée National des Arts Asiatiques-Guimet** for its spectacular Eastern artworks.

By now you will definitely be in need of a rest, so return to the place du Trocadéro for a coffee at the Café Kléber No. 4 (01 47 27 86 65). End the day in the peaceful **Cimetière de Passy** before an unforgettable dinner overlooking the Eiffel Tower at the stylish **Le Jules Verne** (see p117).

Left **Manet bust** Centre **Debussy's grave** Right **Fernandel's grave**

Graves in Cimetière de Passy

1 Edouard Manet
Born in Paris in 1832, Manet became the most notorious artist in the city when works such as *Olympia* and *Le Déjeuner sur l'Herbe (see p12)* were first exhibited. He died in Paris in 1883.

2 Claude Debussy
The French composer (1862–1918) achieved fame through works such as *Prélude à l'Après-midi d'un Faune* and *La Mer*, and was regarded as the musical equivalent of the Impressionist painters.

3 Berthe Morisot
The French Impressionist artist was born in Paris in 1841, posed for Edouard Manet and later married his lawyer brother Eugène. She never achieved the fame of the male Impressionists and died in Paris in 1895.

4 Fernandel
The lugubrious French film actor known as Fernandel was born in Marseille in 1903 and made more than 100 films in a career that lasted from 1930 until his death in Paris in 1971.

5 Marie Bashkirtseff
This Russian artist became more renowned as a diarist after her death from tuberculosis in 1884. Despite living for only 24 years she produced 84 volumes of diaries and their posthumous publication created a sensation due to their intimate nature.

6 Henri Farman
The French aviator was born in Paris in 1874 and died here in 1958. He was the first man to make a circular 1-km (0.5-mile) flight, and the first to fly cross-country in Europe. His gravestone shows him at the controls of a primitive plane.

7 Antoine Cierplikowski
The grave of this fairly obscure artist of the 1920s attracts attention because of its immensely powerful sculpture of a man and woman joined together and seeming to soar from the grave to the heavens.

8 Comte Emanuel de las Cases
Born in 1766, this historian and friend of Napoleon shared the emperor's exile on the island of St Helena and recorded his memoirs. The Comte himself died in Paris in 1842.

9 Gabriel Fauré
The French composer, probably best known today for his *Requiem*, was a great influence on the music of his time. He died in Paris in 1924, at the age of 79.

10 Octave Mirbeau
The satirical French novelist and playwright was also an outspoken journalist. Born in 1848, he died in Cheverchemon in 1917 and his body was brought to Passy for burial.

Around Town – Chaillot Quarter

Price Categories

For a three-course meal for one with half a bottle of wine (or equivalent meal), taxes and extra charges

€ under €30
€€ €30–€40
€€€ €40–€50
€€€€ €50–€60
€€€€€ over €60

Left **Maison Prunier** Right **Le Relais du Parc**

Places to Eat

1 Le Relais du Parc
The fixed-price lunch menu, which changes seasonally, is a bargain. ✪ *55–57 ave Raymond Poincaré, 75016 • Map B3 • 01 44 05 66 10 • Closed Sat L, Sun, Aug • €€€€€*

2 Le Jamin
Former Guy Savoy disciple Alain Pras presides over this elegant, formal restaurant, offering an inventive approach to French classics, and good vegetarian options. ✪ *32 rue de Longchamp, 75016 • Map A3 • 01 45 53 00 07 • Closed Sat L, Sun, Aug • No disabled access • €€€€€*

3 Le Bistrot du Chineur
A tiny, friendly bistro serving good value, thoughtfully prepared cuisine. Advance reservation essential.
✪ *5 impasse des Carrières, 75016 • Map A4 • 01 42 88 17 73 • Closed D, Sat, Sun, Mon • €*

4 L'Astrance
Pascal Barbot serves fusion food at its best. Book a month in advance. ✪ *4 rue Beethoven 75116 • Map B4 • 01 40 50 84 40 • Closed Sat, Sun, Mon • No disabled access • €€€€€*

5 Maison Prunier
Fish dishes reign at this restaurant with 1930s décor. ✪ *16 ave Victor-Hugo, 75016 • Map B3 • 01 44 17 35 85 • Closed Sun, Aug • No disabled access • €€€€€*

6 Comme des Poissons
This tiny Japanese sushi restaurant serves good food at reasonable prices, so book ahead. ✪ *22 rue de la Tour, 75016 • Map A4 • 01 45 20 70 37 • Closed Mon • €*

7 Le Petit Rétro
Cosy atmosphere in this 1900s bistro and affordable prices. *Blanquette de Veau* is delicious. ✪ *5 rue Mesnil, 75016 • Map B3 • 01 44 05 06 05 • Closed Sat, Sun, Aug • No disabled access • €€€*

8 Le Bistrot des Vignes
Unpretentious little bistro of the type everyone hopes to find in Paris. ✪ *1 rue Jean-Bologne, 75016 • Map B4 • 01 45 27 76 64 • Closed Aug, 24 Dec • No disabled access • €€€*

9 La Table Lauriston
Serge Barbey believes in the best ingredients prepared simply. La Table Lauriston is a hit with local gourmets who tuck into his gargantuan steak and rum-doused *baba* in the jewel-toned dining room. ✪ *129 rue Lauriston, 75116 • Map A3 • 01 47 27 00 07 • Closed Sun, Sat L, Aug, 1 wk over Christmas • €€€€*

10 Zebra Square
This is a media hangout as it's next to France's public service radio network. Sunday brunches are popular. ✪ *3 pl Clément-Ader, 75016 • Map A4 • 01 44 14 91 91 • €€€€€*

> **Note:** Unless otherwise stated, all restaurants accept credit cards and serve vegetarian meals

139

Left **Sacré-Coeur** Centre **Espace Montmartre Salvador Dali** Right **Place Pigalle**

Montmartre and Pigalle

PAINTERS AND POETS, *from Picasso to Apollinaire, put the "art" in Montmartre, and it will forever be associated with their Bohemian lifestyles of the late 19th and early 20th centuries.*
There are plenty of artists around today too, painting quick-fire portraits of tourists in the place du Tertre. The area's name comes from "Mount of Martyrs", commemorating the first bishop of Paris, St Denis, who was decapitated here by the Romans in AD 250. Parisians, however, call it the "Butte" (knoll) as it is the highest point in the city. Throngs of tourists climb the hill for the stupendous view from Sacré-Coeur, crowding the main square, but you can still discover Montmartre's charms along the winding back streets, small squares and terraces. Below the hill, Pigalle, once home to dance halls and cabarets, has largely been taken over by sleazy sex shows along the boulevard de Clichy.

Streetside painter, Montmartre

🔟 Sights

1. Sacré-Coeur
2. Espace Montmartre Salvador Dali
3. Musée de Montmartre
4. Place du Tertre
5. Cimetière de Montmartre
6. Musée d'Erotisme
7. Moulin Rouge
8. Au Lapin Agile
9. Place des Abbesses
10. Moulin de la Galette

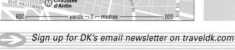
Sign up for DK's email newsletter on traveldk.com

Sacré-Coeur
See pp22–3.

Espace Montmartre Salvador Dalí
The Dalí works here may not be the artist's most famous or best, but this museum is still a must for any fan of the Spanish Surrealist (see p144). More than 300 of his drawings and sculptures are on display amid high-tech light and sound effects, including Dalí's voice, which create a "surreal" atmosphere. There are also bronzes of his memorable "fluid" clocks (see p37). ⊗ 11 rue Poulbot, 75018 • Map F1 Open 10am–6pm daily (Jul–Aug to 8pm) Admission charge • www.daliparis.com

Musée de Montmartre
The museum is set in Montmartre's finest townhouse, known as Le Manoir de Rose de Rosimond after the 17th-century actor who once owned it. From 1875 it provided living quarters and studios for many artists. Using drawings, photographs and memorabilia, the museum presents the history of the Montmartre area, from its 12th-century convent days to the present, with an emphasis on the Bohemian lifestyle of the belle époque. There is even a re-created 19th-century bistro. ⊗ 12 rue Cortot, 75018 • Open 11am–6pm Tue–Sun • Closed 1 Jan, 25 Dec Admission charge • www.museedemontmartre.fr

Place du Tertre
At 130 m (430 ft), Montmartre's old village square, whose name means "hillock", is the highest point in the city. Any picturesque charm it might once have had is now sadly hidden under the tourist-trap veneer of overpriced restaurants and portrait artists hawking their services, although the fairy lights at night are still atmospheric. No. 21 houses the Old Montmartre information office, with details about the area. Nearby is the church of St-Pierre de Montmartre, all that remains of the Benedictine abbey which stood here from 1133 until the Revolution. ⊗ Map F1

Cimetière de Montmartre
The main graveyard for the district lies beneath a busy road in an old gypsum quarry, though it's more restful than first appears when you actually get below street level. The illustrious tombs, many with ornately sculpted monuments, packed tightly into this intimate space reflect the artistic bent of the former residents, who include composers Hector Berlioz and Jacques Offenbach, writers Stendhal and Alexandre Dumas, Russian dancer Nijinsky and the film director François Truffaut. ⊗ 20 ave Rachel, 75018 • Map E1

Sculpture of writer Marcel Aymé

The Montmartre Vineyards

It's hard to imagine it today, but Montmartre was once a French wine region said to match the quality of Bordeaux and Burgundy. There were 20,000 ha (50,000 acres) of Parisian vineyards in the mid-18th century, but today just 1,000 bottles of wine are made annually from the remaining 2,000 vines in Montmartre, and sold for charity.

Musée de l'Erotisme

With more than 2,000 items from around the world, this museum presents all forms of erotic art from painting, sculpture, photos and drawings to objects whose sole purpose seems to be titillation. It's all tastefully presented, however, reflecting the sincere interest of the three collectors who founded the museum in 1997 to explore the cultural aspects of eroticism. The displays range from spiritual objects of primitive cultures to whimsical artworks. ◈ *72 blvd de Clichy, 75018* • *Map E1* • *Open 10am–2am daily* • *Admission charge* • *www.musee-erotisme.com*

Moulin Rouge

The Moulin Rouge ("red windmill") is the most famous of the *belle époque* dance halls which scandalized respectable citizens and attracted Montmartre's artists and Bohemians. Henri de Toulouse-Lautrec immortalized the era with his sketches and posters of dancers such as Jane Avril, some of which now grace the Musée d'Orsay *(see p13)*. Cabaret is still performed here *(see p58)*. ◈ *82 blvd de Clichy, 75018* • *Map E1* • *Shows daily at 9pm & 11pm (dinner at 7pm)* • *www.moulinrouge.fr*

Au Lapin Agile

This *belle époque* restaurant and cabaret was a popular hangout for Picasso, Renoir, and poets Apollinaire and Paul Verlaine. It took its name from a humorous painting by André Gill of a rabbit *(lapin)* leaping over a cooking pot, called the "Lapin à Gill". In time it became known by its current name ("nimble rabbit") *(see p58)*. ◈ *22 rue des Saules, 75018* • *Map F1* • *Open 9pm–2am Tue–Sun* • *www.au-lapin-agile.com*

Au Lapin Agile

Moulin de la Galette

Place des Abbesses

This pretty square lies at the base of the Butte, between Pigalle and the place du Tertre. Reach it via the metro station of the same name to appreciate one of the few original Art Nouveau stations left in the city. Designed by the architect Hector Guimard, it features ornate green wrought-iron arches, amber lanterns and a ship shield, the symbol of Paris, on the roof. Along with Porte Dauphine, it is the only station to retain its original glass roof. A mural painted by local artists winds around the spiral staircase at the entrance. But don't walk to the platform, take the elevator – it's the deepest station in Paris, with 285 steps. ⊛ Map E1

Moulin de la Galette

Montmartre once had more than 30 windmills, used for pressing grapes and grinding wheat; this is one of only two still standing. During the siege of Paris in 1814 its owner, Pierre-Charles Debray, was crucified on its sails by Russian soldiers. It became a dance hall in the 19th century and inspired paintings by Renoir and Van Gogh (see p144). It is now a restaurant, but it can be admired from outside, and rue Lepic is worth a visit for its shops and restaurants. ⊛ 83 rue Lepic, 75018 • Map E1

A Day in Montmartre

Morning

⏲ As with all the city's busy attractions, the sooner you get to **Sacré-Coeur** (see pp22–3) the more you will have it to yourself – it opens at 8am. Later in the morning, enjoy the bustle of Montmartre with tourists having their portraits painted by the area's street artists in the **place du Tertre** (see p141). There are plenty of places to choose for a coffee, but the one most of the artists frequent is the Clairon des Chasseurs (3 pl du Tertre • 01 42 62 40 08).

For art of a more surreal kind, pay a visit to the **Espace Montmartre Salvador Dalí** (see p141). Head down rue des Saules to continue the artistic theme with lunch at La Maison Rose (2 rue de l'Abreuvoir • 01 42 57 66 75). Utrillo once painted this pretty pink restaurant.

Afternoon

After lunch, the **Musée de Montmartre** (see p141) is nearby, as are the Montmartre Vineyards, and the little Cimetière St-Vincent where you will find Maurice Utrillo's grave.

Head back up to rue Lepic to see the **Moulin de la Galette** before heading towards the boulevard de Clichy. Here you will see the sleazy side of Pigalle life, although the **Musée de l'Erotisme** is a more tasteful interpretation.

🍷 To the east is a great bar for an apéritif, La Fourmi (74 rue des Martyrs • 01 42 64 70 35). Then end the day with a show at the world-famous **Moulin Rouge** cabaret.

Left **Dalí sculpture** Centre **Pablo Picasso** Right **Moulin de la Galette, Renoir**

TOP 10 Artists who Lived in Montmartre

1 Pablo Picasso
Picasso (1881–1973) painted *Les Demoiselles d'Avignon* in 1907 while living at the Bateau-Lavoir. It is regarded as the painting which inspired the Cubism movement, which he launched with fellow residents Georges Braque and Juan Gris.

2 Salvador Dalí
The Catalan painter (1904–89) came to Paris in 1929 and held his first Surrealist exhibition that year. He kept a studio in Montmartre, and his work is now celebrated in the Espace Montmartre Salvador Dalí *(see p141)*.

3 Vincent Van Gogh
The Dutch genius (1853–90) lived for a time on the third floor of 54 rue Lepic. Many of his early paintings were inspired by the Moulin de la Galette windmill *(see p143)*.

4 Pierre-Auguste Renoir
Renoir (1841–1919) is another artist who found inspiration in the Moulin de la Galette, when he lived at 12 rue Cortot. For a time he laid tables at Au Lapin Agile *(see p142)*.

5 Edouard Manet
Manet (1832–83) frequented Montmartre's artist haunts and scandalized the art world with his paintings of nudes, including the famous *Olympia (see p13)*.

6 Maurice Utrillo
Utrillo (1883–1955) often painted the Auberge de la Bonne-Franquette, an atmospheric depiction of old Montmartre. His mother was the artist Suzanne Valadon and they both lived at 12 rue Cortot, now the Musée de Montmartre *(see p141)*.

7 Henri de Toulouse-Lautrec
More than any other artist, Toulouse-Lautrec (1864–1901) is associated with Montmartre for his sketches and posters of dancers at the Moulin Rouge and other dance halls. They epitomize the era to this day *(see p13)*.

Toulouse-Lautrec

8 Raoul Dufy
The painter Dufy (1877–1953) lived at Villa Guelma on the boulevard de Clichy from 1911 to 1953, when he was at the height of his career.

9 Amedeo Modigliani
The Italian painter (1884–1920) and sculptor arrived in Paris in 1906, when he was 22, and was greatly influenced by Toulouse-Lautrec and the other artists on the Montmartre scene.

10 Edgar Degas
Edgar Degas was born in Paris in 1834 and lived in the city for the whole of his life, most of the time in Montmartre. He died here in 1917 and is buried in the Montmartre cemetery *(see p141)*.

ft **Art Brut, Halle Saint Pierre** Right **Rue de Poteau market**

🔟 Places to Escape the Crowds

St-Jean l'Evangéliste de Montmartre
his 1904 church is a clash of tyles, from Moorish to Art Nou-eau. ◈ *21 rue des Abbesses, 75018 • Map E1 • Open daily • Free*

Montmartre City Hall
On display in this building re two Utrillo paintings. ◈ *1 pl ules-Joffrin, 75018 • Metro Jules Joffrin*

Hameau des Artistes
This little hamlet of artists' tudios is private, but no one will ind if you take a quiet look round. *11 ave Junot, 75018 • Map E1*

Musée de la Vie Romantique
Vriter George Sand was a equent visitor to this house, which now devoted to her works. ◈ *16 rue Chaptal, 75009 • Map E1 • Open 10am–6pm Tue–Sun • Adm harge for temporary exhibitions*

Musée Gustave Moreau
The former home of Symbol-t artist Moreau now displays a rge collection of his works. ◈ *14 rue de La Rochefoucauld, 75009 • Map E2 • Open 10am–12:45pm, -5:15pm Wed–Mon • Admission charge www.musee-moreau.fr*

Halle Saint Pierre
A fascinating cultural centre at exhibits naive folk art as well s Art Brut. ◈ *2 rue Ronsard, 75018 • Map F1 • 01 42 58 72 89 • Open am–6pm daily (noon–6pm Aug) Closed public hols • Admission charge*

Cité Véron
This cul-de-sac is home to the Académie des Arts Chorégraphiques, a prestigious dance school. ◈ *92 blvd de Clichy, 75018 • Map E1*

Square Suzanne-Buisson
Named after a World War II Resistance fighter, this square is a romantic spot. ◈ *Map E1*

Rue de Poteau Market
This great food market is a long way from the tourist crowds. ◈ *Metro Jules Joffrin*

Crypte du Martyrium
This simple, peaceful 19th-century chapel is said to be on the spot where St Denis, patron saint of Paris, was beheaded by the Romans in AD 250. ◈ *11 rue Yvonne-Le-Tac, 75018 • Map E1 • 01 42 23 48 94 • Open 3–6pm Fri*

Left **Au Lapin Agile** Right **Moulin Rouge**

Cabarets and Clubs

Au Lapin Agile
Poets and artists not only drank in this cabaret club, some such as Renoir and Verlaine also laid tables. Picasso even paid his bill with one of his Harlequin paintings (see p142).

Moulin Rouge
As old as the Eiffel Tower (1889) and as much a part of the Parisian image, today's troupe of 60 Doriss Girls are the modern versions of Jane Avril and La Goulue (see p142). ◈ 82 boulevard de Clichy, 75018 • Map E1

Autour de Midi et Minuit
Tuck into delicious bistro food before heading into the small vaulted cellar for a jazz concert.
◈ 11 rue Lepic, 75018 • Map E1
• Closed Sun, Mon, end Feb, Aug

Le Carmen
This trendy hangout offers excellent cocktails and hosts themed nights featuring live music.
◈ 34 rue Duperré, 75009 • Map E1 • 01 45 26 50 00 • Closed Sun, Mon, Aug & Dec

La Nouvelle Eve
One of the lesser-known cabaret venues. Its intimate nature does not undermine the professionalism of the shows.
◈ 25 rue Fontaine, 75009 • Map E1

Le Bus Palladium
This 60s club hosts concerts with an alternative/rock vibe. ◈ 6 rue Pierre Fontaine, 75009 • Map E1 • 01 45 26 80 35 • Closed Sun, Mon

Cabaret Michou
Outrageous drag artists and a legendary compère whose behaviour can never be predicted, this is close to the original spirit of Montmartre cabaret.
◈ 80 rue des Martyrs, 75018 • Map E1

Folies Pigalle
This former strip club is now a leading dance venue and popular among the gay community.
◈ 11 pl Pigalle, 75018 • Map E1

La Machine du Moulin Rouge
This venue next to the Moulin Rouge hosts both club nights and concerts. ◈ 90 boulevard de Clichy, 75018 • Map E1

Le Divan du Monde
World music is played here live and DJ, with regular dance events and concerts too. ◈ 75 rue des Martyrs, 75018 • Map E1

For more jazz clubs in Paris See pp62–3

Price Categories

For a three-course	€ under €30
meal for one with half	€€ €30–€40
a bottle of wine (or	€€€ €40–€50
equivalent meal), taxes	€€€€ €50–€60
and extra charges	€€€€€ over €60

eft **Café Burq**

10 Places to Eat

1 Café Burq
A genuine Montmartre bistro ith a trendy clientele. Roasted amembert with honey is a avourite. ⊗ 6 rue Burq, 75018 • Map 1 • 01 42 52 81 27 • Closed L, Sun, 1 k Christmas • No disabled access • €€

2 Le Miroir
The emphasis here is on assic French fare with a seasonal enu. ⊗ 94 rue des Martyrs, 75018 Map E1 • 01 46 06 50 73 • No disabled ccess • Closed Sun D, Mon • €€€

3 Table d'Eugène
This chic restaurant serves astronomic cuisine for a very easonable price. ⊗ 18 rue Eugène ue, 75018 • 01 42 55 61 64 • Closed un, Mon • €€

4 Chez Jean
This restaurant boasts fine ontemporary cuisine and a ichelin star. ⊗ 8 rue St-Lazare, 5009 • Map E1 • 01 48 78 62 73 Closed Sat, Sun, Aug • €€€€

5 Le Pétrelle
A restaurant with an offbeat, ccentric decor, an intimate tmosphere and a menu using nly local produce. ⊗ 34 rue Pétrelle, 5009 • Map F1 • 01 42 82 11 02 • Closed un, Mon, 1st week May, Aug • €€€

6 Rose Bakery
The square quiches, carrot akes and sticky puddings have ade this eatery legendary. ⊗ 46 e des Martyrs, 75009 • Map F2 • 01 42 2 12 80 • Closed D, Mon • €

7 Charlot "Roi des Coquillages"
Art Deco brasserie, specializing in seafood. ⊗ 81 boulevard de Clichy, 75009 • Map E1 • 01 53 20 48 00 • No disabled access • €€€

8 Le Cul de Poule
Bistro offering modern French dishes and a good selection of wines. ⊗ 53 rue des Martyrs, 75009 • Map F2 • 01 53 16 13 07 • Closed Sun L, a few weeks from Dec–Jan • €€

9 Hotel Amour
The cosy restaurant in this hip hotel serves Anglo-inspired food. ⊗ 8 rue de Navarin, 75009 • Map F2 • 01 48 78 31 80 • €€

10 Chamarré de Montmartre
Creative Mauritanian-French fusion food is served on a terrace at this fine dining restaurant. ⊗ 52 rue Lamarck, 75018 • Map E1 • 01 42 55 05 42 • No disabled access • €€€€

Note: Unless otherwise stated, all restaurants accept credit cards and serve vegetarian meals.

147

Left **Bois de Boulogne** Centre **Cimetière Père-Lachaise** Right **Parc Monceau**

Greater Paris

CENTRAL PARIS HAS MORE THAN ENOUGH *on offer to keep any visitor occupied, but if time permits you should make at least one foray out of the centre, whether your interest is in the sumptuous Palace of Versailles, former home of the "Sun King" Louis XIV, or in the Magic Kingdom of Disneyland® Paris. The excellent metro system makes for easy day trips to the area's two main parks, the Bois de Boulogne and the Bois de Vincennes, for a wide range of outdoor activities, from boating to riding or in-line skating, or just strolling amid pleasant greenery. In contrast to these bucolic pleasures is the cutting-edge modern architecture of La Défense. Visually stunning, it comprises Paris's stylish business district to the west of the city, with added attractions in its exhibition centres. Two large cemeteries outside the centre are worth a visit for their ornate tombs.*

🔟 Sights

1 Versailles
2 Disneyland® Paris
3 La Défense
4 Bois de Vincennes
5 Bois de Boulogne
6 Parc de la Villette
7 Montparnasse
8 Cimetière du Père Lachaise
9 Parc Monceau
10 Musée Marmottan-Claude Monet

Sculptures, Versailles

Preceding pages **Versailles gardens**

Versailles

The top day-trip from Paris as to be Versailles. This stunning chateau, begun by Louis XIV in 664, is overwhelming in its opulence and scale. Plan what you want to see and arrive early, as even a full day may not be long enough. Much of the palace is only accessible by guided tour *(see p154)*. The Grand Apartments will, however, be closed for part of 2013. ● *Versailles, 78000 • RER line to Versailles-Rive Gauche • Château open Apr–Oct: 9am–6:30pm Tue–Sun; Nov–Mar: 9am–5:30pm Tue–Sun; gardens open 8am–8:30pm daily (to 6pm winter) Closed public hols • Admission charge www.chateauversailles.fr*

Disneyland® Paris

Visitors with children will probably have no choice about whether they visit the Paris branch of Disneyland or not. However, even parents will enjoy the hi-tech workings and imagination behind such attractions as "Pirates of the Caribbean" and "The Haunted House" *(see p60)*. The Walt Disney Studios® Park involves visitors interactively through film, with a professional stunt show at the end and special effects rides. ● *Marne-la-Vallée • RER line A to Marne-la-Vallée Chessy/ Disneyland • Open Sep–Jun: 9am–8pm daily; Jul–Aug: 9am–11pm daily (Studios Sep–Jun: 9am–6pm daily; Jul–Aug: 9am–8pm daily); times vary for Walt Disney Studios® Park Admission charge www.disneylandparis.com*

La Défense

French vision and flair coupled with Parisian style are clearly shown by this modern urban development. This business and government centre was purposely built to the west of the city to allow the centre to remain unmarred by skyscrapers. More than just offices, however, the area is also an attraction in its own right, with stunning sights such as the Grande Arche, a cube-like structure with a centre large enough to contain Notre-Dame, and surrounded by artworks, a fountain, cafés and restaurants. ● *Metro Esplanade de la Défense or RER line A to Grande-Arche-de-la-Défense*

Bois de Vincennes

Southeast of the city lies the Bois de Vincennes, which has several lakes, boating facilities, lovely formal gardens, a Buddhist centre and a summer amusement park. The Château de Vincennes was a royal residence before Versailles and has the tallest keep in Europe. The more energetic can walk here all the way from the Bastille along the Promenade Plantée, formerly a railway viaduct. ● *Vincennes, 94300 • Metro Château de Vincennes/RER Vincennes • Park: open dawn–dusk daily; château: Sep–Apr: 10am–5pm; May–Aug: 10am–6pm • Closed public hols • www.chateau-vincennes.fr*

Grande Arche, La Défense

The Treaty of Versailles

France, Great Britain, the USA, Italy and the German Republic negotiated this agreement after World War I at Versailles, which required Germany to demilitarize parts of its territory, reduce the size of its army, abolish conscription, cease trading in military equipment and to pay compensation. The Treaty was signed on 28 June 1919.

Bois de Boulogne

This enormous park is the Parisians' favourite green retreat, especially on summer weekends when its 865 ha (2,135 acres) can become crowded. There is plenty to do, apart from simply walking and picnicking, such as cycling, riding, boating or visiting the various attractions. These include parks within the park, two race courses *(see p51)* and an art and folk museum. The park is open 24 hours a day, but avoid after dark. ◈ *Map A2*

Parc de la Villette

More than just a park, this landscape was created in 1993 to a futuristic design. It provides the usual park features of paths and gardens, but modern sculptures, zany park benches and

several major hi-tech attractions offer a different edge. These include the interactive science museum, the Cité des Sciences e de l'Industrie, a 60-seater mobile hydraulic cinema, an Omnimax cinema, play areas for younger children and a music institute *(see p60)*. ◈ *30 ave Corentin-Cariou, 75019 • Metro Porte de Pantin • 01 40 03 75 75 • Opening times vary depending on the attraction • Admission charge for certain attractions • www.villette.com*

Montparnasse

Montparnasse's location is highly visible due to the 209-m (685-ft) Tour du Montparnasse which offers spectacular views. Five minutes' walk away is the area's main draw, the Cimetière du Montparnasse, where the great writers Maupassant, Sartre de Beauvoir, Baudelaire and Samuel Beckett are buried *(see p156* For breathtaking views of Paris by night visit the rooftop restaurant "Le Ciel de Paris". ◈ *Metro Gare Montparnasse • Tour du Montparnasse: open 9:30am–11:30pm daily (winter until 10:30pm); admission charge • Cemetery open 8:30am–5:30pm daily; free • www.tourmontparnasse56.com*

Parc de la Villette

Cimetière du Père Lachaise

This is the most visited cemetery in the world, largely due to rock fans who come from around the world to see the grave of the legendary singer Jim Morrison of the Doors. There are about one million other graves here, in some 70,000 different tombs, including those of Chopin, Oscar Wilde, Balzac, Edith Piaf, Colette, Molière and Delacroix (see 156). There are maps posted round the cemetery to enable you to find these notable resting places, or a more detailed plan can be bought at the kiosks round the grounds. ✆ 16 rue du Repos • Metro Père-Lachaise • Open 8am–5:30pm Mon–Sat, 9am–5:30pm Sun • 01 55 25 82 10) • Free

Parc Monceau

This civilized little park is no further from the city centre than Montmartre, yet it goes unnoticed by many visitors. It was created in 1778 by the Duc de Chartres and is still frequented by well-heeled residents. The grounds are full of statues and an air of well-being (see p38). ✆ Blvd de Courcelles, 75008 • Metro Monceau

Musée Marmottan-Claude Monet

Paul Marmottan was an art historian and his 19th-century mansion now houses the world's largest collection of works by Claude Monet (see p13), including his Impression Soleil Levant which gave the Impressionist movement its name. The collection was donated by the artist's son in 1966, and includes the artist's collection of works by Renoir and Gauguin. ✆ 2 rue Louis-Boilly, 75016 • Metro Muette • Open 10am–6pm Tue–Sun (to 8pm Thu) • Adm charge • www.marmottan.com

A Taste of Greater Paris

Morning

🕐 You won't cover Greater Paris in a day, and Disneyland® Paris and Versailles (see p151) both need at least a day.

If you want variety, go to Montparnasse by metro. In front of the busy mainline station, is the Tour Montparnasse – take a trip to the top to admire the view and then enjoy a coffee break in the Panoramic Bar.

When you leave, walk down boulevard Edgar Quinet. On your right is the entrance to the Cimetière du Montparnasse. An hour should be plenty of time here.

Walk towards the Vavin metro station to the historic café/brasserie La Coupole (see p157), to have lunch.

Afternoon

Take the metro at Vavin, changing at Réaumur-Sébastopol, to Cimetière du Père Lachaise and explore the city's other great cemetery. Spend one or two hours searching out the famous names buried here and admiring the architecture of the monuments. Have a coffee afterwards at a neighbourhood café, Le Saint Amour (2 ave Gambetta • 01 47 97 20 15 • Metro Père-Lachaise). From Père-Lachaise it is again just one change on the metro, at Nation, to the Bois de Vincennes, where you can spend the late afternoon in the park and admire the château.

Left **Marble courtyard** Right **Palace gardens**

🔟 Versailles Sights

1 The Hall of Mirrors
The spectacular 70-m (233-ft) long Galerie des Glaces (Hall of Mirrors) has been magnificently restored. It was in this room that the Treaty of Versailles was signed in 1919, to formally end World War I.

2 Chapelle Royale
The Royal Chapel is regarded as one of the finest Baroque buildings in the country. Finished in 1710, the elegant, white marble Corinthian columns and numerous murals make for an awe-inspiring place of prayer.

3 Salon de Venus
In this elaborate room decorated mainly in marble, a statue of Louis XIV, the creator of Versailles, stands centre stage, exuding regal splendour beneath the fine painted ceiling.

4 Queen's Bedroom
Nineteen royal infants were born in this opulent room, which has been meticulously restored to exactly how it appeared when it was last used by Marie-Antoinette in 1789.

5 Marble Courtyard
Approaching the front of the palace across the vast open forecourt, visitors finally reach the splendour of the black-and-white marble courtyard, which is the oldest section of the palace. The north and south wings were added later.

6 L'Opéra
The opulent opera house was built in 1770 for the marriage of the *dauphin*, the future Louis XVI, to Marie-Antoinette. The floors were designed so that they could be raised to stage level during special festivals.

7 Le Trianon
In the southeast corner of the gardens Louis XIV and Louis XV had the Grand and Petit Trianon palaces built as "private' retreats. Marie-Antoinette was given Petit Trianon by Louis XVI.

8 Palace Gardens
The palace gardens feature many walkways, landscaped topiary, fountains, pools, statues and the Orangery, where exotic plants were kept in the winter. The magnificent Fountain of Neptune is situated to the north of the North Wing.

9 Salon d'Apollon
Louis XIV's throne room is, naturally, one of the palace's centrepieces, and features a suitably regal portrait of the great Sun King. Dedicated to the god Apollo, it strikingly reflects the French monarchy's divine self-image.

10 Stables of the King
The magnificent stables have been restored and they now house the famous Bartabas equine academy.

Left **Boating on lake** Right **Cycling in the Bois de Boulogne**

Bois de Boulogne Features

1 Parc de Bagatelle
Differing garden styles feature in this park, including English and Japanese, though the major attraction is the huge rose garden, best seen in June.

2 Pré Catelan
This park-within-a-park is at the very centre of the Bois. Its lawns and wooded areas include a magnificent 200-year-old beech tree and the idyllic, eponymous restaurant *(see p157)*.

3 Jardin d'Acclimatation
The main children's area of the Bois incorporates a small amusement park, a zoo with a farm and a pets' corner, and a Herb Museum aimed especially at children *(see p60)*.

4 Lakes
Two long, thin lakes adjoin each other. The larger of the two, confusingly called Lac Inférieur (the other is Lac Supérieur) has boats for hire and a motor boat to take you to the islands.

5 La Grande Cascade
This man-made waterfall was a major undertaking when the park was built, requiring concrete to be shipped down the Seine.

6 Stade Roland Garros
The legendary home of French clay-court tennis hosts the glamorous French Open each year in June.

7 Château de Longchamp
At the same time as he re-designed central Paris *(see p45)*, Baron Haussmann landscaped the Bois de Boulogne. This château was given to him as a thank-you from Napoleon III.

8 Shakespeare Garden
Inside Pré Catelan park is a little garden planted with all the trees, flowers and herbs mentioned in the plays of Shakespeare. There is a lovely open-air theatre.

Shakespeare Garden

9 Jardin des Serres d'Auteuil
This 19th-century garden has a series of greenhouses where ornamental hothouse plants are grown. In the centre is a palm house with tropical plants.

10 Horse-Racing
The Bois is home to two race courses. To the west is the Hippodrome de Longchamp, where flat racing takes place including the Prix de l'Arc de Triomphe *(see p57)*; in the east, the Hippodrome d'Auteuil holds steeplechases.

For more on the Bois de Boulogne **See p152**

Left **Père Lachaise cemetery** Centre **Jim Morrison's grave** Right **Edith Piaf's tomb**

⁰⁄₁₀ Graves

1 Jim Morrison, Père Lachaise Cemetery

The American lead singer of The Doors rock band spent the last few months of his life in Paris and died here in 1971. Fans still hold vigils at his grave, which is covered with scrawled messages from all over the world.

2 Oscar Wilde, Père Lachaise Cemetery

The Dublin-born author and wit died in 1900, after speaking his alleged last words in his Paris hotel room: "Either that wallpaper goes, or I do." His tomb is unmissable, with a huge monument by Jacob Epstein.

3 Frédéric Chopin, Père Lachaise Cemetery

The Polish composer was born in 1810 but died in Paris at the age of 39. The statue on his tomb represents "the genius of music sunk in grief".

4 Edith Piaf, Père Lachaise Cemetery

The "little sparrow" was born in poverty in the Belleville district of Paris in 1915, less than 1,500 m (5,000 ft) from where she was buried in 1963 in a simple black tomb *(see p63)*.

5 Marcel Proust, Père Lachaise Cemetery

The ultimate chronicler of Paris, the writer was born in the city in 1871. He is buried in the family tomb *(see p47)*.

6 Samuel Beckett, Montparnasse Cemetery

The Irish-born Nobel Prize-winning writer settled in Paris in 1937, having previously studied here. He died in 1989 and his gravestone is a simple slab, reflecting the writer's enigmatic nature *(see p47)*.

7 Jean-Paul Sartre and Simone de Beauvoir, Montparnasse Cemetery

Joined together in death as in life, even though they never lived together, their joint grave is a remarkably simple affair. Both of these philosophers were born, lived and died in Paris.

8 Guy de Maupassant, Montparnasse Cemetery

The great French novelist and short-story writer died in Paris in 1893, and his grave with its luxuriant growth of shrubs stands out because of the open book carving *(see p46)*.

9 Charles Baudelaire, Montparnasse Cemetery

The poet who shocked the world with his frank collection of poems *Les Fleurs du Mal* was born in Paris in 1821 and died here in 1867.

10 Charles Pigeon Family, Montparnasse Cemetery

This charming and touching grave shows Charles Pigeon and his wife in bed, reading by the light of the gas lamp he invented.

For Greater Paris cemeteries **See pp152–3**

Price Categories

For a three course meal for one with half a bottle of wine (or equivalent meal), taxes and extra charges

€ under €30
€€ €30–€40
€€€ €40–€50
€€€€ €50–€60
€€€€€ over €60

Left **Le Dôme**

10 Places to Eat

1 Le Pré Catelan
Tucked away in the Bois de Boulogne *(see p152)* is this high-class dining pavilion. Romantic setting and elegant service.
◈ Route de Suresnes, Bois de Boulogne, 75016 • Metro Porte Maillot • 01 44 14 41 14 • Closed Sun, Mon, 2 weeks Feb, 1 week Oct, Aug • €€€€€

2 Gordon Ramsay au Trianon
Celebrity chef Gordon Ramsay's protegé Simone Zanoni is the chef at this two Michelin-starred restaurant. ◈ 1 blvd de la Reine, Versailles • RER line C to Versailles • 01 30 84 55 56 • Closed L, Sun, Mon, Aug • €€€€€

3 Le Resto du Roi
Close to the chateau, this informal bistro serves classic dishes. Specialities include duck foie gras with fresh fig compote or salmon smoked with birch branches. ◈ 1 ave de Saint-Cloud, Versailles • 01 39 50 42 26 • Closed Mon • €

4 La Coupole
Near the Cimetière de Montparnasse *(see p152)*, this Parisian landmark has an eclectic menu. ◈ 102 blvd du Montparnasse, 75014 • Map E6 • 01 43 20 14 20 • €€€€

5 La Closerie des Lilas
With its piano bar and terrace, this is a Montparnasse institution. The brasserie is cheaper and the steak tartare is recommended. ◈ 171 blvd du Montparnasse, 75006 • Map E6 • 01 40 51 34 50 • €€€€

6 Le Dôme
Montparnasse's prime fish restaurant, once frequented by Sartre. Great food and grand decor. ◈ 108 blvd du Montparnasse, 75014 • Map E6 • 01 43 35 25 81 • Closed Aug • €€€€€

7 La Gare
If visiting the Bois de Boulogne, include La Gare on the itinerary. This stylish brasserie in a former railway station has a summer terrace. ◈ 19 chaussée de la Muette, 75016 • Metro La Muette • 01 42 15 15 31 • €€€

8 Le Baratin
A local favourite in Belleville, this bistro serves modern French cuisine with excellent wines. The fixed-price lunch is particularly popular. ◈ 3 rue Jouye-Rouve, 75020 • 01 43 49 39 70 • Closed Sun & Mon • No disabled access • No vegetarian options • €

9 Le Chapeau Melon
This natural wine shop by day transforms into a charming diner by evening. There is a daily fixed menu with a great selection of wines. ◈ 92 rue Rébeval, 75019 • 01 42 02 68 60 • Closed Mon & Tue • €€

10 Relais d'Auteuil
At the southern end of the Bois de Boulogne is this gourmet restaurant. Sea bass in a pepper crust is just one delicious speciality. ◈ 31 blvd Murat, 75016 • Metro Michel-Ange-Molitor • 01 46 51 09 54 • Open Sat–Tue L • Closed Aug • €€€€€

> **Note:** Unless otherwise stated, all restaurants accept credit cards and serve vegetarian meals

STREETSMART

PARIS TOP 10

Left **Parisian hotel** Centre **Parisian restaurant** Right **French perfume**

🔟 Planning Your Trip

1 When to Go

April in Paris may be a cliché but it is still a good time to visit. Spring and autumn are both pleasant and there are plenty of parks and tree-lined boulevards to enjoy. Although certain restaurants close in August, when most Parisians take their holidays, there is still plenty to see and do.

2 Choosing an Area

The Left Bank is a good choice if you like a Bohemian atmosphere of cafés and student life. The Marais has many museums, shops and restaurants and the Opéra and Louvre quarters are central to everything. To save money, stay just outside the centre and use the excellent yet cheap metro.

3 Choosing a Hotel

If space is important, ask about the size of the rooms: some can be very cramped. It is also worth checking whether the rooms face busy, noisy roads and what is the hotel's nearest metro station. Ask if there is an elevator to all floors, as in some older buildings this may not be the case.

4 Choosing a Restaurant

If you like to eat well, or want to try a particular restaurant, phone and book a few weeks ahead of your visit. If you decide to take pot luck, however,

the city is full of good places to eat. Remember many restaurants close at weekends and in August.

5 What to See

Don't expect to see the whole of Paris on a weekend visit – you would not even see the whole of the Louvre in this time (see pp8–11). Even on a longer visit, don't be over-ambitious: leave time for wandering the streets or relaxing in a bar or café, the way the Parisians do. It's all part of the experience.

6 What to Pack

The weather can be unpredictable, so allow for unexpected cold or wet spells at almost any time of year by bringing a pullover, umbrella and comfortable shoes. Parisians are casual but chic, so take a few smart outfits for dining out. Only the most expensive restaurants require men to wear a tie.

7 How much Money to Take

You can use the major credit cards (Visa, MasterCard, American Express) almost everywhere, and there are cash dispensers (ATMs) all over Paris which display symbols of cards they accept. Make sure you have a few euros in cash when you arrive, however, to pay for metro tickets or a taxi. *Bureaux de change*

offices also abound throughout the city.

8 Passports and Visas

No visa is required for citizens of EU countries, the USA, Canada, Australia or New Zealand if you are staying for less than three months, although your passport will need to be valid for at least three months beyond the end of your stay. Citizens of other countries should consult their French embassy or consulate for information before travelling.

9 Customs

For EU citizens there are no limits on goods that can be taken into or out of France, provided they are for your personal use. Outside the EU, you may import the following allowances duty-free: 200 cigarettes or equivalent in tobacco; 4 litres of wine, or 2 litres of wine plus 1 litre of spirits; 60ml of perfume and 250ml of eau de toilette; €350 worth of other items.

10 Travelling with Children

Parisians dislike *enfants terribles*, so always try to ensure good behaviour. Some hotels allow kids to sleep free in family rooms (see p179). Children are seldom seen in restaurants at night, but there are plenty of child-friendly alternatives.

◣ SORTIE

FORUM DES HALLES

Left **Metro exit sign** Right **Restaurant prices**

Things to Avoid

1 Crime

Paris is a reasonably safe city. Muggings are rare, but theft and pick-pocketing are common so take sensible precautions. Avoid Les Halles, the Bois de Boulogne and Vincennes after dark, and quiet sections of the metro and the RER after 9pm.

2 Health Costs

EU travellers with a European Health Insurance Card (EHIC) get free or reimbursed healthcare, otherwise it is best to have private insurance. For minor problems, ask a pharmacist (look for the green cross). If one is closed, the address of the nearest open pharmacy will be shown in the window.

3 Beggars

Do not confuse the genuine homeless known as "SDFs") with organized beggars at the top tourist spots who should be avoided and ignored. Metro buskers are usually "legit" and often talented.

4 Pickpockets

Pickpockets do frequent busy tourist places and public transport so keep a watchful eye on your belongings. Men should never keep their wallet in a back pocket and women should make sure their handbags are closed and held firmly in front of them if possible.

5 Taking the Wrong Metro

To avoid taking the wrong route, check the number of the line you want on a map and the name of the end station for the direction in which you wish to travel. All signs in metro stations work in this way and the system is simple. There is always a panel on the wall just before you reach the platform; this panel will have a list of the train's destinations, so you can double check *(see p164)*. The RER can be quite confusing and is best avoided for trips in the city centre.

6 Transport Fines

Hold on to your metro, RER or bus ticket for the whole of your journey in case an inspector asks to see it. Remember to validate or show your ticket when boarding a bus.

7 Tourist Traps

In general, avoid the tourist-targeted brasseries with their multilingual *menus touristiques*, flags of the world and photographs of the food on offer. The places where the locals eat will be far better.

8 Hidden Charges in Cafés or Bars

When paying a bill, check if service is included – it usually is. If you want to save money, take your drink or snack at the counter. Prices are lower and no tip is expected.

9 Over-Tipping

Restaurants and cafés normally include a 10–15 per cent service charge, so only leave a further small gratuity for very good service. Taxi drivers should get 10–15 per cent but this is not obligatory. Porters can be tipped €2–3 per bag and chambermaids a similar amount per day, usually left at the end of your stay.

10 Queues

Paris's top sights have made strenuous efforts to reduce their notorious queues for tickets. Almost all sights now sell their tickets in advance at their websites and sometimes for specific times (such as the Eiffel Tower). Otherwise, arrive early or take advantage of late-night openings *(nocturnes)*.

Queues to enter Notre-Dame

Left **Eurostar train** Centre **Ice cream parlour in Gare du Nord** Right **Orlyval high-speed train**

TOP 10 Arriving in Paris

1 Eurostar
Eurostar trains arrive at Gare du Nord, slightly north of the city centre. The station is served by three metro lines and three RER lines, and has a taxi rank outside, usually manned by assistants to help newly arrived visitors.

2 Gare du Nord Facilities
Gare du Nord is a large station with several places to eat and drink and shops selling books, newspapers and snacks. The metro station is reached from the concourse and is clearly signposted. There is also a tourist office by the Grandes Lignes exit.

3 CDG Airport
Roissy-Charles-de-Gaulle Airport is the arrival point for most international flights, 23 km (14 miles) northeast of the city centre. Its main terminals are some distance apart, so check which one you require when returning. A 24-hour English-language information service is available. ◐ CDG information: 39 50.

4 Connections from CDG Airport
CDG is connected to central Paris by Air France and Roissy bus services, and (the easiest option) the RER train line B3. This links with Gare du Nord, Les Halles and St Michel. Taxis take

about 30 minutes to the city centre, sometimes more, and cost about €55.

5 Orly Airport
Orly is 14 km (8.5 miles) south of the city centre and is used by French domestic services and some international airlines. It has two terminals: Orly-Sud is mainly for international flights; Orly-Ouest is for domestic flights. English-language information is available 6am–11:30pm. ◐ Orly information: 39 50.

6 Connections from Orly Airport
Air France coaches run to and from Etoile, Invalides and Montparnasse metro and mainline stations. The high-speed Orlyval shuttle train serves both Orly terminals from Antony on RER line B4. Metro signs to Orly on RER C refer to Orly town – avoid. Taxis take about 30 minutes and cost about €30.

7 Beauvais Tillé Airport
Beauvais Tillé Airport is some 70 km (43 miles) north of Paris and is used by low-cost airlines. There is a connecting bus link with Porte Maillot metro

station; allow at least an hour for the journey.

8 Arriving by Road
All motorways from whichever direction eventually link with Paris's Boulevard Périphérique (Inner Ring Road). Access to central Paris is via different exits (portes), so drivers should always check their destination before setting off and know which exit they will need.

9 Parking
To park on the street you will need the nerves and ability of a local. Meters take the pre-paid carte only, which is available from tobacconists (tabac). Otherwise use one of the many underground car parks in the city, which are clean and safe. For prepaid parking visit www.parkings deparis.com.

10 Arriving by Bus
The main operator, Eurolines, has services from the UK, Ireland, Germany and several other European countries. Coaches arrive at Gare Routière International, east of the city centre but are linked to the metro from the Galliéni station on Line 3

Eurolines long-distance bus

162 ⮕ *For information on getting around Paris* **See p164**

Left **Paris tourist office sign** Right **Parisian listings magazines**

10 Sources of Information

1 French Tourist Offices

The French Tourist Office has branches in many major international cities.

2 Office de Tourisme de Paris

The main office is near the Pyramides metro station. It is well stocked with brochures, and has hotel and tour reservation services.

PARIS
Convention and Visitors Bureau
Tourist Office

• 25 rue des Pyramides, 75001 • Map E3 • Open 10am–7pm Mon–Sat, 11am–7pm Sun (9am–7pm Jun–Oct) • Closed 1 May • www.parisinfo.com

3 Espace du Tourisme d'Île de France

This tourist facility serves Paris and the wider Île de France region, and is the best source of advice and information on visiting places outside the city. It has offices at airports and train stations and a useful website. • www.nouveau-paris-ile-de-france.fr

4 Websites

Two official sites are the Paris City Hall (www.paris.fr) and the city tourist office (www.parisinfo.com), with lots of information and links in French and English. Most major attractions such as the Musée du Louvre (www.louvre.fr) also have their own sites.

5 Magazines

If you are able to read French, try the free, weekly A Nous Paris, which is available in metro stations, and the Sortir insert in the weekly magazine Télérama.

6 Officiel des Spectacles & Pariscope

These two events guides can be bought at newspaper stands and are ideal if you want more general information about current exhibitions.

7 Paris Free Voice

This monthly magazine is published by the American Church and aimed at US residents in Paris. Available from English-language book-shops, it is a good source of information on what is happening in the city. It also has a website. • www.parisvoice.com

8 Bonjour Paris electronic newsletter

This email newsletter and website, entirely in English, provides fascinating articles and up-to-date information on cultural activities as well as restaurant openings and closings in the city. The newsletter is released at least once a week to provide the most current information. • www.bonjourparis.com

9 Libraries

Public libraries are found all over Paris and all of them are free to enter. Most have selections of newspapers and magazines, as well as notices that may be useful to visitors. Only Paris residents, however, can borrow material.

10 Newspapers

Foreign newspapers are available on the day of publication in many newsagents. The International Herald Tribune is published from Paris. French-speakers can also keep in touch with world events via France's national publications such as Le Monde or Libération, or the city's own paper, Le Parisien.

French Tourist Offices Overseas

www.franceguide.com

UK
Lincoln House,
300 High Holborn,
London WC1V 7JH
• 0906 8244 123
(60p/min)

USA
825 Third Ave, 29th
floor, New York, NY
110022

Australia
25 Bligh St, Level 13,
Sydney, NSW 2000
• 02 9231 5244

Canada
1800 Ave McGill College,
Suite 1010, Montréal,
QUE H3A 3J6
• 514 288 2026

Left **Metro sign** Centre **Locator map outside a metro station** Right **Walking in Paris**

Getting Around Paris

Metro
The Paris metro system is cheap and efficient. The network is comprehensive and the service is very frequent. The service operates from roughly 5:30am–12:30am (until 1:30–2am Fri, Sat and the evening before bank holidays) and exact times for each line are given at stations.
⊛ www.ratp.fr

RER
The RER train system (5am–12:30am; to 1:30am Fri, Sat and the evening before public holidays) has only five lines, but the network goes further into the suburbs. Metro tickets are only valid on RER trains in Zone 1. If travelling further, you must buy a separate RER ticket (subject to change).

Buses
Buses run from approximately 6:30am–8:30pm, although some services operate through the night (Noctilien Buses). A Grand Plan de Paris available from metro stations shows all bus routes. Metro tickets are valid in Zones 1 and 2,

Parisian bus

but you cannot switch between bus and metro on the same ticket. Bus stops show the line route.

Taxis
Remember that taxis may not always stop if you hail them on the street. The best method is to head for one of the 470 taxi ranks (look for the taxi icon on a blue background), or ask your hotel or restaurant to call for one. Many drivers will not take more than three people, to avoid front-seat passengers. Fares are not expensive but there may be a charge for extra luggage.

Arrondissements
Paris is divided into 20 arrondissements (districts), which radiate out in a clockwise spiral from the centre. The first is abbreviated to 1er (Premier) and follow on as 2e, 3e (Deuxième, Troisième) etc. The postal address for the first district is 75001, and again these follow on – the second district is 75002.

Asking Directions
The Parisians' reputation for rudeness is unjustified. Most are polite and will try to help even if you do not speak French (many Parisians speak English). Politeness and an effort to speak French are always appreciated, so be sure to begin with "Excusez-moi" ("Excuse me").

Cycling
Paris is an excellent city for cyclists. You can hire bikes from shops such as Decathlon and GoSport, or try the self-service scheme Vélib'. Bi stands are found every 300 metres (330 yards) and payment is by cred card (chip and pin cards only) at the access term nals, which operate in eight different language
⊛ www.velib.paris.fr

Rollerblading
Parisians are mad about rollerblading and on Friday nights and Sunday afternoons orga nized balades (outings) often take place, beginni at Montparnasse.
⊛ www.pari-roller.com

Boat
The Batobus runs fo roughly 11 months a ye and its eight stops link the major sights on the river. Boats run every 1 30 minutes, from 10am 7pm (until 9pm Jun–Sep 10:30am–4:30pm winter One-day, two-day and fi day passes are great val if you plan on making mc than one journey. ⊛ 08 05 01 01, www.batobus.cc

Walking
Central Paris is fairl compact, and even a wa from the Arc de Triomph to the Bastille should or take an hour. Be sure to look up to see the beautiful old buildings – and down to avoid the evidence of Parisian do

Left **Canal tour boat** Centre **Pedestrian walk sign** Right **Bus tour**

10 Guided Tours

1 Boat Tours
The long-established Bateaux-Mouches operate daily with regular day and evening dinner cruises.
Bateaux-Mouches: 01 42 25 96 10, www.bateaux-mouches.fr • Bateaux Parisiens: 01 76 64 14 66, www.bateauxparisiens. com • Vedettes de Paris: 01 44 18 19 50, www. vedettesdeparis.com • Les Vedettes du Pont Neuf: 01 46 33 98 38, www. vedettesdupontneuf.fr

2 Walking Tours
Tours are available in a wide range of themes and in several languages. Secrets of Paris, Paris Walks and Context travel are three of the leading English-language companies. Also check out the website www.paris-expat.com
Context travel: www. contexttravel.com • Paris Walks: 01 48 09 21 40, www.paris-walks.com • Secrets of Paris: www.secretsofparis.com

3 Cycle Tours
Several companies offer guided cycling tours, with multilingual guides, including night-time tours and medieval Paris tours. For the less energetic, Segway Tours hire out electric scooters. *® Paris Vélo: 01 48 87 60 01, www.parisvelosympa.com • Fat Tire Bike Tours: 01 56 58 10 54, www.fattirebike tours.com • City Segway Tours: 01 56 58 10 54, www.citysegwaytours.com*

4 Canal Tours
Less well-known than river trips, these tours take you into the fascinating backwaters of the Paris canal system. A fabulous light show by artist Keiichi Tahara is displayed on the underground section of the Canal St-Martin.

CANAUXRAMA
VISITE des CANAUX
PORT de L'ARSENAL
Tel. 42.39.15.00

Sign for Paris canal tour

® Canauxrama and Navettes de la Villette: 01 42 39 15 00, www.canauxrama.com • Paris Canal: 01 42 40 96 97, www.pariscanal.com

5 Bus Tours
Numerous bus tours are available – the main tourist office on rue des Pyramides *(see p163)* is the best place to begin. Tours usually last up to two hours but many of the companies allow you to hop on and off at any of their stops.

6 Gourmet Tours
Promenades Gourmandes offers tours of Paris markets, food shops and other foodie haunts (English available). Or try a personalized, self-guided itinerary from Edible Paris. *® Edible Paris: www.edible-paris. com • Promenades*

Gourmandes: 01 48 04 56 84, www.promenades gourmandes.com

7 Wine Tours
O-Chateau organizes day trips and tours from Paris to several wine regions including Champagne. They also offer tasting cruises along the Seine. *® 68 rue Jean-Jacques Rousseau, 75001 • Map M1 • 01 44 73 97 80 • www.o-chateau.com*

8 Shopping and Fashion Tours
Pay a guide to direct you to the best shops. You can then choose from a range of themes including Made in France, along the Left Bank and Unique Boutique in the Marais district. *® Chic Shopping Paris: 06 77 65 08 01, www. chicshoppingparis.com*

9 Themed Tours
American company Paris Through Expatriate Eyes runs several tours, revealing many secrets even Parisians don't know. Visit www.parisinfo.com for other tour operators. *® Paris Through Expatriate Eyes: 06 70 98 13 68, www.paris-expat.com*

10 Sports Tour
Sports fans can take a guided one hour tour of the huge and world-famous arena, the Stade de France. *® Stade de France: 08 92 70 09 00 • Tours 11am, 1pm, 3pm, 5pm (except on event days) • www.stadefrance.com*

Left **Paris bus** Centre **Budget hotel** Right **Eating at the bar**

⑩ Paris on a Budget

1 Public Transport
There is a bewildering array of discount travel passes available *(see p168)*, so be sure to study them to find the best one for you. Visitors can buy one-, two-, three- and five-day passes (called a Paris Visite ticket), with options for different zones and savings on the entrance fees to some sights. ◈ *www.ratp.fr*

2 Hostels, Apartments and Camping
It is perfectly feasible to find accommodation in central Paris for €40–50 per night. Even cheaper options include the following hostel groups. ◈ *www.hostelbookers.com* • FUAJ: 01 44 89 87 27, *www.fuaj.com* • Camping du Bois de Boulogne: 01 45 24 30 00, *www.campingparis.fr* • St Christopher's Inn: *www.st-christophers.co.uk* • Perfectly Paris Apartments: *www.perfectlyparis.com*

3 Bed-and-Breakfast
Several companies offer rooms with Parisian families on a bed-and-

Paris metro sign

breakfast basis. Most are located either centrally or close to a metro station, and can cost as little as €30 per person per night, if sharing. ◈ *Alcove & Agapes: 01 44 85 06 05, www.bed-and-breakfast-in-paris.com* • Good Morning Paris: 01 47 07 28 29, *www.goodmorningparis.fr*

4 Cheap Eats
For a coffee or snack, standing at the bar is cheaper than sitting down. In restaurants, the *prix-fixe* (fixed-price) menus offer good deals and the *plat du jour* (dish of the day) is usually inexpensive. If you want to sample fine dining, do it at lunchtime when it's often cheaper.

5 Cheap Seats
Half-price theatre and concert tickets are available for same-day performances only from kiosks at place de la Madeleine *(see p97)*. Cinemas usually offer discounts in the mornings, and on Wednesdays.

6 Cheap Treats
All national museums, including the Louvre, Musée Picasso and Musée d'Orsay, are free on the first Sunday of each month. Early evening admission for the various *nocturnes* (late-night openings) is also cheaper. The Paris City Passport, available from tourist offices, offers reductions for certain sights, shops and tours.

7 Sightseeing Passes
The Paris Museum Pass gives unlimited visits to museums and monuments throughout Paris, and a two-day pass costs €39 for adults. The Paris Pass provides access to many attractions along with free transport on the metro, buses and RER. A two-day adult pass costs €104. Visit the websites for further details and other available rates. ◈ *www.parismuseumpass.fr; www.parispass.com*

8 Breakfast
Most hotels charge separately for breakfast and what is on offer varies widely, from bread and jam to a lavish buffet. You can save money by opting out and choosing a small snack in a café or boulangerie instead.

9 Churches
Although church interiors are free, there may be a charge for towers, crypts etc. If passing a church, take a look to see if any free or inexpensive lunchtime or evening concerts are being advertised.

10 Concessions
State-run national museums are free all year round for everyone under 18 and for those under 26 who are from the EU (ID may be required). Other groups such as senior citizens, also enjoy special rates

Left **Paris taxi** Right **Musée d'Orsay**

10 Paris for the Disabled

1 Tourist Office Leaflets

The main tourist office in Paris (see p163) has information leaflets on facilities for the disabled. Their website also has useful addresses.
Ⓢ www.parisinfo.com

2 Useful Organizations

Both the Association des Paralysés de France (APF) and the Groupement pour l'Insertion des Personnes Handicappées Physiques (GIHP) provide information on disabled facilities in Paris. Ⓢ APF: 17 blvd Auguste Blanqui, 75013, 01 40 78 69 00, www.apf.asso.fr • GIHP: 32 rue du Paradis, 75010, 01 43 95 66 36, www.gihpnational.org

3 Guided Tours

The Paris City Hall organizes numerous specialized tours of the city's parks, gardens and cemeteries for people with disabilities, including special visits for the blind.
Ⓢ City Hall: 01 43 28 47 63

4 Itineraries

For those with wheelchairs who want to go it alone in central Paris, APF have detailed information on negotiating various quarters of the city (see above for address). Paris comme sur des roulettes is also a useful guide with maps colour coding the quality of the pavements on given routes, access to public conveniences etc.
Ⓢ Editions Dakota, 45 rue St-Sébastien, 75011 (€8.99), or from FNAC and large newsagents.

5 Travel Agents

Tourism for All, in the UK, has a useful list of specialist tour operators. Sage Travelling offers a variety of packages and assistance. Ⓢ Tourism for All: 0303 303 0146, outside UK +44 1539 814 683, www.tourismforall. org.uk • Sage Travelling: 1-888-645-7920, www. sagetraveling.com

6 Metro/RER

Few stations are easily accessible for wheelchairs and most require a station member of staff to operate lifts to avoid either stairs or escalators. Line 14, however, is wheelchair accessible. Main metro and RER stations have a leaflet on transport facilities, called Handicaps et Déplacements en Région Ile-de-France.

7 Buses

Paris buses are being equipped with access for wheelchairs, and all buses already have seats reserved for disabled and elderly persons, war veterans and pregnant women.

8 Taxis

It is a legal requirement for taxi drivers to help people with disabilities to get in and out of their vehicle, and to carry guide dogs as passengers. This does not mean that all taxis are able to carry wheelchairs, so do check when booking.
Ⓢ Taxi G7 has a special service for clients in wheelchairs: 01 47 39 00 91

9 Hotels

Many older hotels are unsuitable for people with mobility problems as they are without elevators, so it is essential that you check before booking. Newer hotels and the modern hotel chains are usually wheelchair accessible, but always ask when making a reservation.

10 Attractions

While some of the older museums and monuments are not accessible for people in wheelchairs, most museums and galleries are, and they also increasingly cater for those with special needs. Wheelchair uses enter the Louvre on an open lift under the pyramid. APF publishes a guide to disabled access in Paris's museums, theatres and cinemas (see Useful Organizations).

Wheelchair access sign

Left **Metro carnet tickets** Centre **Navigo Découverte** Right **Paris Visite**

TOP 10 Tickets

1 Metro Tickets
Metro tickets can be bought in batches of 10 *(un carnet)*, which offer considerable savings on the price of a single ticket. Each ticket is valid for one journey in the central zones, no matter how many changes are made. They must be stamped when you enter the metro and retained until you leave *(see p161)*. If staying for a few days, consider buying a *Navigo Découverte* (photo ID needed) or a *Paris Visite* card, which offer savings at some attractions too *(see p166)*.

2 Bus Tickets
One type of ticket serves all bus and metro routes and Zones 1 and 2 of the RER network. As with the metro, you must time-stamp your ticket when boarding the bus and keep it until the end of the journey. You will be fined if you are not in possession of a valid ticket.

3 RER Tickets
Using metro and bus tickets in Zone 1 of the RER network makes for a convenient way to get around. See the station maps for the extent of these zones.

4 SNCF Train Tickets
Tickets issued by the RATP (Régie Autonome des Transports Parisiens) are not valid on the mainline SNCF (Société Nationale des Chemins de Fer) services, France's national rail network. To find out about services to suburban stations, including Versailles *(see p151)*, ring the General Information and reservations line. ◎ *SNCF information: 3635 (special number)* • *www.sncf.com*

5 Theatre Tickets
These can be bought at the box office of the theatre, by telephone or at ticket agencies (including FNAC stores). Some theatres offer reduced-price tickets for students or stand-by seats 15 minutes before the performance. There is also a half-price ticket kiosk *(see p166)*.

6 Cinema Tickets
Prices are average for a European city, but ask about discounts that may be available for students, over-60s and families. Admission prices on Wednesdays are sometimes reduced. Larger cinemas take credit card reservations over the phone and online.

7 Clubs
Admission prices are high at all Paris clubs and are often increased at weekends or after midnight, but women can sometimes get in at a reduced rate or for free. The admission charge may include a first drink, but subsequent drinks will usually be pricey.

8 Tickets for Attractions
Some concessionary and discount tickets are available *(see p166)*. The Museum Pass saves queueing if you are planning to visit many of the major museums *(see pp34–5)*. Some museum have online booking, and the Louvre has automatic ticket machines *(see p8)*. Turning up early is another option.

9 Ticket Touts
Like elsewhere, Paris has its ticket touts, and the usual rules apply. It may get you tickets for an in-demand event, but be wary of forgeries and exorbitantly increased prices. Some Parisians carry a sign outside venues saying; *"cherche une place"* ("looking for a seat"), which sometimes gets a ticket at face-value from someon with one to spare.

10 Ticket Agencies
Tickets for concerts and theatre shows are sold at the main tourist information centre at 25 rue des Pyramides and a ticket agencies around the city, including at several branches of the FNAC chain of CD/book/ video stores, and at the Virgin Megastore. There is a booking fee for usin agencies. ◎ *FNAC, 74 ave des Champs-Elysées* • *Map C3* • *Open 10am–11:45pm Mon–Sat, noon–11:45pm Sun*

10 Shopping

Shopping Hours
Department stores
d chain boutiques are
ually open from
30am–7pm Monday to
turday. Late-night shop-
g is on Thursdays until
m. Private boutiques
ten don't open until 10
11am, and may be
sed during holidays,
Mondays and/or
tween noon and 2pm,
t many open on Sun-
ys. Most food shops are
en on Sunday morning.

Taxes
Different rates of
les tax (TVA) apply to
ost goods, varying
tween 5–25 per cent
d are generally included
the stated price. No
funds are available on
rchases of food, wine
tobacco. On other
ods, tax can be refund-
to non-EU citizens who
end more than €175 in
e shop. Ask the store
r the appropriate form.

Food
Shops such as Maille,
édiard, Fauchon and
durée sell beautifully
ckaged delicacies. Ask
have your pungent
ench cheeses vacuum
cked (sous vide). Place
Madeleine has several
p-quality delis (see p98),
try one of the street
arkets for fresh produce.

Clothes
Paris is one of the
orld centres of fashion
d is home to all the top
mes (see p108), but

don't forget to look out for
the independent designers
and labels often found
nowhere else, such as
Antoine et Lili (see p88).
For vintage clothes try
Espace Kiliwatch (64 rue
Tiquetonne) and Didier
Ludot in the Palais-Royal's
arcades (see p96).

Lingerie
French fashion isn't all
on the surface. Designers
also produce beautiful
lingerie or you can try
specialist firms such as
Lejaby, Lise Charmel,
Aubade (available from
good department stores)
or Carine Gilson (18 rue
de Grenelle).

Perfume and Cosmetics
The Marionnaud and
Sephora chains offer a
huge variety of scents and
make-up brands. Prices
are usually reasonable too.
For something different try
Clara Molloy (Memo Bou-
tique, 60 rue des Saints-
Pères) or Les Parfums de
Rosine (Palais-Royal).

Designer shoes

Department and Concept Stores
Galeries Lafayettes, Au
Printemps and Le Bon
Marché are worth a visit
just for their Belle Epoque
interiors (see p54).
Concept stores are recent
arrivals – try L'Eclaireur
(26 Champs-Elysées),
which sells clothes and
hosts art exhibitions and
events, or Merci (see p88).

Bric-a-brac, Books and Prints
The flea market at Saint-
Ouen (see p55) is good
for bric-a-brac, while the
Marché Malassis gallery
stocks a range of 20th-
century treasures. The
bouquinistes by the Seine
sell vintage posters and
postcards. Shakespeare
and Company is the place
for rare books (see p122).

Music
The FNAC chain of
shops stock a huge range
of CDs, books, videos
and computer software.
The Virgin Megastore on
the Champs-Elysées has
several floors and shop-
floor headphones to let
you listen to the stock.

Stationery
French stationery can
be exquisite and even
chains such as Plein Ciel
sell beautiful notebooks,
diaries and address books.
Independent shops
include Magna Carta
(101 rue du Bac), while
Lamartine (118 rue de la
Pompe) sells G. Lalo's
superb products.

For more shops in Paris **See pp54–5**

Left **Bureau de change** Centre **Paris postbox** Right **Newspapers on sale**

TOP 10 Banking & Communications

1 Currency
The euro (€), the single European currency, is now operational in 17 of the 27 member states of the EU, including France. Euro banknotes have seven denominations: 5, 10, 20, 50, 100, 200 and 500. There are also eight coin denominations: €1 and €2, and 50, 20, 10, 5, 2 and 1 cents (also referred to as centimes). Both notes and coins are valid and interchangeable within each of the 17 countries. Check on exchange rates against your own currency at the time of travel.

2 Credit Cards
These are widely accepted throughout Paris and you should have no difficulty paying for most things with plastic. The only exception is American Express because of the heavy commission it incurs. The Visa card is the most widely used.

Parisian public telephone

3 Cash Dispensers (ATMs)
There are cash dispensers all over Paris, and each one indicates the cards it accepts. Many of them also operate in several languages. If you know your PIN number, obtaining cash in this way is very easy.

4 Changing Money
Bureaux de Change exist throughout Paris, especially near tourist hotspots. Many banks also have either a *bureau de change* or foreign desk. "No commission" signs can be misleading, as they probably mean an unfavourable rate.

5 Post Offices
The main post offices in the heart of Paris are at 52 rue de Louvre (open 24 hours) and 71 ave des Champs-Elysées. They do not exchange currency or travellers' cheques but will exchange international postal cheques, giros and money orders. For simple letters and postcards, you can buy stamps at a *tabac* (tobacconist) rather than try to find a post office. Not all of them advertise the service, but if they sell postcards it is worth asking. Some hotels and newsagents also sell postage stamps.

6 Telephones
Paris phone numbers begin with 01 or 09 and have eight subsequent digits, usually written in four sets of two digits. When calling Paris from overseas, drop the zero from "01". Most public telephones require a *télécarte* (phone card), which can be bought from post offices, metro stations, tobacconists and a few other outlets.

7 Mobile Phones
Check the roaming rates with your mobile operator before your trip. Pay as you go SIM cards can be bought for unlocked phones and topped up at tobacconist

8 Internet Cafés
These aren't as common as in some cities. Many cafés also provide Wi-Fi access. The small chain Milk has a café at 31 blvd Sebastopol, 75001: 01 40 13 06 51, or find others at www.cafes-wifi.com.

9 Newspapers and Magazines
A wide choice of the major foreign newspapers is available on the day of publication throughout Paris. The closer you are to the Champs-Elysées, the more you will see. The popular *International Herald Tribune* is published in Paris.

10 Television and Radio
Most hotels subscribe to multilingual cable and satellite channels, which vary the diet of French-language entertainment

eft **Pedestrian stop sign** Centre **Paris police car** Right **Pharmacy sign**

10 Security & Health

1 Crossing the Road
ake care when crossing
aris's roads. French
rivers are not known for
especting pedestrians,
hough a red light will
sually – although not
lways – make them stop.
edestrians do not have
utomatic priority on a
rossing, unless lights
re also in their favour.
On pedestrian crossings,
notorists often have the
ght to turn right, so
lways look before you
tart to cross.

2 Pickpockets
Gangs of pickpockets
o frequent tourist spots
uch as the Eiffel Tower
nd the Arc de Triomphe,
s well as wandering the
netro system. Some are
mateur gangs and easy
o spot, but others are
nore subtle so guard your
elongings at all times.

3 Mugging
Mugging is less of a
roblem in Paris than in
ther big cities, but it can
appen. Try not to travel
lone late at night and
void unlit streets. Try to
void long changes
etween metro lines too:
etter a longer journey
han an unfortunate
xperience. The main
tations you should avoid
t night are Les Halles
nd Gare du Nord.

4 Police
There are a number
f police stations in
entral Paris. These are
listed in the phone book,
or call the Préfecture
Centrale for details. All
crimes should be reported,
if only for insurance
purposes. ◈ *Préfecture
Centrale: 01 53 71 53 71
• Open 24 hours*

5 Women Travellers
Parisian men are
generally courteous. A
firm rebuttal usually halts
unwanted attention. If
not, try to seek the help
of another man: they do
not like to see a woman
being pestered.

6 Insurance
Paris medical treat-
ment is very good but it
can be expensive, so be
sure to have good health
insurance. Visitors from
EU countries should be
equipped with a Euro-
pean Health Insurance
card to avoid emergency
fees. All other nation-
alities should take out
private insurance. Report
all crimes or lost
property, and keep a copy
of the statement you
make to the police.

7 Hospitals
English-speaking
visitors might want to
contact the British or the
American Hospitals, both
open 24 hours a day. Paris
hospitals are listed in the
phone book, or call Hôpital
Assistance Publique.
◈ *British Hospital: 01 46 39
22 22 • American Hospital:
01 46 41 25 25 • Hôpital
Assistance Publique:
www.aphp.fr*

8 Ambulances
If you need an ambu-
lance, dial the emergency
number. Fire stations
also have ambulances
and are qualified to carry
out first aid.

9 Pharmacies
A green cross
indicates a pharmacy
(chemist). They are
usually open between
9am–7pm Monday to
Saturday. At other times,
the address of the duty
pharmacy will probably
be displayed, or contact
the local *gendarmerie*.
Pharmacies will also give
doctors' details.

10 Dentists
These are listed in
the Paris *Pages Jaunes
(Yellow Pages)* under
Dentistes. In a dire
emergency, a service
called SOS Dentistes will
provide a house call, but
be prepared to pay a
large amount for this.
A large dental practice is
at the Centre Médical
Europe. ◈ *SOS Dentistes:
87 blvd Port Royal, 01 43 37
51 00 • Centre Médical
Europe: 44 rue d'Amster-
dam, 01 42 81 93 33*

**Emergency
Numbers**

Police
17

Ambulance (SAMU)
15

Fire Department
18

Left **The Westin Paris** Centre **Renaissance le Parc Trocadero** Right **Meurice**

Luxury Hotels

Hôtel de Crillon
With one of the best locations in Paris, one of the best restaurants and one of the best reputations, the Crillon is for those who enjoy their comforts. From the marble lounge to the light and spacious rooms, the Crillon oozes class and distinction. ◈ *10 pl de la Concorde, 75008 • Map D3 • 01 44 71 15 00 • www.crillon.com • No disabled access • €€€€€*

Four Seasons George V
One of the most luxurious and fashionable hotels in Paris, the George V combines period features with modern amenities. Bedrooms are spacious, beautifully decorated and have marble bathrooms. The restaurant, Le Cinq *(see p109)*, has become one of "the" places to eat. ◈ *31 ave George V, 75008 • Map C3 • 01 49 52 70 00 • www.fourseasons.com/paris • €€€€€*

The Westin Paris
A world away from the usual anonymity of chain hotels, being set in a 19th-century building designed by Charles Garnier and overlooking the Tuileries *(see p95)*. The original atmosphere has been retained, but the rooms offer everything you would expect from a Westin hotel. ◈ *3 rue de Castiglione, 75001 • Map E3 • 01 44 77 11 11 • www.westin.com • €€€€€*

Mandarin Oriental
Centrally located on one of Paris's most fashionable streets, Rue Saint-Honoré, the interiors of this hotel boast Art Deco with Oriental influences. The rooms and suites are luxurious and spacious. ◈ *251 rue Saint-Honoré, 75001 • Map E3 • 01 70 98 78 88 • www.mandarinoriental.com/paris • €€€€€*

Meurice
The sumptuous antique decor of the Meurice may not be original, but you would never know it. The fading hotel has been completely restored, creating spacious guest rooms and state-of-the-art facilities, as well as interiors by Philippe Starck. And the location could not be better. ◈ *228 rue de Rivoli, 75001 • Map E3 • 01 44 58 10 15 • www.lemeurice.com • €€€€€*

Renaissance Le Parc Trocadero
The façade of this 1912 mansion conceals a beautiful flower-filled courtyard, while the interior decor combines the feel of the old with the design of the new. Its restaurant, Le Relais du Parc *(see p139)*, is one of the best dining venues in the area. ◈ *55–59 ave Raymond Poincaré, 75016 • Map B3 • 01 44 05 66 66 • www.parisrenaissance.com • €€€€*

Shangri-La Paris
Housed in the former home of Napoleon's grand-nephew, this fabulous hotel is located in the chic 16th arrondisement. Most of the rooms have impressive views of the Eiffel Tower. ◈ *10 ave d'Iéna, 75116 • Map A3 • 01 80 27 19 35 • www.shangri-la.com • €€€€€*

Hôtel Raphaël
One of the city's finest hotels. The antique decor is reflected in the rooms but they have been fully modernized in terms of facilities. Higher floors have stunning Parisian views. ◈ *17 ave Kleber, 75016 • Map B3 • 01 53 64 32 00 • www.raphael-hotel.com • €€€€€*

Le Royal Monceau
This Paris branch of the Raffles hotel chain features interiors by famous designer Philippe Starck. ◈ *37 ave Hoche, 75008 • Map C2 • 01 42 99 88 00 • www.raffles.com/paris • €€€€€*

Westminster
This hotel was built in the 18th century and was named after the Duke of Westminster who used to stay here. The rooms combine modern facilities with elegant English-style furnishings. ◈ *13 rue de la Paix, 75002 • Map E3 • 01 42 61 57 46 • www.warwickwestminsteropera.com • €€€€*

Note: Unless otherwise stated, all hotels accept credit cards, have en-suite bathrooms and air conditioning

Price Categories

For a standard, double room per night (with breakfast if included), taxes and extra charges.

€ under €100
€€ €100–€150
€€€ €150–€250
€€€€ €250–€350
€€€€€ over €350

ft **Brighton** Right **Hôtel du Panthéon**

10 Hotels in Great Locations

Hôtel Edouard VII
An elegant boutique otel with eclectic design atures and oodles of arm. Most rooms have e bonus of breath-king balcony views over e spectacular Opéra ational de Paris Garnier ee p97). ◎ 39 avenue de)péra, 75002 • Map E3 01 42 61 56 90 • www. Jouard7hotel.com • info@ Jouard7hotel.com • €€€€€

Brighton
Enjoy the rue de voli, within walking stance of many tractions, without ying the usual prices sociated with this cation. This old hotel s been completely furbished, ask for one the rooms with a ew over the Tuileries posite (see p95), or the Eiffel Tower (see 16–17). ◎ 218 rue de voli, 75001 • Map K1 01 47 03 61 61 • www. pritdefrance.com • €€€

Bristol
Prices reflect the xury standards and cation, close to the ubourg St-Honoré. poms are large and ted out with antique rniture and spacious, arble bathrooms, as ell as all the latest odern facilities. There e also two restaurants. 112 rue du Faubourg-St-onoré, 75008 • Map D3 01 53 43 43 00 • www. bristolparis.com • resa@ bristolparis.com • €€€€€

Hôtel du Jeu de Paume
Tucked away on the Ile St-Louis is this beautiful old building with beams. Some rooms overlook a peaceful courtyard. Rooms are small but the friendly atmosphere makes up for everything. ◎ 54 rue St-Louis-en-l'Ile, 75004 • Map Q5 • 01 43 26 14 18 • www.jeudepaume hotel.com • info@jeude paumehotel.com • €€€€

Hôtel des Deux-Iles
To stay on one of the Seine islands is a treat, and to do it in this hotel is a double treat. The bedrooms may be small, due to the building's 17th-century origins, but the cheerful decor, the intimacy (only 17 rooms) and the hidden patio with its flowers and fountain more than compensate. ◎ 59 rue St-Louis-en-l'Ile, 75004 • Map Q5 • 01 43 26 13 35 • www.hoteldes deuxiles.com • No disabled access • €€€

Hôtel d'Orsay
Art-lovers will enjoy this hotel, right by the magnificent Musée d'Orsay (see pp12–15). The hotel's modern bright colours are strikingly offset with antique furniture here and there. Several more expensive suites are also available. ◎ 93 rue de Lille, 75007 • Map J2 • 01 47 05 85 54 • www.paris-hotel-orsay. com • €€€

Hôtel du Panthéon
A small, charming hotel set in an 18th-century building right by the Panthéon (see pp28–9). ◎ 19 place du Panthéon, 75005 • Map N6 • 01 43 54 32 95 • www.hoteldu pantheon.com • reservation @hoteldupantheon.com • €€€€

Pavillon de la Reine
The best hotel in the Marais, right on the place des Vosges (see pp84–7). Lovely rooms, a spa and a quiet courtyard. ◎ 28 pl des Vosges, 75003 • Map R3 • 01 40 29 19 19 • www. pavillon-de-la-reine.com • contact@pavillon-de-la-reine.com • €€€€€

Hôtel de la Place du Louvre
A hotel that provides its guests with a superb view of the Louvre (see pp10–13). The rooms cleverly mix the historical with the modern. ◎ 21 rue des Prêtres-St-Germain-l'Auxerrois, 75001 • Map M2 • 01 42 33 78 68 • www.paris-hotel-place-du-louvre.com • No disabled access • €€€

Hôtel Castille
This elegant hotel near place Vendôme is just a couple of steps away from the original Chanel store. It also boasts an Italian restaurant, L'Assaggio. ◎ 33 rue Cambon, 75001 • Map E3 • 01 44 58 44 58 • www.castille.com • €€€€€

Streetsmart

Left **Hôtel Bellechasse** Centre **Aviatic Hôtel** Right **Hôtel d'Aubusson**

Romantic Hotels

1 Hôtel d'Aubusson
The rooms in this 17th-century building are spacious and many of them have beams. In winter there is a log fire in the guests' lounge. ◉ 33 rue Dauphine, 75006 • Map M4 • 01 43 29 43 43 • www.hoteldaubusson. com • €€€€

2 Hôtel Particulier Montmartre
Housed in a former private residence, this hotel's rooms are individually decorated in stunning Baroque style. ◉ 23 ave Junot, Pavillon D, 75018 • Map E1 • 01 53 41 81 40 • www.hotel-particulier-montmartre.com • No disabled access • €€€€€

3 Aviatic Hôtel
A stylish hotel that bubbles with the delightful atmosphere of the Left Bank. Ask them to pack a picnic for you for a romantic stroll around the nearby Jardin du Luxembourg (see p119). ◉ 105 rue de Vaugirad, 75006 • Map D6 • 01 53 63 25 50 • www.aviatic.fr • welcome@aviatic.fr • No disabled access • €€€

4 L'Hôtel
This hotel has come up in the world since Oscar Wilde expired here, having uttered the famous words, "My wallpaper and I are fighting a duel to the death. One or the other of us has to go." Fashionable as it has become, with stylish

decor by Jacques Garcia and a Michelin-starred restaurant, the hotel still has a quirky charm. ◉ 13 rue des Beaux-Arts, 75006 • Map E4 • 01 44 41 99 00 • www.l-hotel.com • €€€€€

5 Hôtel Bellechasse
The fabulously opulent rooms at this hotel were designed by Christian Lacroix. Special packages, such as Pour Une Nuit, include a 3pm checkout, champagne and other indulgent treats. The hotel is located just a few minutes' walk from the Musée d'Orsay. ◉ 8 rue de Bellechasse, 75007 • Map J2 • 01 45 50 22 31 • www.lebellechasse.com • No disabled access • €€€€€

6 Five Hotel
Fibre-optic lighting creates a glittering atmosphere in many of this boutique hotel's 24 rooms. Guests can choose from nine colours, ranging from tranquil black to cheerful plum-and-pink, and five "olfactory ambiences" by Esteban. The Five has already established a reputation as the perfect lovers' getaway. ◉ 3 rue Flatters, 75005 • 01 43 31 74 21 • www.thefivehotel.com • €€

7 Hôtel Costes
Book a first-floor room overlooking the courtyard for a romantic place to stay. Low lighting and dark furniture add to the mood, as does the Oriental-style swimming

pool and trendy restaurant. ◉ 239 rue St-Honoré, 75001 • Map E3 • 01 42 44 50 00 • www.hotelcostes. com • €€€€€

8 Le Relais Christine
This historic mansion with a spa offers a back street haven from the St-Germain bustle. Opt for terraced room overlooking the secluded garden and take breakfast in the vaulted room which was once an abbey's refectory. ◉ 3 rue Christine, 75006 • Map M4 • 01 40 51 60 80 • www.relais-christine. com • No disabled access • €€€€

9 Hôtel Lancaster
Pampering is paid for here, but the investment pays off with huge room in a 19th-century mansion just a stroll from the Champs-Elysées. ◉ 7 rue de Berri, 75008 • Map C3 • 01 40 76 40 76 • www. hotel-lancaster.fr • reservations@hotel-lancaster.fr • €€€€€

10 Hôtel Caron de Beaumarchais
Wooden beams, candle light, a log fire, authentic decor and sparkling crystal chandeliers evoke the essence of 18th-century romance. Rooms are beautiful and guests are truly pampered. ◉ 12 rue Vieille-du-Temple, 75004 • Map R2 • 01 42 34 12 • www.caronde beaumarchais.com • hotel carondebeaumarchais.com • No disabled access • €€

Price Categories

For a standard, double room per night (with breakfast if included), taxes and extra charges.

€ under €100
€€ €100–€150
€€€ €150–€250
€€€€ €250–€350
€€€€€ over €350

Left **Hôtel des Grandes Écoles** Right **Hôtel Lenox Montparnasse**

10 Budget Hotels

1 Hôtel des Grandes Écoles
A secret hideaway in a lovely part of Paris, the three buildings that make up this 51-room hotel are set around a garden. The rooms are attractively decorated and the location is perfect as a base for exploring the Latin Quarter. ◈ 75 rue du Cardinal-Lemoine, 75005 • Map P6 • 01 43 26 79 23 • www.hotel-grandes-ecoles.com • No air conditioning • €€

2 Hôtel Lenox Montparnasse
The flower-filled Lenox is close to Montparnasse Cemetery (see p151). The rooms are clean, with modern facilities. Some are on the small side so ask for a larger room if you don't like being too cramped: there is also a top-floor suite. ◈ 15 rue Delambre, 75014 • Map D6 • 01 43 35 34 50 • www.hotellenox.com • No disabled access • €€€

3 Hôtel Saint-André-des-Arts
This charmingly modest hotel offers ancient exposed beams and a Left Bank location at bargain prices. The rooms are tiny, but for a cheap bolt-hole and truly Parisian Bohemian feel, it can't be beaten. ◈ 66 rue St-André-des-Arts, 75006 • Map M4 • 01 43 26 96 16 • hsaintand@wanadoo.fr • No air conditioning • No disabled access • €

4 Hôtel Amour
Situated just below Montmartre, this extremely trendy vintage hotel and bistro has medium-sized rooms decorated with cutting edge photography and pop art (bare bottoms and more much are in evidence). As it is on a quiet residential street, guests can experience Parisian Bohemia without the usual crowds. ◈ 8 rue Navarin, 75009 • Map F1 • 01 48 78 31 80 • www.hotelamourparis.fr • €€€

5 Grand Hôtel Lévêque
The only thing grand about this hotel is its name, but it remains a favourite for budget accommodation in Paris. Almost all rooms have fans, phone, TV and a hairdryer. ◈ 29 rue Cler, 75007 • Map C4 • 01 47 05 49 15 • www.hotel-leveque.com • info@hotel-leveque.com • No disabled access • €

6 Hôtel du Cygne
This lovely hotel is housed in a restored 17th-century building and has 20 rooms. It is centrally located, just a five-minute walk away from Forum Les Halles. Free Wi-Fi is available in all the rooms. ◈ 8 rue du Cygne, 75001 • Map N1 • 01 42 60 14 16 • Not all en-suite • No air conditioning • No disabled access • €€

7 Le Caulaincourt Square Hôtel
Part budget hotel, part hostel, with a friendly atmosphere and access to the sights of Montmartre. ◈ 2 square Caulaincourt, 75018 • Map E1 • 01 46 06 46 06 • www.caulaincourt.com • No air conditioning • No disabled access • €

8 Mama Shelter
Created by well-known designer Philippe Starck, this trendy hotel offers stylish and affordable rooms. The lively restaurant is very popular with guests. ◈ 109 rue de Bagnolet, 75020 • 01 43 48 48 48 • www.mamashelter.com • €€

9 St Christopher's Inn Paris
This hostel offers mixed as well as single-sex dorms, private twins with shared bathrooms and private doubles. ◈ 159 rue de Crimée, 75019 • Map H1 • 01 40 34 34 40 • www.st-christophers.co.uk/paris-hostels • Not all en-suite • €

10 Ermitage Hôtel
A wonderful family-run hotel in Montmartre. Some rooms have views over the city, others overlook a garden, and the furniture is antique or retro. ◈ 24 rue Lamarck, 75018 • Map E1 • 01 42 64 79 22 • www.ermitage sacrecoeur.fr • No credit cards • No air conditioning • No disabled access • €€

Left **Hôtel de Seine** Right **Hôtel de Banville**

Medium-Priced Hotels

1 La Régence Étoile Hôtel

Very reasonably priced for its standard and location (a short walk from the Arc de Triomphe), the Régence has plush public areas and modern bedrooms with TVs, direct-dial phones, mini-bars and safe. ⓢ *24 ave Carnot, 75017 • Map B2 • 01 58 05 42 42 • www.laregenceetoile.com • No disabled access • €€€*

2 Hôtel d'Angleterre

Hemingway once stayed in this long-established hotel. Most rooms are a good size with high ceilings, and some are decorated with antiques. The standard rooms are small so book a superior one at extra cost. ⓢ *44 rue Jacob, 75006 • Map N5 • 01 42 60 34 72 • www.hotel-dangleterre.com • No air conditioning • No disabled access • €€€*

3 L'Abbaye Saint–Germain

This 16th-century former convent has a cobbled courtyard in a quiet location near St-Sulpice *(see p41)*. It is perfect for exploring much of the Left Bank, and is a haven to return to afterwards. The 44 rooms are all different, the best being the top-floor suites with their rooftop views. ⓢ *10 rue Cassette, 75006 • Map K5 • 01 45 44 38 11 • www.hotel-abbaye.com • hotel-abbaye@wanadoo.fr • No disabled access • €€€€*

4 Hôtel de Seine

Timbered rooms indicate the old-world nature of this mansion, close to the Jardin du Luxembourg. Some rooms have balconies. ⓢ *52 rue de Seine, 75006 • Map L5 • 01 46 34 22 80 • www. hoteldeseine.com • No disabled access • €€€*

5 Hôtel Notre-Dame Maître Albert

Situated in a quiet street opposite Notre-Dame, close to the Latin Quarter and the Marais, this hotel combines modern design with beams and stone walls. ⓢ *19 rue Maitre-Albert, 75005 • Map N5 • 01 43 26 79 00 • www.hotel-charme-notredame.com • No disabled access • €€€*

6 Hôtel Le Clos Médicis

Built in 1773 for the Médici family, ancient beams and artworks now combine with modern design. Rooms are small, but compensations are the garden, adjacent bar, and the location in a quiet street off boulevard St-Michel. ⓢ *56 rue Monsieur-le-Prince, 75006 • Map M5 • 01 43 29 10 80 • www.hotelclosmedicis paris.com • message@ closmedicis.com • 1 room suitable for disabled guests • €€€*

7 Hotel des Trois Poussins

This hotel is in the Pigalle area but is well away from the sleazy side. Some rooms are small, but the higher they go, the better the view. ⓢ *15 rue Clauzel, 75009 • Map E1 • 01 53 32 81 81 • www.les3poussins.com • h3p@les3poussins.com • €€€*

8 Le Citizen

This eco-hotel with modern decor boasts lovely views over the fashionable Canal St-Martin. There are 12 comfortable rooms. A wide choice of restaurants is available nearby. ⓢ *96 quai de Jenmapes, 75010 • Map H2 • 01 83 62 55 50 • www.lecitizenhote. com • €€€*

9 Hôtel Saint-Paul

This 17th-century building has antique furniture, beams and some four-poster beds. Several rooms have great views over Paris and the Sorbonne *(see p119)*. ⓢ *43 rue Monsieur-le-Prince, 75006 • Map M5 • 01 43 26 98 64 • www.hotelsaintpaul paris.fr • contact@hotel saintpaulparis.com • €€€*

10 Hôtel de Banville

This wonderful 1928 mansion may be away from the centre but it oozes class and is filled with antiques. Several bedrooms have balconies ⓢ *166 boulevard Berthier, 75017 • Metro Porte de Clichy • 01 42 67 70 16 • www.hotelbanville.fr • €€€€*

Note: *Unless otherwise stated, all hotels accept credit cards, have en-suite bathrooms and air conditioning*

Price Categories

For a standard, double room per night (with breakfast if included), taxes and extra charges.

€	under €100
€€	€100–€150
€€€	€150–€250
€€€€	€250–€350
€€€€€	over €350

Left **Hotel Résidence Lord Byron** Right **Hôtel Chopin**

10 Famous-Name Hotels

Hôtel Esmeralda
The proximity to Notre-Dame gives the hotel its name. Ask for a room with a cathedral view, and be prepared for a Bohemian atmosphere. The area is noisy and the rooms are not modernized, although they all have en-suite bathrooms. ✎ 4 rue St-Julien-le-Pauvre, 75005 • Map P4 • 01 43 54 19 20 • www.hotel-esmeralda.fr • No air conditioning • No disabled access • €€

Résidence Lord Byron
Located just off the Champs-Elysées, this is an inexpensive hotel in an expensive area, with a pleasant courtyard garden for summer breakfasts. Top floor rooms have good views. ✎ 5 rue Chateaubriand, 75008 • Map C2 • 01 43 59 89 98 • www.hotel-lordbyron.fr • lordbyron@hotel-lordbyron.fr • €€€

Hôtel Balzac
Fashionably chic, this luxurious hotel has a restaurant and a basement bar, both popular with the locals. The hotel's 57 rooms and 3 apartments are simply but tastefully decorated, with terraced suites offering great views of the Eiffel Tower. ✎ 6 rue Balzac, 75008 • Map C2 • 01 44 35 18 00 • www.hotelbalzac.com • reservation-balzac@jjwhotels.com • €€€€€

Hôtel Chopin
Hidden away in one of the city's passages (see p50), the Chopin opened in 1846. At this price don't expect the best facilities, but it is a pleasant place to stay and the rooms are comfortable. Ask for an upper room for more light. ✎ 46 passage Jouffroy, 10 blvd Montmartre, 75009 • Map F2 • 01 47 70 58 10 • www.hotelchopin.fr • No air conditioning • No disabled access • €€

Hôtel Langlois
Originally opened in 1897, this quaint belle époque hotel has large, individually decorated rooms, all en-suite, and a modern lift. It is located near the Gustave Moreau Museum and the Opéra National de Paris Garnier is within walking distance. ✎ 63 rue Saint-Lazare, 75009 • 01 48 74 78 24 • www.hotel-langlois.com • No disabled access • €€

Hôtel Flaubert
Terrific value, slightly out of the centre but not far from the metro. New owners have smartened it up and the lush garden is a delight. Room sizes vary. ✎ 19 rue Rennequin, 75017 • Map C1 • 01 46 22 44 35 • www.hotelflaubert.com • paris@hotelflaubert.com • €€

Hôtel Baudelaire Opéra
The French writer Baudelaire lived here in 1854, and today it makes a good bargain find in this central area. Rooms are brightly decorated, although most of them are small. ✎ 61 rue St-Anne, 75002 • Map H4 • 01 42 97 50 62 • www.hotel-baudelaire.com • resa@hotel-baudelaire.com • No air conditioning • No disabled access • €€€

Plaza Athénée
Surrounded by designer shops (see p108) is this venerable but thoroughly modernized hotel. Alain Ducasse has a restaurant in the hotel (see p109). ✎ 25 ave Montaigne, 75008 • Map C3 • 01 53 67 66 65 • www.plaza-athenee-paris.com • €€€€€

Hôtel Galileo
Tasteful decor and a walled garden, all just a short walk from the Arc de Triomphe. ✎ 54 rue Galilée, 75008 • Map B2 • 01 47 20 66 06 • www.galileo-paris-hotel.com • €€€€

Grand Hôtel Jeanne d'Arc
You could pass a whole weekend in Paris without wandering far from this well-equipped hotel, surrounded as it is by Marais attractions. ✎ 3 rue de Jarente, 75004 • Metro St-Paul • 01 48 87 62 11 • www.hoteljeannedarc.com • information@hoteljeannedarc.com • No air conditioning • €€

Recommend your favourite hotel on traveldk.com

177

Left **Hotel Square** Centre **Hôtel du Quai Voltaire** Right **Le Notre-Dame St-Michel**

🔟 Rooms with a View

1 Hôtel Bourgogne et Montana
Stylish hotel, with the Musée d'Orsay (see pp12–15) and the Invalides close by. Rooms have empire-style furnishings with Kenzo-designed wallpaper. Some top-floor rooms have views across the Seine. 🕙 3 rue de Bourgogne, 75007 • Map D4 • 01 45 51 20 22 • www.bourgogne-montana.com • No disabled access • €€€€

2 Artus Hôtel
Indulge yourself in the food shops of the Rue de Buci (see p123), then indulge yourself even more back in this hotel – especially if you have booked the suite with a Jacuzzi from which there are views of the Latin Quarter. 🕙 34 rue de Buci, 75006 • Map L4 • 01 43 29 07 20 • www.artushotel.com • info@artushotel.com • No disabled access • €€€€

3 Hotel Square
Ultra-chic boutique hotel with 22 rooms and views over Paris. The Zebra Square is a cool restaurant (see p139). 🕙 3 rue de Boulainvilliers, 75016 • Map A5 • 01 44 14 91 90 • www.hotelsquare.com • reservation@hotelsquare.com • €€€€€€

4 Hôtel du Quai Voltaire
Impressionist artist Camille Pissarro (1830–1903) painted the view of the Seine and Notre-Dame visible from most of the guest rooms here. Rooms are small, but the warm welcome and the location more than make up for that. 🕙 19 quai Voltaire, 75007 • Map K2 • 01 42 61 50 91 • www.quaivoltaire.fr • No air conditioning • No disabled access • €€

5 Hôtel des Grands Hommes
Great upper floor views of the Panthéon (see pp28–9) from this intimate 32-room hotel in an 18th-century house. The rooms are reasonably sized. 🕙 17 pl du Panthéon, 75005 • Map N6 • 01 46 34 19 60 • www.hoteldesgrandshommes.com • No disabled access • €€€€

6 Terrass Hôtel
Located in Montmartre, the Terrass has fabulous views over Paris which can be enjoyed from its rooftop terrace. Most rooms in this early 19th-century building have air conditioning. There is a bar, restaurant and other facilities. 🕙 12–14 rue Joseph-de-Maistre, 75018 • Map E1 • 01 44 92 34 14 • www.terrass-hotel.com • reservation@terrass-hotel.com • €€€€

7 Le Notre-Dame St-Michel
A great location right by the Seine with magnificent views of Notre-Dame, the bright decor by Christian Lacroix here makes up for the size of the rooms. There are also three suites. 🕙 1 quai St Michel, 75005 • Map N4 • 01 43 54 20 43 • www.hotelnotredameparis.com • info@hotelnotredameparis.com • No disabled access • €€€€

8 Les Rives de Notre-Dame
The view of Notre-Dame from this 10-room hotel is arguably the best in Paris. The spacious and modern rooms have charming wooden beams. 🕙 15 quai St-Michel, 75005 • Map N4 • 01 43 54 81 16 • www.rivesdenotredame.com • hotel@rivesdenotredame.com • No disabled access • €€€€

9 Hôtel Régina
Across the rue de Rivoli from the Louvre (see pp8–11) with views of the Tuileries and the Louvre, this is a splendid old hotel. 🕙 2 pl des Pyramides, 75001 • Map K • 01 42 60 31 10 • www.regina-hotel.com • €€€€€

10 Radisson Blu Le Metropolitan
Five upper suites offer striking views onto the Eiffel Tower; the best has a giant bull's-eye window. Lower-floor rooms have good, but less spectacular balcony views. 🕙 10 place de Mexico, 75016 • Map A • 01 56 90 40 04 • www.radissonblu.com • €€€€

Note: Unless otherwise stated, all hotels accept credit cards, have en-suite bathrooms and air conditioning

Price Categories

For a standard, double room per night (with breakfast if included), taxes and extra charges.

€	under €100
€€	€100–€150
€€€	€150–€250
€€€€	€250–€350
€€€€€	over €350

Left **Relais St-Germain** Right **Fleurie**

🔟 Family-Friendly Hotels

1 Hôtel Baltimore
Part of the Accor hotel chain and situated between the Trocadéro and the Arc de Triomphe, the Baltimore caters well for families with good facilities and a friendly attitude. Rooms and suites are elegant. ◈ 88 bis avenue Kléber, 75016 • Map B3 • 01 44 34 54 54 • www.accorhotels. com • €€€€

2 Relais St-Germain
A delightful hotel in a 17th-century town house right in the heart of the Left Bank. The Musée du Louvre, Musée d'Orsay and Notre-Dame cathedral are all within walking distance, and the Jardin du Luxembourg is nearby for when the children simply want to play in the park. ◈ 9 carrefour de l'Odéon, 75006 • Map L4 • 01 43 29 12 05 • www.hotel-paris-relais-saint-germain.com • No disabled access • €€€€

3 Relais du Louvre
Right by the Louvre, this great family hotel offers a self-catering apartment for five, plus several family suites and communicating rooms, as well as a host of "extras" for small children. ◈ 19 rue des Prêtres-Saint-Germain-l'Auxerrois, 75001 • Map N2 • 01 40 41 96 42 • www.relaisdulouvre.com • contact@relaisdulouvre. com • No disabled access • €€€

4 Fleurie
Children under 12 sleeping in their parents' room stay free in this smart but lively St-Germain hotel. A small charge is made for over 12s. Satellite TV, Wi-Fi and air conditioning in each room, and a huge buffet breakfast. ◈ 32–4 rue Grégoire de Tours, 75006 • Map L4 • 01 53 73 70 00 • www.hotel-de-fleurie.fr • bonjour@hotel-de-fleurie.fr • No disabled access • €€€

5 Pullman Paris Montparnasse
Facilities here include family rooms with two double beds. Children's entertainment is laid on during Sunday brunch. ◈ 19 rue du Commandant René Mouchotte, 75014 • Map D6 • 01 44 36 44 36 • www.pullmanhotels.com • €€€

6 Hôtel de l'Université
This 17th-century St-Germain mansion has several apartments with two rooms and small terraces. ◈ 22 rue de l'Université, 75007 • Map K3 • 01 42 61 09 39 • www.hoteluniversite. com • hoteluniversite@ wanadoo.fr • €€€

7 Hôtel des Arts
This hotel is an excellent choice for families on a budget, with triple rooms and cots available. The hotel is in one of Paris's passages (see p50).

◈ 7 Cité Bergère, 6 rue du Faubourg Montmartre, 75009 • Map F2 • 01 42 46 73 30 • www.hoteldesarts. fr • contact@hoteldesarts.fr • No air conditioning • No disabled access • €

8 Hôtel St-Jacques
Numerous Left Bank attractions are near this comfortable hotel with triple-bed rooms and cots available. All rooms are en-suite and have a TV. ◈ 35 rue des Écoles, 75005 • Map N5 • 01 44 07 45 45 • www.paris-hotel-stjacques.com • hotelsaintjacques@ wanadoo.fr • €€€

9 Hôtel Residence Romance Malesherbes
A collection of intriguing studios with kitchenettes makes up for the slightly out-of-centre location. Parc Monceau and a good market are nearby. ◈ 129 rue Cardinet, 75017 • Map D1 • 01 44 15 85 00 • www.hotel-romance.com • hotel@hotel-romance.com • No air conditioning • No disabled access • €€€

10 Hotel Ibis Bastille Opéra
Right in the heart of the Bastille district, this no-frills chain hotel offers triple-bed rooms or doubles with a child's bed. Rooms are small but well-equipped and are cheaper at weekends. ◈ 15 rue Breguet, 75011 • Map H5 • 01 49 29 20 20 • www.ibishotel.com • €€

For Paris for children **See pp60–61**

General Index

General Index

General Index

Acknowledgements

Authors

Donna Dailey and Mike Gerrard are award-winning journalists, specializing in travel, food and wine, and have written more than 30 guidebooks between them. Mike Gerrard's *Time for Food* guide to Paris for Thomas Cook won the Benjamin Franklin Award for best new guidebook in 2001. Their work has appeared in international publications such as the *Times*, *Washington Post* and *Global Adventure*.

Produced by Book Creation Services Ltd, London

Project Editor Zoë Ross
Art Editor Alison Verity
Designer Anne Fisher
Picture Research Monica Allende
Proofreader Stewart J Wild
Index Hilary Bird
Revisions Team
Kim Laidlaw Adrey, Claire Baranowski, Sonal Bhatt, Anna Brooke, Louise Cleghorn, Simon Davis, Nicola Erdpresser, Fay Franklin, Anna Freiberger, Rhiannon Furbear, Lydia Halliday, Kaberi Hazarika, Lily Heise, Victoria Heyworth-Dunne, Conrad van Dyk, Paul Hines, Laura Jones, Kim Laidlaw Adrey, Louise Rogers Lalaurie, Maite Lantaron, Delphine Lawrance, Carly Madden, Nicola Malone, Sam Merrell, Jane Oliver-Jedrzejak, Helen Partington, Quadrum Solutions, Rada Radojicic, Tamiko Rex, Philippa Richmond, Ellen Root, Laura de Selincourt, Beverly Smart, Graham Tearse, Beatriz Waller, Sophie Warne, Dora Whitaker.
Additional Contributor Rosa Jackson
Main Photographer Peter Wilson
Additional Photography
Kim Laidlaw Adrey, Max Alexander, Marta Bescos, Michael Crockett, Robert O'Dea, Britta Jaschinski, Oliver Knight, Neil Lukas, Eric Meacher, Rough Guides/James McConnachie, Jules Selmes, Tony Souter, Steven Wooster.

Illustrator Chris Orr & Associates

Cartography Dominic Beddow, Simonetta Giori (Draughtsman Ltd)At Dorling Kindersley:
Senior Editor Marcus Hardy
Senior Art Editor Marisa Renzullo
Cartography Co-ordinator Casper Morris
Senior DTP Designer Jason Little
Production Joanna Bull, Marie Ingledew
Publishing Manager Kate Poole
Senior Publishing Manager Louise Bostock Lang
Director of Publishing Gillian Allan

Special Assistance
The authors would like to thank Euros and Room Service for help with their travel arrangements.

Picture Credits
a-above; b-below/bottom; c-centre; f-far; l-left; r-right; t-top

Works of art on the pages detailed have been reproduced with the permission of the following copyright holders:

Eiffel Tower illuminations Pierre Bideau 16-7; *Sculpture Palais Royale Courtyard* Pol Bury @ADAGP, Paris and DACS, London 2011 96b; *Espace Montmartre* Salvador Dali © Kingdom of Spain, Gaia - Salvador Dali Foundation, DACS, London 2011 140tc; *Sculpture* Salvador Dali © Kingdom of Spain, Gaia - Salvador Dali Foundation, DACS, London 2011 144tl; *L'Sofa* Salvador Dali © Kingdom of Spain, Gaia - Salvador Dali Foundation, DACS, London 2011 37c; *L'Ecoute* Henri de Miller ©ADAGP, Paris and DACS, London 2011 78tr; *Stravinsky Fountain* Niki de Saint Phalle and Jean Tinguely ©ADAGP, Paris and DACS, London 2011 27r, 39r, 74tl. The publishers would like to thank the following individuals, companies and picture libraries for permission to reproduce their photographs:

Acknowledgements

P, London: 56tl, 56b; AGENCE
PUBLIC: 168tc; AKG, London:17tr,
l, 21tr, 29cr, 44tl, 44tr, 45t,
c, 47c, 47b, 58b, 63t, 63b,128tc,135t,
na Lisa by Leonardo da Vinci 6ca, 11t,
l, The Raft of the Medusa by
eodore Gericault 9t,
onardo da Vinci portrait 11c, Picnic on
e Grass by Manet 12b, Empress
sephine by Pierre Paul Prud'hon 20tc,
oture by Anton von Werner 23cr,
bleau de Guerre Interprete by Vallotton
b, Erich Lessing: 10t, 10b,107tl,
e Lace-Maker by Vermeer 9c, Van
gh Bedroom in Arles by Van Gogh
13c, 36tl, Statues of Dancers by
gas 13tr, Cafe des Hauteurs by
ulouse-Lautrec 13cr, Blue Waterlilies by
net 13b, © Succession H Matisse/
CS, London 2011 Sorrow of the King
Matisse,

AMY IMAGES: Bildarchiv Monheim
bH/Florian Monheim 3tl, 19c; Chad
ers 135tr, Matthew Richardson 171tc;
CAZA RESTAURANT: 127tl; MAX
EXANDER: 4-5; ANTOINE ET LILI:
r; ART ARCHIVE: Musée Carnavalet
is/ Dagli Orti Interior of Pantheon
urch Paris by Boilly 28-29c, Musee
Orsay, Paris/Dagli Orti Blue Dancers by
gas 14tl, La Belle Angela by Gaugin
r, Cathedral at Rouen by Monet 15t,
nce at Moulin de la Galette by
noir 15b, 144b, General Ferdinand
h 111b; L'ATELIER DE JOEL
BUCHON: Gerard Bedeau 65cr;
ELIER MAITRE ALBERT: Eric
ssaud 127tr; AVIATIC HOTEL: 174c.

HOTEL BANVILLE: 176tr; BRIDGEMAN
ART LIBRARY: 26–27b, 45b, 46tr, 47t,
Musee d'Armee, Paris 114tr, The
Succession of Louis XIII by Gianni 44b,
Roger Viollet, Paris 114tl.
CAVEAU DE LA HUCHETTE Gary Wiggins
performing 62b; CHRISTOPHE CAZARRE:
165 tr; CINEAQUA: 134tc; CORBIS: 33t.
GALERIE NIKKI DIANA MARQUARDT:
91tr; A GAZZETTA: 93; GETTY IMAGES:
The Bridgeman Art Library/Felix Benoist
80t; The Bridgeman Art Library/Giradon/
Musee Marmottan Portrait of Napoleon
Bonaparte (1769-1821) (oil on canvas),
Jean Pierre Franque (1774-1860) 29tr;
RONALD GRANT ARCHIVE: 59t, 59c,
59b.
LA HALLE SAINT PIERRE: Untitled
Stavroula Feleggakis 145tl. HOTEL LE
BELLECHASE: 174tl. HOTEL
D'AUBUSSON: 174tr. LE JULES VERNE:
Eric Laignel 64tc. LA MAISON DRUNIER:
139tl; MUSEE NATIONALE DE LA MODE
ET DU TEXTILE: Diego Zitelli 94tr. MUSEE
DU QUAI BRANLY: 112b.
PYLONES: 72tl. LE RELAIS DU PARC:
139tc; RESTAURANT LA ROSE DE
FRANCE: 73tl; SENDERENS: Roberto
Frankenburg 99tl; LE SOUS-BOCK: Tarek
Nini 79tc; STARWOOD HOTELS AND
RESORTS: 62tl. TOPHAM PICTUREPOINT:
21b, 46t, 56tr,57b,144tc,144b, 150cr,
154tl, 154 tr, 162tl, J.Brinon/STR 107tr,
Daniel Frasnay 63b.
All other images are © DK. For further
information see www.dkimages.com.

Special Editions of DK Travel Guides

DK Travel Guides can be purchased
n bulk quantities at discounted prices
or use in promotions or as premiums.
We are also able to offer special
ditions and personalized jackets,
orporate imprints, and excerpts from
l of our books, tailored specifically to
eet your own needs.

To find out more, please contact:
(in the United States)
SpecialSales@dk.com
(in the UK) travelspecialsales
@uk.dk.com
(in Canada) DK Special Sales at
general@tourmaline.ca
(in Australia) business.development
@pearson.com.au

Phrase Book

In Emergency

Help!	**Au secours!**	oh sekoor
Stop!	**Arrêtez!**	aret-ay
Call a doctor!	**Appelez un médecin!**	apuh-lay uñ medsañ
Call an ambulance!	**Appelez une ambulance!**	apuh-lay oon oñboo-loñs
Call the police!	**Appelez la police!**	apuh-lay lah poh-lees
Call the fire brigade!	**Appelez les pompiers!**	apuh-lay leh poñ-peeyay

Communication Essentials

Yes/No	**Oui/Non**	wee/noñ
Please	**S'il vous plaît**	seel voo play
Thank you	**Merci**	mer-see
Excuse me	**Excusez-moi**	exkoo-zay mwah
Hello	**Bonjour**	boñzhoor
Goodbye	**Au revoir**	oh ruh-vwar
Good night	**Bonsoir**	boñ-swar
What?	**Quel, quelle?**	kel, kel
When?	**Quand?**	koñ
Why?	**Pourquoi?**	poor-kwah
Where?	**Où?**	oo

Useful Phrases

How are you?	**Comment allez-vous?**	kom-moñ talay voo
Very well,	**Très bien,**	treh byañ
Pleased to meet you.	**Enchanté de faire votre connaissance.**	oñshoñ-tay duh fehr votr konay-sans
Where is/are…?	**Où est/sont…?**	oo ay/soñ
Which way to…?	**Quelle est la direction pour…?**	kel ay lah deer-ek-syoñ poor
Do you speak English?	**Parlez-vous anglais?**	par-lay voo oñg-lay
I don't understand.	**Je ne comprends pas.**	zhuh nuh kom-proñ pah
I'm sorry.	**Excusez-moi.**	exkoo-zay mwah

Useful Words

big	**grand**	groñ
small	**petit**	puh-tee
hot	**chaud**	show
cold	**froid**	frwah
good	**bon**	boñ
bad	**mauvais**	moh-veh
open	**ouvert**	oo-ver
closed	**fermé**	fer-meh
left	**gauche**	gohsh
right	**droit**	drwah
entrance	**l'entrée**	l'on-tray
exit	**la sortie**	sor-tee
toilet	**les toilettes**	twah-let

Shopping

How much does this cost?	**C'est combien s'il vous plaît?**	say kom-byañ seel voo play
I would like …	**je voudrais…**	zhuh voo-dray
Do you have?	**Est-ce que vous avez?**	es-kuh voo zavay
Do you take credit cards?	**Est-ce que vous acceptez les cartes de crédit?**	es-kuh voo zaksept-ay leh kart duh kreh-dee
What time do you open?	**A quelle heure êtes-vous ouvert?**	ah kel urr voo zet oo-ver

What time do you close?	**A quelle heure êtes-vous fermé?**	ah kel urr voo zet fer-meh
This one.	**Celui-ci.**	suhl-wee-see
That one.	**Celui-là.**	suhl-wee-lah
expensive	**cher**	shehr
cheap	**pas cher, bon marché,**	pah shehr, boñ mar-shay
size, clothes	**la taille**	tye
size, shoes	**la pointure**	pwañ-tur
white	**blanc**	bloñ
black	**noir**	nwahr
red	**rouge**	roozh
yellow	**jaune**	zhohwn
green	**vert**	vehr
blue	**bleu**	bluh

Types of Shop

antique shop	**le magasin d'antiquités**	maga-zañ d'oñteekee-tay
bakery	**la boulangerie**	booloñ-zhuree
bank	**la banque**	boñk
bookshop	**la librairie**	lee-brehree
cake shop	**la pâtisserie**	patee-sree
cheese shop	**la fromagerie**	fromazh-ree
chemist	**la pharmacie**	farmah-see
department store	**le grand magasin**	groñ maga-zo
delicatessen	**la charcuterie**	sharkoot-ree
gift shop	**le magasin de cadeaux**	maga-zañ du kadoh
greengrocer	**le marchand de légumes**	mar-shoñ duh lay-goom
grocery	**l'alimentation**	alee-moñta-syoñ
market	**le marché**	marsh-ay
newsagent	**le magasin de journaux**	maga-zañ du zhoor-no
post office	**la poste, le bureau de poste, le PTT**	pohst, booroh duh pohst, peh-teh teh
supermarket	**le supermarché**	soo pehr-marshay
tobacconist	**le tabac**	tabah
travel agent	**l'agence de voyages**	l'azhoñs duh vwayazh

Sightseeing

abbey	**l'abbaye**	l'abay-ee
art gallery	**la galerie d'art**	galer-ree dart
bus station	**la gare routière**	gahr roo-tee-yehr
cathedral	**la cathédrale**	katay-dral
church	**l'église**	l'aygleez
garden	**le jardin**	zhar-doñ
library	**la bibliothèque**	beebleeo-tek
museum	**le musée**	moo-zay
railway station	**la gare (SNCF)**	gahr (es-en-say-ef)
tourist information office	**renseignements touristiques, le syndicat d'initiative**	roñsayn-moñ toorees-teek, sandee-ka d'eenee-syateev
town hall	**l'hôtel de ville**	l'ohtel duh ve

Staying in a Hotel

Do you have a vacant room?	**Est-ce que vous avez une chambre?**	es-kuh voo-zavay oon shambr
double room,	**la chambre à deux**	shambr ah d

h double bed	**personnes, avec**	*pehr-son avek*
	un grand lit	*un gronñ lee*
n room	**la chambre à**	*shambr ah*
	deux lits	*duh lee*
gle room	**la chambre à**	*shambr ah*
	une personne	*oon pehr-son*
m with a	**la chambre avec**	*shambr avek*
, shower	**salle de bains,**	*sal duh bañ,*
	une douche	*oon doosh*
ave a	**J'ai fait une**	*zhay fay oon*
ervation.	**réservation.**	*rayzehrva-syoñ*

ting Out

ve you	**Avez-vous une**	*avay-voo oon*
a table?	**table libre?**	*tahbl duh leebr*
nt to	**Je voudrais**	*zhuh voo-dray*
erve	**réserver**	*rayzehr-vay*
able.	**une table.**	*oon tahbl*
bill	**L'addition s'il**	*l'adee-syoñ seel*
ase.	**vous plaît.**	*voo play*
tress/	**Madame,**	*mah-dam,*
ter	**Mademoiselle/**	*mah-*
	Monsieur	*demwahzel/ muh-syuh*

nu	**le menu, la carte**	*men-oo, kart*
d-price	**le menu à**	*men-oo ah*
nu	**prix fixe**	*pree feeks*
er charge	**le couvert**	*koo-vehr*
le list	**la carte des vins**	*kart-deh vañ*
ss	**le verre**	*vehr*
le	**la bouteille**	*boo-tay*
le	**le couteau**	*koo-toh*
	la fourchette	*for-shet*
	la cuillère	*kwee-yehr*
on	**le petit**	*puh-tee*
akfast	**déjeuner**	*deh-zhuh-nay*
ch	**le déjeuner**	*deh-zhuh-nay*
ner	**le dîner**	*dee-nay*
in course	**le plat principal**	*plah prañsee-pal*
ter, first	**l'entrée, le hors**	*l'oñ-tray, or-*
irse	**d'oeuvre**	*duhvr*
of the day	**le plat du jour**	*plah doo zhoor*
e bar	**le bar à vin**	*bar ah vañ*
	le café	*ka-fay*

nu Decoder

ed	**cuit au four**	*kweet oh foor*
f	**le boeuf**	*buhf*
r	**la bière**	*bee-yehr*
ed	**bouilli**	*boo-yee*
ad	**le pain**	*pan*
er	**le beurre**	*burr*
	le gâteau	*gah-toh*
ese	**le fromage**	*from-azh*
ken	**le poulet**	*poo-lay*
s	**les frites**	*freet*
colate	**le chocolat**	*shoko-lah*
ee	**le café**	*kah-fay*
sert	**le dessert**	*deh-ser*
k	**le canard**	*kanar*
	l'oeuf	*l'uf*
	le poisson	*pwah-ssoñ*
h fruit	**le fruit frais**	*frwee freh*
c	**l'ail**	*l'eye*
ed	**grillé**	*gree-yay*
	le jambon	*zhoñ-boñ*
ice cream	**la glace**	*glas*
b	**l'agneau**	*l'anyoh*
on	**le citron**	*see-troñ*
t	**la viande**	*vee-yand*
	le lait	*leh*

mineral water	**l'eau minérale**	*l'oh meeney-ral*
oil	**l'huile**	*l'weel*
onions	**les oignons**	*leh zonyoñ*
fresh orange juice	**l'orange pressée**	*l'oroñzh press-eh*
fresh lemon juice	**le citron pressé**	*see-troñ press-eh*
pepper	**le poivre**	*pwavr*
pork	**le porc**	*por*
potatoes	**les pommes de terre**	*pom-duh tehr*
rice	**le riz**	*ree*
roast	**rôti**	*row-tee*
salt	**le sel**	*sel*
sausage, fresh	**la saucisse**	*sohsees*
seafood	**les fruits de mer**	*frwee duh mer*
snails	**les escargots**	*leh zes-kar-goh*
soup	**la soupe, le potage**	*soop, poh-tazh*
steak	**le bifteck, le steack**	*beef-tek, stek*
sugar	**le sucre**	*sookr*
tea	**le thé**	*tay*
vegetables	**les légumes**	*lay-goom*
vinegar	**le vinaigre**	*veenaygr*
water	**l'eau**	*l'oh*
red wine	**le vin rouge**	*vañ roozh*
white wine	**le vin blanc**	*vañ bloñ*

Numbers

0	**zéro**	*zeh-roh*
1	**un, une**	*uñ, oon*
2	**deux**	*duh*
3	**trois**	*trwah*
4	**quatre**	*katr*
5	**cinq**	*sañk*
6	**six**	*sees*
7	**sept**	*set*
8	**huit**	*weet*
9	**neuf**	*nerf*
10	**dix**	*dees*
11	**onze**	*oñz*
12	**douze**	*dooz*
13	**treize**	*trehz*
14	**quatorze**	*katorz*
15	**quinze**	*kañz*
16	**seize**	*sehz*
17	**dix-sept**	*dees-set*
18	**dix-huit**	*dees-weet*
19	**dix-neuf**	*dees-nerf*
20	**vingt**	*vañ*
30	**trente**	*tront*
40	**quarante**	*karoñt*
50	**cinquante**	*sañkoñt*
60	**soixante**	*swasoñt*
70	**soixante-dix**	*swasoñt-dees*
80	**quatre-vingts**	*katr-vañ*
90	**quatre-vingt-dix**	*katr-vañ-dees*
100	**cent**	*soñ*
1,000	**mille**	*meel*

Time

one minute	**une minute**	*oon mee-noot*
one hour	**une heure**	*oon urr*
half an hour	**une demi-heure**	*urr duh-me urr*
one day	**un jour**	*urr zhorr*
Monday	**lundi**	*luñ-dee*
Tuesday	**mardi**	*mar-dee*
Wednesday	**mercredi**	*mehrkruh-dee*
Thursday	**jeudi**	*zhuh-dee*
Friday	**vendredi**	*voñdruh-dee*
Saturday	**samedi**	*sam-dee*
Sunday	**dimanche**	*dee-moñsh*

877 833-5617 BofA
001 607 597-2395

Index of Main Streets